Frommer's®

Portable

Savannah

5th Edition

by Darwin Porter & Danforth Prince

WILEY
Wiley Publishing, Inc.

Published by:

WILEY PUBLISHING, INC.

111 River St.
Hoboken, NJ 07030-5774

ISBN 978-0-470-88728-8 (paper); ISBN 978-1-118-08286-7 (ebk); ISBN 978-1-118-08268-3 (ebk); ISBN 978-1-118-08284-3 (ebk)

Editor: Jennifer Swetzoff and Alexia Travaglini
Production Editor: Lindsay Conner
Cartographer: Guy Ruggerio
Photo Editor: Richard Fox
Production by Wiley Indianapolis Composition Services

Front cover photo: An Antebellum home in picture-perfect Savannah © Mike Briner / Alamy Images

For information on our other products and services or to obtain technical support, please contact our Customer Care Department within the U.S. at 877/762-2974, outside the U.S. at 317/572-3993 or fax 317/572-4002.

Wiley also publishes its books in a variety of electronic formats. Some content that appears in print may not be available in electronic formats.

Manufactured in the United States of America

5 4 3 2 1

CONTENTS

LIST OF MAPS   vi

1 THE BEST OF SAVANNAH   1

1 Frommer's Favorite Savannah Experiences......................2
2 Best Hotel Bets..4
3 Best Restaurant Bets 6

2 SAVANNAH IN DEPTH   9

1 Savannah Today..9
2 Savannah History 10
3 Savannah's Architecture & Art 17
4 Savannah in Popular Culture: Books, Films & Music 22
5 Eating in Savannah...24

3 PLANNING YOUR TRIP TO SAVANNAH   27

1 Getting There & Around..27
2 Neighborhoods in Brief 29
3 When to Go...32
    Savannah Calendar of Events....................................32
4 Money & Costs..34
    What Things Cost in Savannah 34
5 Specialized Travel Resources 35

4 WHERE TO STAY IN SAVANNAH   38

1 Along the Riverfront 38
    Family-Friendly Hotels..42

2 In the Historic District 43

3 Nearby Hotels & Inns 52

5 WHERE TO EAT IN SAVANNAH 54

1 Along or Near the Riverfront 54

2 In the Historic District 57

Family-Friendly Restaurants 63

3 In & Around the City Market 66

4 In the Victorian District 67

5 On the South Side 68

6 EXPLORING SAVANNAH 69

Sightseeing Suggestions 69

1 Historic Homes 70

A Visit to the U.S. Custom House 73

2 Museums 73

3 Historic Churches & Synagogues 75

Gateway to Historic Savannah 77

4 The Forts: Civil War Memories 78

5 Cemeteries 79

6 Black History Sights 79

Martinis in the Cemetery 80

7 Literary Landmarks 83

8 Especially for Kids 83

A Visit to the Murder House 84

9 Organized Tours 84

10 Sports & Outdoor Activities 87

Exploring the Savannah National Wildlife Refuge 88

7 SAVANNAH STROLLS 91

Walking Tour 1: Savannah's Historic Squares 91

Walking Tour 2: The Riverwalk 98

8 SHOPPING IN SAVANNAH 104

1 Shopping A to Z 104

9 SAVANNAH AFTER DARK 110

1 The Performing Arts...110
2 Live Music Clubs 110
3 Bar Hoppin' & Pub-Crawlin' 111
4 Gay & Lesbian Bars 114
5 Dinner Cruises 115

10 DAY TRIPS & OVERNIGHTS FROM SAVANNAH 116

1 Tybee Island 116
  Strolling Around Isle of Hope....................................118
2 Hilton Head..121
  Hilton Head's Wonderful Wildlife 128
3 St. Simons Island 153
4 Daufuskie Island 162
5 Beaufort 163
6 Sea Island 171

11 FAST FACTS & WEBSITES 173

1 Fast Facts: Savannah 173
2 Airline Websites..175

INDEX 176

LIST OF MAPS

Greater Savannah 30

Where to Stay in
Savannah 39

Where to Eat in Savannah . . . 55

Savannah Attractions 71

Walking Tour: Savannah's
Historic Squares 93

Walking Tour:
The Riverwalk 99

Tybee Island 117

Hilton Head 134

St. Simons 159

Beaufort 167

ABOUT THE AUTHORS

Veteran travel writers **Darwin Porter** and **Danforth Prince** have produced dozens of previous titles for Frommer's, including many guides to Europe, plus the Caribbean, Bermuda, and The Bahamas. They're also the authors of Frommer's *The Carolinas and Georgia* and *Portable Charleston*. Porter, a noted celebrity biographer, is a native of North Carolina and has lived in both Georgia and South Carolina. He is joined by Danforth Prince, formerly of the Paris bureau of *The New York Times* and today the president of Blood Moon Productions.

HOW TO CONTACT US

In researching this book, we discovered many wonderful places—hotels, restaurants, shops, and more. We're sure you'll find others. Please tell us about them, so we can share the information with your fellow travelers in upcoming editions. If you were disappointed with a recommendation, we'd love to know that, too. Please write to:

Frommer's Portable Savannah, 5th Edition
Wiley Publishing, Inc. • 111 River St. • Hoboken, NJ 07030
frommersfeedback@wiley.com

AN ADDITIONAL NOTE

Please be advised that travel information is subject to change at any time—and this is especially true of prices. We therefore suggest that you write or call ahead for confirmation when making your travel plans. The authors, editors, and publisher cannot be held responsible for the experiences of readers while traveling. Your safety is important to us, however, so we encourage you to stay alert and be aware of your surroundings. Keep a close eye on cameras, purses, and wallets, all favorite targets of thieves and pickpockets.

FROMMER'S STAR RATINGS, ICONS & ABBREVIATIONS

Every hotel, restaurant, and attraction listing in this guide has been ranked for quality, value, service, amenities, and special features using a **star-rating system.** In country, state, and regional guides, we also rate towns and regions to help you narrow down your choices and budget your time accordingly. Hotels and restaurants are rated on a scale of zero (recommended) to three stars (exceptional). Attractions, shopping, nightlife, towns, and regions are rated according to the following scale: zero stars (recommended), one star (highly recommended), two stars (very highly recommended), and three stars (must-see).

In addition to the star-rating system, we also use **seven feature icons** that point you to the great deals, in-the-know advice, and unique experiences that separate travelers from tourists. Throughout the book, look for:

(Finds)　Special finds—those places only insiders know about

(Fun Facts)　Fun facts—details that make travelers more informed and their trips more fun

(Kids)　Best bets for kids, and advice for the whole family

(Moments)　Special moments—those experiences that memories are made of

(Overrated)　Places or experiences not worth your time or money

(Tips)　Insider tips—great ways to save time and money

(Value)　Great values—where to get the best deals

The following **abbreviations** are used for credit cards:

AE American Express	**DISC** Discover	**V** Visa
DC Diners Club	**MC** MasterCard	

TRAVEL RESOURCES AT FROMMERS.COM

Frommer's travel resources don't end with this guide. Frommer's website, **www.frommers.com**, has travel information on more than 4,000 destinations. We update features regularly, giving you access to the most current trip-planning information and the best airfare, lodging, and car-rental bargains. You can also listen to podcasts, connect with other Frommers.com members through our active reader forums, share your travel photos, read blogs from guidebook editors and fellow travelers, and much more.

The Best of Savannah

If you have time to visit only one city in the Southeast, make it Savannah. It's that special.

The movie *Forrest Gump* may have put the city squarely on the tourist map, but nothing changed the face of Savannah more than the 1994 publication of John Berendt's *Midnight in the Garden of Good and Evil*. The impact has been unprecedented, bringing in millions in revenue as thousands flock to see the sights from the bestseller and the 1997 movie directed by Clint Eastwood. In fact, Savannah tourism has nearly doubled since the publication of what's known locally as The Book. Even after all this time, some locals still earn their living off The Book's fallout, hawking postcards, walking tours, T-shirts, and in some cases their own careers, as in the case of the Lady Chablis, the drag queen in The Book who plays herself in The Film. She still performs on Jefferson Street at Club One.

Also giving new publicity to Savannah are Paula Deen's appearances on the *Food Network* and her restaurant in the city. Many visitors, especially foodies, visit Savannah, hoping to encounter Deen personally, catching her pulling taffy or trying out new recipes for her cookbooks.

"What's special about Savannah?" we asked an old-timer. "Why, here we even have water fountains for dogs," he said.

The free spirit, the passion, and even the decadence of Savannah resemble those of Key West or New Orleans rather than the Bible Belt down-home "Red State" interior of Georgia. In that sense, it's as different from the rest of the state as New York City is from upstate New York.

Savannah—pronounce it with a drawl—conjures up all the clichéd images of the Deep South: live oaks dripping with Spanish moss, stately antebellum mansions, mint juleps sipped on the veranda, magnolia trees, peaceful marshes, horse-drawn carriages, ships sailing up the river (though no longer laden with cotton), and even General Sherman, no one's favorite military hero here.

Today, the economy and much of the city's day-to-day life still revolve around port activity. For the visitor, however, the big draw is Old Savannah, a beautifully restored and maintained historic area.

For this, we can thank seven Savannah women who, after watching mansion after mansion be demolished in the name of progress, managed in 1954 to raise funds to buy the dilapidated Isaiah Davenport House—hours before it was slated for demolition. The women banded together as the Historic Savannah Foundation, and then went to work buying up architecturally valuable buildings and reselling them to private owners who promised to restore them. As a result, more than 800 of Old Savannah's 1,100 historic buildings have been restored and painted in their original colors—pinks and reds and blues and greens. This "living museum" is now the largest urban National Historic Landmark District in the country—some 2½ square miles, including 21 1-acre squares that survive from General James Oglethorpe's dream of a gracious city.

1 FROMMER'S FAVORITE SAVANNAH EXPERIENCES

- **Experiencing 19th-Century Ambience**   Savannah is one of the top two cities in the Deep South (the other being Charleston) where you can experience what elegant life was like in the 19th century by checking into a B&B in a restored historic building. If you're a man sitting in one of these Victorian parlors, surrounded by wall paintings of bygone belles, you'll feel a little bit like Rhett Butler come to call on Scarlett O'Hara. Typical of these is the Eliza Thompson House (see p. 48), built around 1847 in Savannah's antebellum heyday.
- **Wandering the Isle of Hope**   Spanish conquistador Hernando de Soto came here 4 centuries ago looking for gold. The island later became a place of refuge for Royalists escaping the guillotine of the French Revolution. Today, the Isle of Hope, 10 miles south of Savannah, is an evocative and nostalgic reminder of Savannah's yesteryears. You can go for a stroll in a setting of oaks lining the bluff, plenty of Spanish moss, and Georgia pine, dogwood, magnolia, azalea, and ferns. See p. 118.
- **Having a Picnic Among Plantation Ruins**   There is no more evocative site in the Savannah area for a picnic than Wormsloe State Historic Site at 7601 Skidaway Rd., 10 miles southeast of town. A picnic here can be combined with an exploration of the Isle of Hope. Now ruins, these grounds were once part of a 900-acre estate that belonged to Noble Jones, an 18th-century Colonial who came to Savannah with James Oglethorpe in 1733. Nature

Impressions

Savannah is America's Mona Lisa. Gaze your fill, look all you will. (For once it's quite polite to stare.) You may never fathom the secret of her smile, but like those who love and live with her, you will know the endless rich rewards of trying.

—Writer Anita Raskin

trails are cut through the property, and there are picnic tables. The property is reached along a beautiful oak-lined drive that makes you think you're on the road to Tara.

- **Pursuing Grits, Game & Gumbo**   In the state of Georgia, only the much larger city of Atlanta equals Savannah in the number of fine restaurants. Since the mid–18th century, Savannah and the Low Country have been known for their abundance and variety of food, and lavish eating and drinking have long been local customs. The surrounding area was (and is) rich in game and fish, including marsh hen, quail, deer, and crab. Adding to these hunters' trophies is the bounty of local gardens, full of old favorites including collard greens, beets, turnips, peas, okra, and corn. That corn is ground into grits as well, and the okra is used to thicken gumbos, for which every Savannahian seems to have a favorite recipe.

- **Finding Your Own *Forrest Gump* Bench**   Arm yourself with a box of chocolates and set out to discover your own historic Savannah square like Tom Hanks's character did in the film *Forrest Gump,* where he began to spin out his adventures. Find the square of your choice, perhaps Chippewa Square (see p. 93)—where Forrest actually sat—sit down, enjoy those chocolates, and watch the world go by. Savannah revolves around its historic squares, and it's said that if you sit on a bench long enough, everybody in Savannah will eventually pass by.

- **Enjoying a Martini in Bonaventure Cemetery**   In *Midnight in the Garden of Good and Evil,* Mary Harty invites John Berendt, the author of The Book, for martinis in this moss-draped cemetery (see p. 80). It has since become a tradition to partake of this quaint custom. On the former grounds of an oak-shaded plantation, you can enjoy your libation amid the long departed. Of course, the proper way to drink a martini, as in The Book, is from a silver goblet. Your seat? None other than the bench-gravestone of poet Conrad Aiken.

- **Taking a Pub-Crawl Along the Riverfront** It's always party time at the friendly old taverns along the riverfront in Savannah. On any night, you can stroll along the cobblestone streets searching for your favorite hangout, perhaps one with live music. If not, count on the locals or visitors to supply amusement. Many of the beautiful former houses represent one of the Deep South's best recycling programs. On St. Patrick's Day, people drive down from South Carolina or up from Florida just to go pubbing here for a grand celebration where the color green reigns supreme, even in the beer.

- **Spending a Day at the Beach on Tybee Island** East of the city, Tybee Island (see p. 116), with its golden sands, is a great place to unwind. Sun worshipers, joggers, surf casters, kite flyers, swimmers, and sightseers come to escape the oppressive heat of Savannah's summers. You'll be following the footsteps of Blackbeard, who often took refuge here. It is believed that many of the pirate's treasures are still buried at Tybee. To cap off a perfect day, head for Fort Screven, a Civil War fort. Then climb to the top of the lighthouse for a panoramic view of coastal Georgia.

- **Camping It Up at Club One** From Clint Eastwood to Demi Moore, from Meg Ryan to Bruce Willis, it seems like every movie star or celebrity heads to this rollicking joint when they're in town. 'Tis true that some Savannahians refer to Club One as a gay club, and there are those who would never darken its door. But the club undeniably attracts a wide spectrum of humanity because it's known for having the best entertainment in Savannah. Sometimes even the fabled Lady Chablis, empress of Savannah, appears here. This drag queen gained prominence in John Berendt's book, *Midnight in the Garden of Good and Evil,* and plays herself in The Film (even though Diana Ross reportedly wanted to). The dancing here is the hottest in Savannah. See p. 114.

2 BEST HOTEL BETS

- **Best in Opulence** Built in 1888, the **Mansion on Forsyth Park** (© **888/213-3671** or 912/238-5158; www.mansiononforsythpark. com) is the most spectacular in Savannah. This luxurious hotel is also home to one of the city's top places to eat, 700 Drayton Restaurant. See p. 40.

- **Best River Street Rejuvenation** Of all the cotton warehouses along the Savannah River that were converted into hotels, shops, and restaurants, none was restored better than the **River Street Inn** (© **800/253-4229** or 912/234-6400; www.riverstreetinn.com). A flourishing storage warehouse for cotton until the boll weevil came, the building dates from 1817, when it was constructed from ballast stones brought over from England. Today, it is the epitome of comfort and charm with memorable views of the river. See p. 42.

- **Best B&B in the Historic District** Savannah's most classic and charming inn, **Ballastone Inn** (© **800/822-4553** or 912/236-1484; www.ballastone.com), an 1838 building, has been given the glamour treatment. You're housed in a 19th-century-style interior, but with far greater comforts than the antebellum wealthy of Savannah used to experience. Polished hardwood floors, elaborate draperies, and well-polished antiques set the stage for a grand B&B experience. See p. 43.

- **Best Deals on Suites** Originally a pickle factory, **Staybridge Suites** (© **800/225-1237** or 912/721-9000; www.ichotelsgroup.com) has some of the most elegant and affordable suites in town. Antique brick walls, a dramatic fireplace, and exposed wood evoke a ski lodge. See p. 51.

- **Best Rescue of a Decaying Building** Dating from 1873, the **Hamilton-Turner Inn** (© **888/448-8849** or 912/233-1833; www.hamilton-turnerinn.com) has been beautifully restored after falling into decay. Today, the four-story French Empire house is one of the most upscale B&Bs in Savannah. The building earned notoriety in John Berendt's *Midnight in the Garden of Good and Evil,* but those high-rolling party days are over. It's now a serene oasis. See p. 44.

- **Best & Most Opulent B&B** Built in 1892, the **Kehoe House** (© **800/820-1020** or 912/232-1020; www.kehoehouse.com) is no longer a funeral parlor but an inn of such grace that it ranks among the finest in Georgia. Its fabrics, furniture, and comfort make it an adult retreat of flawless taste. Tom Hanks stayed here during the filming of *Forrest Gump.* See p. 44.

- **Best Grand Hotel–Style Living** Built in 1890 as the city's grandest hotel, today's **Hilton Savannah DeSoto** (© **800/445-8667** or 912/232-9000; www.desotohilton.com) has kept abreast of the times. The old Grand was demolished in 1967 and replaced with this contemporary and conservatively modern hotel of efficiency and streamlined comfort. It was completely renovated in 2008. Lobby decor was partially inspired by an 18th-century drawing room. See p. 46.

- **Best Moderately Priced Hotel** The most appealing of the city's middle-bracket but large-scale hotels, the **Hampton Inn Historic**

District (© 800/426-7866 or 912/721-1600; www.hampton-inn. com) opened in 1997, rising seven redbrick stories. Although modern, it pays homage to Savannah's past with its big-windowed lobby designed to evoke an 18th-century city salon. See p. 49.

- **Best Value**   Adjacent to Chatham Square, **Bed & Breakfast Inn** (© 888/238-0518 or 912/238-0518; www.savannahbnb.com) lies in one of the oldest and most historic parts of Savannah. Its guest rooms are exceedingly comfortable and some of the most affordable for those wishing to stay in the historic core. Furnishings are a combination of antiques and tasteful reproductions. See p. 51.

3 BEST RESTAURANT BETS

- **Best Restaurant   Elizabeth on 37th** (© 912/236-5547; www. elizabethon37th.net) is the most upscale restaurant in Savannah. Housed in a palatial neoclassical villa from the turn of the 20th century, it's filled with antique furniture from the *Gone With the Wind* era. The food brings a modern interpretation to the South's cuisine— for example, black-eyed peas are served with cauliflower and roasted shitake mushrooms, and the Savannah red rice is enlivened with shrimp, river clams, grouper, sausage, and okra. See p. 67.
- **Best Southern Cuisine   The Lady & Sons** (© 912/233-2600; www.ladyandsons.com) is the domain of bestselling cookbook author and *Food Network* star Paula Deen. Along with her sons, she launched this temple of gastronomy in 1996. Whenever we're in town, we drop in for her chicken potpie topped with puff pastry. It doesn't get much better than Paula's version of this southern staple. See p. 56.
- **Best International Cuisine**   In the Mansion on Forsyth Park, **700 Drayton Restaurant** (© 912/721-5002; www.700drayton. com), is one of Savannah's culinary showcases. Enticing almost every visiting celebrity to Savannah, it dazzles with seductive, market-fresh cuisine. See p. 58.
- **Best Low-Country Cuisine**   Stylish yet casual, **Sapphire Grill** (© 912/443-9962; www.sapphiregrill.com) is best defined as an upscale bistro. Known for having some of the best service in town, the restaurant offers market-fresh cuisine. Try the delectable blueberry barbecue chicken, a savory seafood stew with five kinds of fish in a fennel broth, or a tasting menu with a sampling of the chef's proudest dishes. Christopher Nason's "coastal cuisine" wins raves among food critics. See p. 58.

- **Best Seafood** Many restaurants in Savannah serve good seafood, or else they're soon out of business. But the **Olde Pink House Restaurant** (© 912/232-4286) seems to put more flavor into its offerings than its competitors do. You don't get just fried fish here, but the likes of black grouper stuffed with blue crab and drenched in a Vidalia onion sauce, or crispy scored flounder with a tangy apricot sauce. The setting is both elegant and romantic, making the Pink House even more appealing. See p. 59.

- **Best Prime Rib** Chain restaurants rarely make Frommer's "best of" lists, but there's one exception in Savannah: the **Chart House** (© 912/234-6686; www.chart-house.com). Its prime rib is slow roasted and served au jus. The specially supplied beef is corn fed, aged, and hand cut. Beef eaters will be in heaven here. The chefs prepare a mean lobster as well. See p. 54.

- **Best Organic Cuisine** Mediterranean flavors permeate the atmosphere at **Cha Bella** (© 912/790-7888; www.cha-bella.com), which is housed in a restored industrial site. It appeals to a trendy, young crowd who feasts on farm-to-table locally grown cuisine, such as farm-raised, free-range, and pan-seared chicken with olives and rosemary, or a white shrimp risotto harvested from nearby waters, served with a light lemon chardonnay sauce. The seafood platter is brimming with scallops, shrimp, the catch of the day, and cold-water mussels served over linguini. See p. 60.

- **Best Barbecue** The good people of Savannah don't survive on oyster po'boys or catfish suppers all week. At least once a week, they like barbecue. For that tasty treat, many of them show up at **Wall's** (© 912/232-9754). This is an affordable, casual, family-style restaurant, where the barbecue is something to write home about. The sauce and the slow cooking are part of the secret—not to mention the hickory wood. But of course, no Southern chef reveals all his secrets for barbecue! See p. 65.

- **Best Breakfast** Everybody, or so it seems, shows up at **Clary's Café** (© 912/233-0402) for breakfast. A Savannah tradition since 1903, the cafe today still has a 1950s aura. You might expect James Dean to show up on a motorcycle wearing blue jeans and a leather jacket. The cafe is featured in the film *Midnight in the Garden of Good and Evil*. Among the dozens of breakfast offerings, we usually go for the chef's special: Hoppel Poppel (scrambled eggs with chunks of kosher salami, potatoes, onions, and green peppers). See p. 63.

- **Best Down-Home Favorite** For belly-busting food, **Mrs. Wilkes' Dining Room** (✆ **912/232-5997;** www.mrswilkes.com) is a Savannah tradition. Visitors and locals have been standing in line here since the 1940s for real down-home Southern fare. Mrs. Wilkes' time-tested recipes get a workout every day, feeding generations of the local citizenry on barbecued chicken, red rice and sausage, corn on the cob, squash and yams, and plenty of dishes with okra. Don't leave without trying Mrs. Wilkes' cornbread and collard greens. See p. 64.

Savannah in Depth

Savannah has recently received heaps of praise, with MSN.com naming it "one of the 15 coolest cities in North America" and *Southern Living* magazine calling it "Best Southern City." In this chapter, we'll take you from Savannah's founding in Colonial days, through its many stages of growth, decline, and rebirth, with special attention paid to its unique art and architecture. We'll also learn about the city and its people through a tour of Low Country cuisine.

Despite some close parallels to the history of its neighbor, Charleston, Savannah has played a unique role in the South. There were battles with American Indians, British troops, Yankees, Spaniards, and, ultimately, civil rights advocates. But before Savannah became General Sherman's Christmas gift to Abraham Lincoln, how did it all begin?

---

1 SAVANNAH TODAY

Attracting millions of visitors every year, Savannah is often mentioned as one of the most historic cities in the Southeast. In 1966, the U.S. government designated its downtown area as the Savannah Historic District, making it one of the largest such zones in America.

It's also the largest port along the Savannah River, lying along the U.S. Intracoastal Waterway. And like New Orleans, Savannah is prone to floods because of its flat topography.

Today, the city's population is estimated at approximately 135,000. The majority of residents, some 57%, are African American. Unlike many cities of the Southeast, the Hispanic or Latin population is small—some 2.23%. Savannah is not a rich city, with some 21% of the population below the poverty line.

The port, along with tourism, is the local economy's mainstay. One of the world's largest paper mills, owned by International Paper, is one of the biggest employers. The Gulfstream Aerospace Company, maker of private jets, also has its home base in Savannah.

"We're not as big or as important as Atlanta," a former mayor of Savannah told us, "but we've forgotten more about true Southern hospitality than those good folks will ever know."

2 SAVANNAH HISTORY

COLONIAL DAYS

In 1733, British General James Edward Oglethorpe (1696–1785) landed on the historic bluff above the Savannah River and founded what would become the 13th colony in America. The land was wilderness, but the British wanted to build a buffer zone between their colony in South Carolina and the "Spanish menace" to the south in Florida.

Still in his 30s when he sailed into the port of Savannah, Oglethorpe had already served in the military for 21 years, been a member of parliament for 11 years, and served on a committee that uncovered widespread abuse of prisoners in England's jails. He had also spent 5 months in jail for killing a man in a brawl. After one of Oglethorpe's friends died in debtor's prison, Oglethorpe vowed to prevent similar deaths by establishing a debtor's colony. (His own stay in the slammer must have motivated him as well.) On June 9, 1732, King George II granted a charter to Oglethorpe and 20 others (the "Trustees") for the creation of a new colony to be called Georgia, after the king.

Hundreds of people in London applied to sail west, but only 114 men and women were chosen, as well as a doctor and a pastor. There would be freedom of worship in this new land on America's southeast coast, providing a settler wasn't a slave, a Roman Catholic, or a lawyer.

Seven months after being granted the charter, the colonists sailed from the port at Gravesend, England, aboard an overcrowded vessel called the *Anne.* They were heading west on a rough, wave-tossed voyage into an uncertain future. The crew and passengers were close to starvation when they landed at Savannah.

Like Columbus in the Bahamas, Oglethorpe and his colonists did not discover an unoccupied Savannah, but encountered an already inhabited land of Native Americans. The Low Country area of Georgia, or so it is believed, had actually been inhabited by nomadic Indian tribes since the end of the Ice Age, when vegetation returned to the land and animals roamed its plains. It was a good thing that the Native Americans were friendly, because they could easily have overpowered the weakened colonists.

The Yamacraws, a small tribe, had fled the Spanish conquistadors in Florida and had moved north to settle in Georgia. It was this group of Indians that was on hand to greet Oglethorpe. Instead of attacking, the Yamacraws were hospitable to these invaders who would change their continent forever. The Native Americans not only lived in peace with Oglethorpe's colonists, but they would also later help them fight off invasions by the Spaniards and other hostile tribes.

While in London, Oglethorpe had fantasized about the new place he wanted to found in the Americas. For this dream city, he wanted rectilinear streets that would cross at right angles. The core of town would be filled with squares that would be earmarked as "green lungs," or public parks, so settlers could "breathe the fresh air." Savannah would be laid out in "wards" around these central squares.

Once in Savannah, Oglethorpe also set aside space for markets and public areas. He established a 10-acre Trustees' Garden, modeled after the Chelsea Botanical Garden in London. The garden, however, was doomed to fail because many of the plants were not hardy enough for the hard clay soil of coastal Georgia. The mulberry trees died, denying a home to silkworms, and the vines planted in the vineyards didn't bear grapes.

Oglethorpe viewed himself as the spiritual leader of the colony, and indeed he was called "Father Oglethorpe" by the colonists. His new city was founded only 6 months before a new set of colonists arrived from Europe, many escaping religious persecution. The ban on Catholics was rescinded. Not just Catholics, but Jews and Protestants also arrived, many coming from Iberia, especially Portugal.

By the mid–18th century, colonists in Georgia began to import slaves. They'd seen how their wealthy neighbors to the north in South Carolina were prospering in an economy fueled by slave labor. In a few short years, one out of every three persons in the colony was a slave, working the rich plantations that enveloped Savannah to its west.

Politically, the colonists in Georgia turned back further expansion by the Spanish coming north from Florida. Originally, the Spanish had wanted to make Georgia a colony. Oglethorpe, helped at the time by his Native American friends, thwarted their plans.

The founding father stayed in Savannah until 1743, finally giving up his dream and sailing back to London. The throne felt that Oglethorpe had failed as an administrator, and he was replaced by William Stephens, who was sent to govern in his place. The Trustees originally named by the king held onto their charter until 1752 before finally abandoning it. A political movement at the time wanted to turn their Low Country area into another royal colony like that enjoyed by South Carolina, centered at prosperous Charleston.

By 1754, a royal colony was established. Savannah became one of the leading ports of the Southeast, although it never overtook its major rival, Charleston. That prosperity of Low Country plantations became especially marked when the French and Indian War of 1763 came to an end. Britain won Florida, which ended Spain's attempts to forge colonies along the east coast of America. The slaves began to build cotton plantations and Colonial buildings soon came to dominate the landscape in the Low Country around Savannah.

THE AMERICAN REVOLUTION

At least a decade before the American Revolution, the residents of Savannah began to defy their English rulers. British property was being destroyed, and so-called Liberty Boys often fought openly with Loyalists. The much-hated Stamp Act of 1765 didn't go over well with the colonists, who objected to the tax on every printed item. Savannah even staged its own version of the Boston Tea Party.

The raucous Peter Tondee's Tavern at Whitaker and Broughton streets became the center of a growing rebellion in Georgia led by the Liberty Boys. The name came from their compatriots in Charleston, who had adopted it from Boston's Sons of Liberty. In defiance of royal authority, they flew a flag, featuring a rattlesnake with 13 rattles. Each of these rattles symbolized a different American colony.

These grog-swilling colonists defiantly wore homemade Liberty stocking caps and went so far as to erect a so-called Liberty Pole in front of Tondee's Tavern. The Declaration of Independence was read in Georgia for the first time in front of this tavern, and it was also at Tondee's Tavern that the Liberty Boys first heard the news of the battles of Lexington and Concord. The die was cast: America's war of freedom had begun, even though there were many Loyalists still residing in Georgia.

By June 28, 1776, the battles had come to South Carolina and Georgia as well. The first major victory for the U.S. freedom fighters came on that day, when General William Moultrie defeated an invading fleet of 50 British warships. Although outnumbered and lacking adequate ammunition, the revolutionaries battled the British from a fort hastily assembled on Sullivan's Island.

This early victory was followed by disaster. Before Christmas of 1778, the city of Savannah fell to British troops, with Charleston falling in the spring 2 years later. In their victory, British troops sought vengeance. They executed many patriots and robbed and pillaged from the richest homes in the area.

In October 1781, word reached Savannah that the British "sword of surrender" had been presented to the American forces at Yorktown.

"Mad" Anthony Wayne and his troops arrived to reclaim the city in 1782. The British were defeated, and many die-hard Loyalists in Georgia returned to Mother England, never to be seen again.

After the war, Savannah was made the capital city of Georgia, a position it would lose in 1786 to Augusta, which in time would lose out to Atlanta.

ANTEBELLUM TRIUMPH & TRAGEDY

In the years following the American Revolution, commerce in Savannah boomed. The demand grew for Sea Island cotton. On the Low Country plantations, cotton was king, and Savannah was the port from which to ship it north or abroad.

In 1793, Eli Whitney invented the cotton gin on a plantation near Savannah. A former schoolteacher from the North, Whitney created this new device with the aid of a widow, Catherine ("Caty") Greene, who ran the plantation and had been married to Nathanael Greene of Revolutionary War fame. The cotton gin allowed seeds to be removed with far greater speed and efficiency than by existing methods. Thanks to this invention, Low Country cotton plantations flourished for the next 6 decades.

Both Europe and America focused on Savannah in 1819 when the SS *Savannah* became the first steam-powered vessel to cross the Atlantic. The vessel departed Savannah on May 22 of that year, arriving at the port of Liverpool a record 29 days later. Triumphantly, the ship went on to Glasgow, Stockholm, and even to St. Petersburg in Russia. But in 1821, the vessel was caught in gale winds and capsized off the shores of Long Island.

Disaster struck Savannah in 1796 and 1820, when two major fires left half the city in ruins. The famous Savannah City Market was burned in both instances. As if the fire of 1820 didn't devastate Savannah enough, a yellow fever epidemic broke out and about one-tenth of the city's population died. Yellow fever struck again and again during the 19th century.

Antebellum Savannah was at the peak of its prosperity, fueled by cotton and slavery. But ominous clouds were on the horizon as tension between the North and South grew steadily worse.

THE CIVIL WAR ERA

There was rejoicing on the streets of Savannah as its neighbor South Carolina seceded from the Union on December 20, 1860. The election of President Abraham Lincoln, who was despised in Savannah, had demoralized the city. In 1861, Georgia followed South Carolina in separating itself from the Union, and when Confederate troops fired on Fort Sumter that same year, war was declared. Calling it "the War of Northern Aggression," Savannahians hoped for a quick and easy victory.

Within a few months, federal troops occupied much of the coastal lowlands of the Carolinas and Georgia, leaving only the port cities of Wilmington, Charleston, and Savannah in Confederate hands, albeit blockaded by the Union navy.

On April 11, 1862, Union cannons fired on Fort Pulaski, 15 miles east of Savannah. They overcame the masonry fortification, but Savannah was months from occupation. In just 30 hours, Union forces had captured Pulaski, marking the end of building forts to ward off attacks from the North.

With its port blockaded by the Union, Savannah suffered greatly during the war. Goods were hard to come by, as Savannah had always looked to the sea for its livelihood. But the city endured bravely, with both men and women aiding the war effort.

Except for a few skirmishes and the bombardment of Charleston in 1863, the Carolinas and Georgia escaped heavy fighting until May 1864, when Union General Ulysses S. Grant told General William Tecumseh Sherman to "get into the interior of the enemy's country as far as you can, inflicting all the damage you can against their war resources." Thus began Sherman's famous March to the Sea, the world's first modern example of total war waged against a civilian population. Savannah was the final target.

Sherman fought his way south from Chattanooga, Tennessee, to Atlanta, a key railroad junction, which the Confederates evacuated on September 1, 1864. Leaving Atlanta burning, he departed for the sea on October 17, cutting a 60-mile path of destruction across central and eastern Georgia. "We have devoured the land, and our animals eat up the wheat and corn fields close," Sherman reported. "All the people retire before us, and desolation is behind. To realize what war is, one should follow our tracks." Despite his orders, looting and pillaging were rampant, but there were few attacks on civilians and none against women.

Sherman arrived at Savannah on December 10, in time to make the port city a Christmas present to Lincoln. (Fortunately, he did not burn the city.) In January 1865, he turned northward into South Carolina. He torched 80 square blocks of Columbia in February. Confederate General Joseph E. Johnston made several attempts to slow Sherman's advance. One such attempt was the Battle of Rivers Bridge, between Allendale and Erhardt, South Carolina, in February; the last was the Battle of Bentonville, near Durham in central North Carolina, in March. On April 26, 2 weeks after General Robert E. Lee

surrendered to Grant at Appomattox Courthouse in Virginia, Johnston met Sherman at Durham and handed over his sword. The war in
the Carolinas and Georgia was over.

SCALAWAGS, CARPETBAGGERS & JIM CROW

The Confederate survivors straggled home to face Reconstruction. At
first, Confederate war veterans dominated the state legislatures in
Georgia. They enacted so-called black code laws, which gave some
rights to the newly freed slaves but denied them the vote. This and
other actions infuriated the Republicans who controlled the U.S.
Congress and wanted to see the South punished for its rebellion. In
1867, Congress passed the Reconstruction Act, which gave blacks the
right to vote and divided the South into five districts, each under a
military governor who had near-dictatorial powers. Approximately
20,000 federal troops were sent to the South to enforce the act.

Recalcitrant white officials were removed from state office, and
with their new vote, the ex-slaves helped elect Republican legislatures,
and many blacks won seats. Despite doing some good work, these
legislatures were corrupt. They enacted high taxes to pay for rebuilding and social programs, further alienating the struggling white population.

White Georgians also complained bitterly about "scalawags" (local
whites who joined the Republican Party) and "carpetbaggers" (North-
erners who came South carrying all their possessions in bags made of
carpet). The animosity led to the formation of two secret white organizations—the Knights of the White Camelia and the Knights of the
Ku Klux Klan—that engaged in terrorism to keep blacks from voting
or exercising their other new rights. The former slaves were also disappointed with the Republicans when it became obvious that they
wouldn't receive the promised "40 acres and a mule." Those who did
vote began to cast them for their former masters. Factions also devel-
oped among the local scalawags and the Northern carpetbaggers.

During Reconstruction, blacks from plantations throughout Georgia flooded into Savannah, living in poverty. For the planters, though,
cotton returned as king and would reign supreme until the arrival of
the boll weevil.

All this set the stage for whites to regain control of Georgia in
1871. By 1877, President Rutherford B. Hayes, a Republican, with-
drew federal troops from the South. Reconstruction was over.

During the next 20 years, white governments enacted Jim Crow
laws, which imposed poll taxes, literacy tests, and other requirements

intended to prevent blacks from voting. Whites flocked to the Democratic Party, which restricted its primaries—tantamount to elections throughout the South—to white voters. Blacks who did try to vote faced having the Ku Klux Klan burn crosses on their lawns, or even being lynched. Indeed, "strange fruit" hung from many Southern trees during this period.

Racial segregation became a legal fact of life, from the public drinking fountains to the public schools. The U.S. Supreme Court ratified the scheme in its 1896 *Plessy vs. Ferguson* decision, declaring "separate but equal" public schools to be constitutional. Black schools in the South were hardly equal, but they surely were separate.

Throughout the 19th century, Savannah remained rigidly segregated. In 1878, the first public school for blacks was opened. That was followed in 1891 by the first public college for blacks. Educational segregation remained in place until well into the 20th century.

SAVANNAH IN THE 20TH & 21ST CENTURIES

As Savannah entered a new century, things were looking up. The city was economically powerful, with its ships fanning out to take Georgia exports such as lumber around the world. Then Savannah's men marched off to World War I.

Upon their return, economic devastation set in. The boll weevil attacked the cotton fields in the Low Country plantations around Savannah. King Cotton was dethroned. If that weren't enough, America entered a grave Depression during the Hoover era.

The Democrats remained supreme in Savannah, and racial segregation was a way of life. The city's economy was helped when the Eighth Air Force was founded outside Savannah, restoring some vigor to a sagging economy.

But Savannah was literally falling apart. Its historic buildings were being torn down or left to rot. Finally, in 1955, a group of determined ladies saved the historic Davenport House from the wrecking ball, and Savannah began to take preservation seriously.

Savannah took a back seat in the civil rights movement of the 1950s. The drama, for the most part, was centered in Atlanta, under the leadership of Martin Luther King, Jr.

As late as 1959 and 1960, segregation in Savannah was firmly entrenched and backed by official state law. Unlike much of the more rural South, however, Savannah had a more progressive attitude regarding race relations. Even before the surge of the civil rights movement, there was relative tolerance between the races, as African Americans slowly integrated themselves into the city's social fabric.

Local leaders urged the city to face its problems of race relations with decency and dignity—and without hate. By 1961, Savannah was desegregating its public schools.

In May 1981, antiques dealer Jim Williams shot his lover-assistant, a hustler named Danny Hansford, 21. As a result, through a complicated legal process, Williams became the first person in Georgia to be tried four times for murder before he was finally acquitted.

The case could have slipped into history as another gay murder. However, writer John Berendt drifted into town one day, became intrigued by the story, and eventually wrote his megabestseller, *Midnight in the Garden of Good and Evil.* His original agent turned down the story as too bizarre and "too regional." Buyers of books felt otherwise, and, in time, Clint Eastwood even directed the movie version.

Berendt's book put Savannah on the tourist map, and millions began to visit. Through the interest created by what is locally called "The Book," the city became a tourist attraction that started to compete with its northern neighbor, Charleston.

More recently, Savannah again made headlines when it joined with the Republicans in a sweep of Georgia in the November 2010 elections. The race for governor was particularly tight, but former congressman Nathan Deal, a Republican, beat out former governor Roy Barnes, his Democratic opponent.

---

3 SAVANNAH'S ARCHITECTURE & ART

Charleston still outclasses Savannah when it comes to art and architecture, but not by much.

The greatest collection of Savannah's evocative architecture lies in the Historic District, which you can walk around at your leisure, discovering the area's old buildings, churches, and squares. Some structures are from the Colonial era, others perhaps inspired by the Adam brothers or built in the Regency style. There are plenty of ironwork and antique buildings in brick or clapboard. Even modest townhouses from the 18th century have been restored and are now coveted addresses.

Because many of the city's residents lacked money in the final decades of the 19th century and the beginning of the 20th, antique structures were allowed to stand, whereas many American cities destroyed their heritage and replaced them with modern buildings.

By the time Savannahians got around to tearing down their old structures, a forceful preservation movement was launched—and just in time.

What you won't see, however, as you travel through the Low Country around Savannah, are a lot of plantations where cotton was king. Many of these have "gone with the wind."

THE FIRST CITY

In 1733, during the founding of Savannah, James Oglethorpe faced a daunting challenge. He not only had to secure homes for Trustees and colonists, but he also had to construct forts around the new town of Savannah to fend off possible raids, even though the local Native Americans were friendly.

Since they weren't well built and were later torn down to make way for grander structures, none of the founding fathers' little wooden homes remain today. But the town plan that Oglethorpe envisioned back in London still remains. He wanted an orderly grid composed of 24 squares. In case of rebellion, he also wanted "mustering points" where troops could gather to squelch any problems.

Nine years after the colonists arrived in port, they had enough money and building materials to construct their first church, which quickly became the most elaborate structure in town. Called "The Orphan House," the church took its name from the Bethesda Orphanage founded by the evangelist George Whitefield in 1738. Along with Oglethorpe, Whitefield believed that rum drinking caused a yellow fever–like disease but that beer drinking was acceptable. This philosophy was expounded to the congregation of Georgia's first church. Unfortunately, this landmark building no longer stands.

After the Revolutionary War, the port of Savannah began to grow rich on profits it made shipping sago powder, beef, pork, animal skins, tar, turpentine, and other exports. Money generated from this thriving trade with Europe, especially London, was poured into architecture. Grander homes began to sprout on the squares of Savannah. Still, none of these early structures equaled the glory of the rival city of Charleston. While visiting General Nathanael Greene's family, Eli Whitney invented the cotton gin in 1793, bringing even greater prosperity to the area, which led to even grander building.

Only one structure remains from this post–Revolutionary era. Built by James Habersham, Jr., in a Georgian style, it is covered in pink stucco. Underneath the stucco is a solid brick foundation. Today it is a well-recommended restaurant and bar, known as the Olde Pink House Restaurant (p. 59), open to the general public at 23 Abercorn St.

The reason so little architecture from the post–Revolutionary era survived is that a disastrous fire struck in 1796, burning block after block of the city. In 1820, another devastating fire swept over Savannah, destroying architectural gems that had been erected by builders from both Charleston and the North. The fire erupted just as an epidemic of yellow fever broke out. Thousands of slaves died from the illness, temporarily slowing down building efforts because they provided the hard labor on the construction projects. Work on rebuilding Savannah was further slowed when cholera broke out in 1834.

But through it all, Savannahians survived and prospered and continued to spend money on elaborate structures, many of which remain today, especially those constructed of brick. The Federal style—was very prevalent, as it was along many parts of America's east coast. (Federal-style architecture was created in America between 1780 and 1830, using adaptations of Greek and Roman designs.) Some builders, however, perhaps those with Loyalist hearts, preferred the Georgian style. (Georgian architecture was a neo-Palladian style, prevalent between 1720 and 1840, that often used wood and clapboards. Even columns were made of timber.) Locals also invested heavily in their churches, notably the Independent Presbyterian Church of Savannah, whose architectural beauty rivals some of the finest churches of Charleston.

THE REGENCY STYLE SWEEPS SAVANNAH

With their newfound money, Savannah's cotton planters invited an English architect named William Jay to come to Savannah in 1817. He introduced the Regency style, which became all the rage in Savannah.

Some of Jay's structures still stand today. He built public buildings and fashionable neoclassical mansions for the city's richest residents. His greatest achievement is the Owens-Thomas House, widely considered the best example of English Regency architecture in the United States. Its unique beauty and elegant design is evidenced in the round portico guarding its entrance, shuttered windows, an unusual cast-iron veranda on the south side, a stucco facade, and a black front door.

Inspired by classical buildings, the flourishing Regency style was named for King George IV, who ruled as prince regent from 1811 to 1820. The house overlooks Oglethorpe Square and was standing in 1825 to welcome the Marquis de Lafayette when he was a guest of honor in Savannah. The French war hero addressed a crowd of Savannahians from the cast-iron veranda on the south facade of the building. This landmark building was constructed largely from tabby, a concrete mixture of oyster shells, sand, and lime. The Grecian-inspired veranda on the southern facade was the first major use of cast iron in Savannah. As an architectural device, cast iron later swept the city.

Jay also designed the Telfair Mansion in a neoclassical Regency style. It was constructed in 1818 for Alexander Telfair, the scion of Edward Telfair, a former Georgia governor and Revolutionary War hero. The mansion was bequeathed to the city for use as a museum, and formally opened in 1886. Many notables attended, but most of the crowd's interest focused on Jefferson Davis, the former president of the Confederacy.

The Irish-born architect Charles B. Cluskey (1808–71) arrived in Savannah in 1838 and stayed for almost a decade, becoming known for his antebellum architecture influenced by the Greek Revival style. The elite of Savannah, prospering from neighboring plantations, hired him to design their townhouses, including the Champion-McAlpin-Fowlkes house in 1844. He served as city surveyor of Savannah from 1845 to 1847, when he went to Washington with plans to renovate the White House and Capitol (few of his ideas were carried out, however).

Another antebellum architect, John Norris (1804–76), flourished in Savannah between 1846 and 1860. His most famous landmark is the Savannah Customs House, which was constructed between 1848 and 1852 in the Greek Revival style, with its mammoth portico. In the same general style, he also designed many more notable structures throughout the city, including the Andrew Low House in 1849.

A competitor of his was John B. Hogg, who hailed from South Carolina. Hogg's most notable structure is the Trinity United Methodist Church at 225 W. President St. The church was built of stucco over gray brick, the famous "Savannah grays" form of architecture. The building became known in Georgia as the "Mother Church of Methodism."

As Georgia, along with South Carolina, moved closer to the horror of the Civil War, Savannah architecture stood at the peak of its beauty and charm. A visitor from London claimed, "Savannah puts on a hell of a good show. It's not London but not bad for a colony."

WAR, RECONSTRUCTION & PRESERVATION

Unlike Atlanta, Savannah was not burned to the ground, with no Scarlett O'Hara fleeing into the night to escape the flames. Even in 1864, after all the wartime deprivation suffered by the long blockade of its port, Savannah was still a worthy gift when Sherman presented it as a Christmas present to Lincoln.

The Civil War brought poverty to most Savannahians, and the decades of Reconstruction meant the end of opulence. Oglethorpe's original town plan had stretched from 6 to 24 city squares. Renowned architects avoided building in Savannah, going to richer cities.

The famous "Savannah grays" (bricks) ceased production in the 1880s. Many buildings fell into ruin or decay. Modern structures outside the Historic District were haphazardly constructed, although the Victorian era produced some notable structures to grace the cityscape.

Just when it appeared that Savannah was going to rot away in the hot Georgia sun, the preservation movement of the 1950s came at the 11th hour. Historic Savannah was restored during the latter part of the 20th century and it now awaits your discovery in the 21st century.

THE ART OF SAVANNAH

In antebellum days, portraiture was the most common form of art in the Colonial era. Any moderately well off family commissioned rather idealized portraits of its family members, or at least the gentleman and lady of the house. Most of the portraits were either painted in oil on canvas or in watercolor. In some rare instances, the portraits were done on ivory.

The subjects of the portraits are attired in their "Sunday go-to-meeting" garb. If a setting was used as a backdrop, it was romanticized—for instance, there might have been an elegant drapery, a Grecian column, or a distant view of the ocean.

With the coming of the deprivations caused by the Civil War and the lean poverty years of the Reconstruction era, Savannah was more in survivalist mode than in the mood for painting. But slowly, Savannahians began to find time for art again, although the latest part of the 19th century produced no known national painters.

As time went on, a number of self-taught artists emerged in Savannah and the Low Country. Many of them were black, working in a folk art medium. Sometimes they painted on unpainted clapboard from some abandoned barn or other structure. The Telfair Museum (p. 74) is the major exhibition center for these self-taught artists, exhibiting Low Country art in various temporary exhibitions.

Other artists who distinguished themselves in modern times include Leonora Quarterman (1911–79), who became one of the best-known watercolorists in the South. Her silk-screen prints of coastal scenes in Savannah and Georgia are highly prized by collectors today.

Christopher P. H. Murphy (1902–69), a native of Savannah, became known for drawings that captured both the cityscape and the landscape of the Low Country coastline. His originals and reproductions still come on the market from time to time and are as sought after as those of Ms. Quarterman.

4 SAVANNAH IN POPULAR CULTURE: BOOKS, FILMS & MUSIC

BOOKS

- **Berendt, John.** *Midnight in the Garden of Good and Evil* (1994). This is the book that really put Savannah on the tourist map—with a little help from *Forrest Gump* of course. Characters such as Lady Chablis (a wickedly funny black drag queen) and Danny Hansford (a hustler) are introduced in this brilliantly conceived and seductive story of murder (or was it self-defense?) in the steamy Old South. It has been called both a travel book and a murder mystery. Berendt's book—called "The Book" in Savannah—was a bestseller, but the sappy movie of the same title, directed by Clint Eastwood, didn't fare as well with viewers.
- **Jones, Jacqueline.** *Saving Savannah* (2008). This is a meticulous re-creation of the Civil War in Georgia's rice kingdom. It documents how locals surrendered to Sherman's invading forces rather than face destruction like Atlanta. The book is the best yet to document the struggles and conflicts between blacks and whites during the tumultuous Reconstruction years.
- **Kennett, Lee.** *Marching Through Georgia* (1995). General William Tecumseh Sherman pledged "to make a trail that would be visible for 50 years"—250 miles long and 60 miles wide, from Atlanta to Savannah. This carefully researched book, the story of both soldiers and civilians, tells how he did it.
- **Silver, Murray.** *Behind the Moss Curtain and Other Great Savannah Stories* (2002). A fifth-generation Savannahian, the author gives some interesting insights into the city.

FILMS

Set in Savannah, *Forrest Gump* (1994) was a huge worldwide commercial success, winning six Oscars, including a Best Actor award for Tom Hanks. The movie tells the story of a man with an IQ of 75 and his epic journey through life. The film received rave reviews, except for a dissent here and there—*Entertainment Weekly* called it "a baby boomer version of Disney's America."

Director Clint Eastwood's *Midnight in the Garden of Good and Evil* (1997) is based on John Berendt's spectacular bestseller. Southern Gothic in tone, it depicts the fabulously eccentric personalities of Savannah, including drag queen Lady Chablis. The book is based on the actual killing of Danny Hansford, a local hustler, by art dealer Jim Williams, an event that resulted in four murder trials before a final acquittal.

With Savannah as a setting, *The Legend of Bagger Vance* (2000) is directed by Robert Redford. It stars Will Smith as Bagger Vance and Matt Damon as Rannulph Junuh, the best golfer in the city. Bagger teaches Rannulph the secret of an authentic golf stroke, which also turns out to be the secret to mastering any challenge and finding meaning in life.

Bestselling novelist John Grisham wrote the story, *The Gingerbread Man*, that director Robert Altman turned into a 1998 film. Kenneth Branagh stars as lawyer Rick Magtruder, who has a one-night stand with caterer Mallory Doss (played by Embeth Davidtz) and becomes hooked on her. For those who like strong suspense, heavy plotting, and a dark atmosphere, this one evokes the more famous *Midnight in the Garden of Good and Evil.*

In 2010, two films were shot in Savannah, including *The Conspirator*, a historical drama about the trial of Mary Surratt, the only female co-conspirator in the Abraham Lincoln assassination and the first woman to be hanged by the federal government. The film stars Robin Wright Penn and Kevin Kline. Another recent movie, shot on Tybee Island, is *The Last Song*, starring Miley Cyrus and Greg Kinnear. It's the story of a troubled teenager and her estranged father.

MUSIC

Johnny Mercer, born in Savannah in 1909, is the most famous composer to hail from the city. This noted lyricist and songwriter wrote more than 1,000 songs, many of them hits, including "Blues in the Night" and "One for My Baby."

Jazz legend **Joe Steele** is a seminal figure from the golden age of jazz in the '20s to the Big Band era. Born in 1899, Steele reached the peak of his jazz career from 1932 to 1936 when he played piano in Chick Webb's band. Some of his playing can be heard in the Smithsonian record collection titled "Big Band Jazz."

The career of **Connie Haines** (1921–2008) spanned decades of American music and 200 recordings. She was the first white artist to record for Motown Records, and she appeared before five U.S. presidents and in many films.

Called "The Lady from Savannah," **Irene Reid** (1930–2008) sings in the grand tradition of such performers as Ella Fitzgerald and Sarah Vaughn. She won fame at Harlem's Apollo Theater in 1947, and was a fixture in New York nightclubs such as the Village Gate for years. In 1961, she joined Count Basie. After touring the world with the Basie band, she formed her own group, Ms. Irene Reid & Co. Throughout her life, she appeared on the stage with some of the biggest names in show business, including Flip Wilson, Carmen McRae, Aretha Franklin, and B. B. King.

5 EATING IN SAVANNAH

Savannah is the food capital of the Georgia Low Country and the coastal Sea Islands, the site of many former rice and cotton plantations.

In recent years, Savannah chefs have moved far beyond the "grits-and-greens" type of cookery, creating fresh combinations from traditional ingredients. For example, instead of black-eyed peas cooked in bacon fat, you might get black-eyed-pea salsa. Instead of fried shrimp, you might get smoked shrimp and melon gazpacho. Instead of Southern fried chicken, you might get stuffed breast of chicken with a crabmeat-and-artichoke dressing.

COLONIAL CUISINE

Oglethorpe's Colonials found a Low Country made up of marshes and saltwater creeks. They turned to these for a harvest of shrimp and oysters. For meat, the forests were full of game such as rabbits. The Low Country also yielded marsh hens, doves, pigeons, and

Impressions

The land belongs to the women, and the corn that grows upon it; but meat must be got by the men, because it is they only that hunt. This makes marriage necessary, that the women may furnish corn and the men meat.

—James Oglethorpe on Savannah's
Native Americans (1733)

Impressions

Oh, lady, if yo' want to tas'e somethin' sweet,
Jes' take a li'l onion an' a li'l piece o' met
An' mix 'em wid yo' tender, pure, raw s'rimp.
                                    —Traditional vendor call

quail. Deer were hunted at night by torchlight. By 1800, visitors reported seeing the old City Market (since burned down) overflowing with corn, peas, okra, field greens, beets, squash, turnips, sweet potatoes, eggplant, and beans. The bean of choice was the black-eyed pea, which was African in origin. Combined with rice, it became hoppin' John. Many Savannahians still eat hoppin' John on New Year's Day. Tradition has it that it will bring them luck in the coming year.

The Colonials roasted their meat over fires on spits. Rare meat was considered not only the best tasting but the healthiest. In time, however, beginning in the 1800s, the iron kitchen range was introduced. Cooks started cooking their meat well-done, and even today many Savannahians will only eat it that way.

From the Native Americans Oglethorpe encountered when he landed, the Colonials learned how to make cornbread, which they called hoecake, pone, or dodgers. The seasoning in this first early American version of cornbread? Bear grease. For many Savannahians during the blockade of the Civil War, cornbread and milk were all they had to sustain life.

In the Savannah tradition, meat was preferred if it had "streak of lean and a streak of fat." Some early settlers liked boiled fat—not lean.

When slavery became more prevalent in the colony, many Africans introduced recipes remembered from their distant homelands. Dishes became hotter and spicier, especially with the use of red pepper.

Sometimes vendors came around from door to door (back door, that is) hawking fresh produce or seafood. The shrimp man, for example, sold fresh shrimp carried in a basket on his head.

FAVORITE SAVANNAH FOODS

The Southern love for pork was and is economical. Hogs are easier to raise than cattle, because they more or less take care of themselves by foraging for their food, and cows take longer to raise. A succulent hog can add to its body weight 150 times in just 1 year of life. Savannahians found that all parts of the hog, even the head, could be consumed.

From the hog, they smoked hams, made sausages, dried cracklings for cornbread, and saved the fat for lard, which they used in virtually every dish, most often to season greens and other vegetables. Salt pork preserved the meat during long cold winters and came in most handily during the long siege caused by the Civil War.

BBQ'd pork remains the favorite meat dish of Savannah, followed by fried chicken, of which every Southern chef has a special recipe. Beef lags are a distant third. Even today, many Savannahians do not eat lamb.

Quail is the favorite game bird of Savannah and the Low Country. In fact, it is a staple on most tables and is served grilled, stuffed, or sautéed at breakfast, lunch, or dinner.

The tomato, which is now integral to most Southern meals, from fried green tomatoes to soups, was thought to be poisonous before the Civil War. Some Savannahians believed that it had the power to act as a love potion—hence they called it the "love apple." After the Civil War, the tomato came into favor and started to appear in okra-laced gumbos, in soups, in catsup and, miracle of miracles, to be eaten raw by the most daring of diners.

Although the tomato is botanically a fruit, the Supreme Court in 1893 declared it a vegetable. At the same time, eggplants, peppers, avocados, peas, beans, cucumbers, and squash, though botanical fruit, were also ruled vegetables. All of these found favor with the diners of Savannah. A true Savannahian will eat a fresh tomato only between late May and early August.

Lima beans, sometimes cooked with okra, became the best-known beans for consumption in Savannah. Named for their place of origin, Lima, Peru, the beans became known as "butter beans" in Savannah.

Savannahians love sweet potatoes, and they're fashioned in countless dishes, with sweet-potato pancakes a favorite, especially at Sunday brunches. Southerners also take to greens, especially collards, which are almost invariably cooked in pork stock, served with cornbread used to mop up the "pot liquor."

Grits appear frequently on menus, most often at breakfast. Savannahians like to spice them up in several versions, including cheese grits.

3

Planning Your Trip to Savannah

Savannah is to Georgia what Charleston is to South Carolina—Georgia's grandest and most intriguing city to visit. According to *Travel + Leisure* magazine, it's also one of the 10 most historic cities in America.

Because the city's core is easily walkable, most visitors get the hang of navigating Savannah relatively quickly. And if you get lost, there's no need to worry about asking for directions. Even more than Charlestonians, the people of Savannah are noted for their old-fashioned Southern hospitality. You'll frequently hear them say, "Y'all come back, you hear?" In the pages that follow, we've compiled everything you need to know to handle the practical details of planning your trip. For additional details and more on-the-ground resources in Savannah, please see "Fast Facts & Websites" on p. 173.

1 GETTING THERE & AROUND

GETTING TO SAVANNAH

BY PLANE Depending on where you're coming from, many visitors fly first to **Hartsfield International Airport (ATL),** 13 miles south of downtown Atlanta off I-85 and I-285. From Atlanta, there are many connecting flights into Savannah. There are also direct flights into **Savannah/Hilton Head International Airport (SAV)** on many airlines.

Savannah/Hilton Head International Airport is about 8 miles west of downtown just off I-16. **American** (© **800/433-7300;** www. aa.com), **Delta** (© **800/221-1212;** www.delta.com), **United** (© **800/ 241-6522;** www.united.com), and **US Airways** (© **800/428-4322;** www.usairways.com) have flights from Atlanta and Charlotte, with connections from other points.

BY TRAIN Amtrak (© **800/USA-RAIL** [800/872-7245]; www. amtrak.com) has stops in Atlanta and Savannah. Be sure to ask about Amtrak's money-saving "All Aboard America" regional fares or other current fare specials. Amtrak also offers attractively priced rail-drive packages in the Carolinas and Georgia. The **train station** in Savannah is at 2611 Seaboard Coastline Dr. (© **912/234-2611**), about 4 miles southwest of downtown; cab fare into the city is around $5.

BY CAR Several major interstate highways crisscross Georgia: I-75 bisects the state from Dalton in the north to Valdosta in the south; I-95 runs north-south along the Eastern Seaboard. The major east-west routes are I-16, running between Macon and Savannah, and I-20, running from Augusta through Atlanta and into Alabama. I-85 runs northeast-southwest in the northern half of the state.

In addition to the interstates, U.S. 84 cuts across the southern part of the state from the Alabama state line through Valdosta and Way-cross, and eventually connects to I-95 south of Savannah.

The state-run welcome centers at all major points of entry are staffed with knowledgeable, helpful Georgians who can often advise you on timesaving routes. The speed limit varies from 55 to 70 mph and the seat-belt law is strictly enforced.

Here's a list of approximate mileages to Savannah from other major cities in the East: Atlanta, GA, 248 miles; Charleston, SC, 107 miles; Charlotte, NC, 252 miles; Jackson, FL, 138 miles; Richmond, VA, 467 miles; Orlando, FL, 278 miles; New York, NY, 815 miles; and Washington, DC, 579 miles.

For 24-hour road conditions, call © **800/222-4357. AAA** services are available in Savannah. The Savannah branch office of AAA is located at 712 Mall Blvd. (© **912/352-8222;** www.aaan.com; open Mon, Wed, and Fri 8:30am–5:30pm and Tues and Thurs 10am–7pm).

BY BUS Greyhound (© **800/231-2222;** www.greyhound.com) has good direct service to major cities in Georgia from out of state, including Savannah, with connections to almost any destination.

GETTING AROUND

The grid-shaped Historic District is best seen on foot. Plan on taking leisurely strolls with frequent stops in the many squares.

BY CAR Though you can reach many points of interest outside the Historic District by bus, having your own wheels is much more convenient and it's absolutely essential for sightseeing outside the city proper.

All major car-rental firms have branches in Savannah and at the airport, including **Hertz** (© **800/654-3131** or 912/964-9595 at the airport; www.hertz.com); **Avis** (© **800/831-2847;** www.avis.com), with locations at 422 Airways Ave. (© **912/964-1781**) and at 2215

Travis Field Rd. (© **912/964-0234**); and **Budget** (© **800/527-**
0700; www.budget.com), with offices at 7070 Abercorn St. (© **912/**
966-1771).

BY BUS   You'll need exact change for the $1 fare, plus $1 for a
transfer. For route and schedule information, call **Chatham Area**
Transit (CAT) at © **912/233-5767.**

BY TAXI   The base rate for taxis is $2.00, with a $1.80 additional
charge for each mile. For 24-hour taxi service, call **Adam Cab Co.** at
© **912/927-7466.**

2 NEIGHBORHOODS IN BRIEF

CITY LAYOUT

Every other street—north, south, west, and east—is punctuated by
greenery. The city's grid of 21 scenic squares was laid out in 1733 by
General James Oglethorpe, the founder of Georgia. The design—still
in use—has been called "one of the world's most revered city plans."
It's said that if Savannah didn't have its history and architecture, it
would be worth a visit just to see its layout.

Bull Street is the dividing line between east and west. On the south
side are odd-numbered buildings, and on the north side are even-
numbered buildings.

HISTORIC DISTRICT   The Historic District—the real reason to
visit Savannah—takes in both the Riverfront District and the City
Market, described below. It's bordered by the Savannah River and
Forsyth Park at Gaston Street and Montgomery and Price streets.
Within its borders are more than 2,350 architecturally and historically significant buildings in a 2½-square-mile area. About 75% of
these buildings have been restored.

RIVERFRONT DISTRICT   In this popular tourist district, River
Street borders the Savannah River. Once lined with warehouses holding King Cotton, it has experienced a massive urban renewal, and the
strip now features a row of restaurants, art galleries, shops, and bars.
The source of the area's growth was the river, which offered a prime
shipping avenue for New World goods bound for European ports. In
1818, about half of Savannah fell under quarantine during a yellow-
fever epidemic. River Street never fully recovered and fell into disre-
pair until its rediscovery in the mid-1970s. The urban-renewal project
stabilized the downtown and revitalized the Historic District. Stroll
the bluffs along the river on the old passageway of alleys, cobblestone
walkways, and bridges known as Factors Walk.

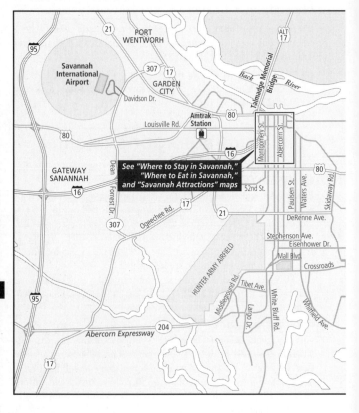

See "Where to Stay in Savannah," "Where to Eat in Savannah," and "Savannah Attractions" maps

CITY MARKET Two blocks from River Street and bordering the Savannah River, the City Market was the former social and business mecca of Savannah. Since the late 18th century, it has endured fires and various devastations, including the threat of demolition. But in a major move, the city of Savannah decided to save the district. Today, former decaying warehouses are filled with restaurants and shops offering everything from antiques to collectibles, including many Savannah-made products. Every cuisine from seafood and pizza to French and Italian cuisine is served here. Live music often fills the nighttime air. Some of the best jazz in the city is presented here in various clubs. The market lies at Jefferson and West Julian streets, bordered by Franklin Square on its western flank and Ellis Square on its eastern side.

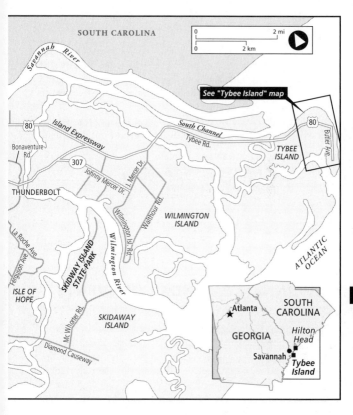

VICTORIAN DISTRICT   The Victorian District, south of the Historic District, holds some of the finest examples of post–Civil War architecture in the Deep South. The district is bordered by Martin Luther King Jr. Boulevard and by East Broad, Gwinnett, and Anderson streets. Houses in the district are characterized by gingerbread trim, stained-glass windows, and imaginative architectural details like Gothic towers. In all, the district encompasses an area of nearly 50 blocks, spread across some 165 acres. The entire district was added to the National Register of Historic Places in 1974. Most of the two-story homes are wood frame and were constructed in the late 1800s on brick foundations. The district, overflowing from the historic inner core, became the first suburb of Savannah.

3 WHEN TO GO

CLIMATE

Judging by the average high and low temperatures in Savannah, Low Country coastal areas tend to be warmer year-round than farther inland. Winter temperatures seldom drop below freezing. Spring and fall are the longest seasons, and the wettest months are December to April.

Spring is a spectacular time to visit Savannah. Many areas become a riot of color as azaleas, dogwoods, and camellias burst into bloom.

Savannah Average Temperatures & Rainfall

	Jan	Feb	Mar	Apr	May	June	July	Aug	Sept	Oct	Nov	Dec
High (°F)	60	62	70	78	84	89	91	90	85	78	70	62
High (°C)	16	17	21	26	29	32	33	32	29	26	21	17
Low (°F)	38	41	48	55	63	69	72	72	68	57	57	41
Low (°C)	3	5	9	13	17	21	22	22	20	14	14	5
Rain (in.)	3.6	3.2	3.8	3.0	4.1	5.7	6.4	7.5	4.5	2.4	2.2	3.0

SAVANNAH CALENDAR OF EVENTS

FEBRUARY

Georgia Days Colonial Faire and Muster. Georgians turn out to celebrate the founding of their colony in Savannah on February 12, 1733, by James Oglethorpe. Various events are staged, including costumed demonstrators depicting skills used by the early settlers. Tickets cost $2 for adults and $1 for children. Call © 912/651-2125 or go to www.georgiahistory.com for more information. First Saturday and Sunday in February.

Savannah Irish Festival. This Irish heritage celebration promises fun for the entire family, with music, dancing, and food. There's a children's stage and a main stage. Contact the Irish Committee of Savannah at © 912/604-8298 or go to www.savannahirish.org for more information. Mid-February.

MARCH

St. Patrick's Day Celebration on the River. The river flows green and so does the beer in one of the largest celebrations held on River Street each year. Enjoy live entertainment, lots of food, and tons of fun. Contact the Savannah Waterfront Association at © 912/234-0295 or visit www.riverstreetsavannah.com for more information. St. Patrick's Day weekend.

Savannah Music Festival. Featuring everything from indigenous music from the South to world premieres, this annual music festival attracts fans from all over America. Chamber music and even ballet troupes perform before appreciative audiences. For more information, call © **912/234-3378** or visit www.savannahmusic festival.org. Begins mid-March.

The Savannah Tour of Homes & Gardens. During this annual festival, now more than 70 years old, each day a different district of historic Savannah is featured on a tour, including private homes and gardens not available to visitors the rest of the year. For more information, call © **912/234-8054** or visit www.savannahtour ofhomes.org. Mid-March.

MAY

Memorial Day at Old Fort Jackson. The commemoration includes a flag-raising ceremony and a memorial service featuring "Taps." Contact the Coastal Heritage Society at © **912/651-6840** or visit www.chsgeorgia.org for more information. Late May.

JUNE

Juneteenth. This event highlights the contributions of more than 200,000 African Americans who fought for their freedom and the freedom of future generations. This event is a celebration of the Emancipation Proclamation. Although this promise of freedom was announced in January, it was not until the middle of June (actual date unknown) that the news reached Savannah, thus prompting the remembrance of "Juneteenth." For more information, contact the Savannah Convention & Visitors Bureau at © **877/728-2662** or visit www.savannahvisit.com. Mid-June.

SEPTEMBER

Savannah Jazz Festival. This festival features national and local jazz and blues legends. A jazz brunch and music at different venues throughout the city are among the highlights. For details, call © **912/525-5050** or visit www.savannahjazzfestival.org. Late September.

NOVEMBER

Cane Grinding and Harvest Festival. More than 75 craftspeople from four states sell and demonstrate their art at this annual festival. Music is provided by the Savannah Folk Music Society. Contact Oatland Island at © **912/395-1212** or go to www. oatlandisland.org for more information. Mid-November.

DECEMBER

Christmas 1864. Fort Jackson hosts the dramatic re-creation of its evacuation on December 20, 1864. More than 60 Civil War reenactors play the part of Fort Jackson's Confederate defenders, who were preparing to evacuate ahead of Union General William Tecumseh Sherman. Contact Old Fort Jackson at (✆ **912/232-3945** or go to www.chsgeorgia.org/jackson/home.htm for more information. Early December.

Holiday Tour of Homes. The doors of Savannah's historic homes are opened to the public during the holiday season. Each home is decorated, and a different group of homes is shown every day. Contact the Savannah Downtown Neighborhood Association at (✆ **912/236-8362** or visit www.dnaholidaytour.net for more information. Early December.

4 MONEY & COSTS

You won't have any problem finding ATMs that are connected to the major national networks. For specific locations of **Cirrus** machines, call (✆ **800/424-7787** or go to www.mastercard.com; for the **PLUS** network, visit www.visa.com.

What Things Cost in Savannah	US$
Taxi from Savannah airport to downtown	25.00
One-way bus fare	1.00
Double room at AVIA Savannah (expensive)	179.00
Double room at the River Street Inn (moderate)	139.00
Double room at Bed & Breakfast Inn (inexpensive)	99.00
Lunch for one at Outback Steakhouse (moderate)	15.00
Lunch for one at Clary's Café (inexpensive)	12.00
Dinner for one, without wine, at 700 Drayton (very expensive)	50.00
Dinner for one, without wine, at the Pirates' House (moderate)	17.00
Dinner for one, without wine, at Wall's (inexpensive)	15.00
Bottle of beer	4.00
Coca-Cola	2.00
Cup of coffee in a cafe	2.50
Admission to Telfair Mansion and Art Museum	15.00
Movie ticket	10.00
Theater ticket to Savannah Theater	33.00

If you run out of funds on the road, you can have a friend or relative send you some money through **MONEYGRAM,** www.moneygram. com, which allows you to transfer funds from one person to another in less than 10 minutes from thousands of locations. An American Express phone representative will give you the names of four or five offices nearby.

---

5 SPECIALIZED TRAVEL RESOURCES

TRAVELERS WITH DISABILITIES Many hotels and restaurants in Georgia provide easy access for persons with disabilities, and some display the international wheelchair symbol in their brochures. However, it's always a good idea to call ahead.

The **Governor's Developmental Disabilities Council** (✆ 888/ 275-4233 or 404/657-2126) may also be of help. The Georgia Department of Industry, Trade & Tourism publishes a guide, *Georgia on My Mind,* that lists attractions and accommodations with access for persons with disabilities. To receive a copy, contact **Tour Georgia,** 75 5th St., Technology Sq., Atlanta, GA 30308 (✆ 800/VISIT-GA [847-4842], ext. 1903; www.exploregeorgia.org).

For transportation within Georgia, individuals with disabilities can contact **Handicapped Driver Services** (✆ 877/437-8267 or 457-9851; www.hdsvans.com) or **Wheelchair Getaways, Inc.** (✆ 800/ 642-2042; www.wheelchairgetaways.com).

Amtrak (✆ 800/USA-RAIL [872-7245]; www.amtrak.com), with 24 hours' notice, provides porter service, special seating, and a substantial discount.

Many travel agencies offer customized tours and itineraries for travelers with disabilities. **Flying Wheels Travel** (✆ 877/451-5006 or 507/451-5005; www.flyingwheelstravel.com) offers escorted tours and cruises that emphasize sports and private tours in minivans with lifts. **Access-Able Travel Source** (✆ 303/232-2979; www.access-able. com) offers extensive access information and advice for those with disabilities traveling around the world. **Accessible Journeys** (✆ 800/ 846-4537 or 610/521-0339; www.disabilitytravel.com) caters specifically to slow walkers and wheelchair travelers and their families and friends.

Organizations that offer travel assistance to people with disabilities include **MossRehab** (✆ 800/225-5667; www.mossresourcenet.org), which provides a library of accessible-travel resources online; and **SATH** (Society for Accessible Travel & Hospitality; ✆ 212/447-7284; www.sath.org; annual membership $45 adults, $30 seniors and students), which offers a wealth of travel resources for people with all types of disabilities and informed recommendations on destinations, access guides, travel agents, tour operators, vehicle rentals, and companion services. **AirAmbulanceCard.com** is now partnered with SATH and allows you to pre-select top-notch hospitals in case of an emergency. The **American Foundation for the Blind (AFB;** ✆ **800/ 232-5463;** www.afb.org), is a referral resource for the blind or visually impaired that includes information on traveling with Seeing Eye dogs.

For more on organizations that offer travel resources to people with disabilities, go to **www.frommers.com**.

LGBT TRAVELERS Homophobia is rampant in "red state" Georgia, which does not approve, according to voter turnout, of same-sex marriage. Nor does it approve, in the words of one gay bartender, "of homosexuals in general." That said, Savannah and Atlanta are the most gay-friendly places to travel in Georgia. Even so, open displays of affection between same-sex couples may be met with glares of hostility.

The **International Gay and Lesbian Travel Association (IGLTA;** ✆ **954/630-1637;** www.iglta.org) is the trade association for the gay and lesbian travel industry and offers an online directory of gay- and lesbian-friendly travel businesses; go to their website and click "Travel."

SENIOR TRAVEL Nearly all major U.S. hotel and motel chains now offer a senior discount, so ask for the reduction *when you make the reservation;* there may be restrictions during peak days. When you check in, be sure to have proof of your age (a driver's license or passport, for example). Among the chains that offer the best discounts are **Marriott Hotels** (✆ **800/228-9290;** www.marriott.com) for those 62 and older and **La Quinta Inns & Suites** (✆ **800/753-3757;** www.lq.com) for ages 55 and older.

AARP, 601 E. St. NW, Washington, DC 20049 (✆ **888/687-2277;** www.aarp.org), is an organization for seniors that offers a wide variety of travel benefits.

FAMILY TRAVEL The Savannah Convention & Visitors' Bureau offers, without charge, their 115-page *Savannah Travel Planner* that's loaded with ideas about how to effectively choreograph a trip to Savannah. A subsection of this travel planner, "Savannah for Kids," places special emphasis on the museums and Tybee Island beach-oriented destinations that children love. Look for insights into family-friendly approaches to local forts, historic sites, wetland and wildlife refuges, and museums in and around the city. The brochure also includes maps scaled for both pedestrians and motorists as well as information about tours, events, and attractions. You can pick up a copy of this planning guide at the Savannah Convention & Visitors' Bureau, 301 Martin Luther King Jr. Blvd., Savannah, GA 31401; by calling **877/728-2662;** or by visiting www.savannahvisit.com.

Where to Stay in Savannah

The undisputed stars of Savannah lodging are the small inns in the Historic District, most in restored homes that have been renovated with modern conveniences while retaining their original charm. Staying in one of these converted historic properties is sure to enhance your visit.

Savannah's hotel and B&B rates are like the weather—subject to change. High season is from April to October. You will find that the cheapest rates will usually be on weekdays during low season, which is January, February, and sometimes late August. The price ranges listed below include both high and low seasons. Very expensive hotels often have some smaller, more moderately priced units. It always pays to ask.

1 ALONG THE RIVERFRONT

EXPENSIVE

AVIA Savannah Hotel ★★★ This is the best boutique hotel in town. Set in a building that used to churn out copies of the old *Savannah Daily News*, today the space is devoted to "the art of living well," and it lives up to its motto. Public rooms are filled with "plunder," including chandeliers rescued from a Victorian mansion about to be demolished. The magnet is the second-floor pool deck where some of the best bodies in Savannah can be seen sprawled on Gullah-style wicker furniture. The bedrooms—called "private enclaves" here—are ultra streamlined, almost to the point of severity, with crisp linens on lush beds, plus bathrooms with walk-in showers, soaking tubs, and designer toiletries. It's almost as if Philippe Starck designed the rooms (he didn't). An Italian visitor pronounced the wine bar *molto romantico*, and we concur.

14 Barnard St., Savannah, GA 31401. ☎ **866/644-2842** or 912/233-2116. www.aviahotels.com. 151 units. $179–$209 double; $199–$289 suite. AE, DISC, MC, V. Parking $16–$20. **Amenities:** Wine bar; concierge; fitness center; room service (at night only). *In room:* A/C, TV, hair dryer, minibar, MP3 docking station, Wi-Fi (free).

AVIA Savannah Hotel **3**
The Azalea Inn **27**
Ballastone Inn **16**
Bed & Breakfast Inn **22**
Catherine Ward House Inn **29**
Dresser Palmer House **24**
East Bay Inn **10**
Eliza Thompson House **21**
Foley House Inn **17**
Forsyth Park Inn **26**
Four Points by Sheraton Historic
  Savannah **2**
The Gastonian **23**
Hamilton-Turner Inn **20**

Hampton Inn Historic District **11**
Hilton Savannah DeSoto **19**
Hyatt Regency Savannah **4**
The Kehoe House **14**
The Mansion on Forsyth Park **28**
Marriott Riverfront Hotel **7**
The Marshall House **13**
The Mulberry Inn **8**
Olde Harbour Inn **6**
Planters Inn **12**
The President's Quarters **15**
The River Street Inn **5**
Staybridge Suites **9**
Thunderbird Inn **18**
The Westin Savannah Harbor
  Golf Resort & Spa **1**
Whitaker-Huntington Inn **25**

Hyatt Regency Savannah ★   There was an outcry from Savannah's historic preservation movement when this place went up in 1981. Boxy and massively bulky, it was renovated in 2007 but it still stands in unpleasant contrast to the restored warehouses flanking it along the legendary banks of the Savannah River. Today it is grudgingly accepted as one of the biggest and flashiest hotels in town. It has a soaring atrium as well as glass-sided elevators. The comfortable rooms, international and modern in their feel, feature good-sized bathrooms and some have balconies overlooking the atrium. The only downside is the fact that most rooms seem to have paper-thin walls. Prices vary according to the views—rooms without a view are quite a bargain. There is a restaurant on-site, but chances are you'll find better food by dining outside the hotel at one of the independent restaurants recommended later in this book (see the "Where to Eat in Savannah" chapter).

2 W. Bay St., Savannah, GA 31401. ℂ **800/223-1234** or 912/238-1234. Fax 912/944-3678. www.hyatt.com. 351 units. $169–$409 double; $400–$600 suite. AE, DC, DISC, MC, V. Parking $18. **Amenities:** Restaurant; bar; exercise room; indoor pool; room service. *In room:* A/C, TV, hair dryer, Wi-Fi ($10 per day).

The Mansion on Forsyth Park ★★★   This is the most opulent and spectacular hotel in Savannah. Its core, known as the Kayton Family Mansion, was built in 1888 of terra-cotta bricks in a high-ceilinged, neo-Romanesque style. This place is more like a (tasteful) version of a Las Vegas blockbuster hotel than anything else in southeastern Georgia. Part of its allure derives from the rotating series of more than 400 paintings that sheath the walls of both the public areas and the upper hallways. Expect a plush environment with gilded cove moldings; Beaux Arts marble statues of, among others, turn-of-the-20th-century rococo goddesses at their baths; lavish antique chandeliers; and Versace copies of 19th-century French armchairs upholstered in faux zebra or leopard skin. The hotel's focal point is a courtyard and a small but artfully postmodern swimming pool. Bedrooms are avant-garde and plush, and among the most spacious in Savannah.

700 Drayton St., Savannah, GA 31401. ℂ **888/213-3671** or 912/238-5158. Fax 912/721-1123. www.mansiononforsythpark.com. 126 units. $169–$300 double; from $400 suite. AE, DC, DISC, MC, V. Parking $20. **Amenities:** Restaurant; 2 bars; exercise room; outdoor pool; room service; spa. *In room:* A/C, TV, minibar, Wi-Fi (free).

Marriott Riverfront Hotel ★   At least the massive modern bulk of this place is far enough from the 19th-century restored warehouses of River Street not to clash with them aesthetically. Towering eight stories, with an angular facade sheathed in orange-and-yellow brick, it doesn't quite succeed at being a top-rated luxury palace. Nonetheless, it attracts lots of corporate business travelers and conventions to its comfortable, modern rooms, which aren't style setters but are generous in space. The Magnolia Spa has on-site facilities.

100 General McIntosh Blvd., Savannah, GA 31401. © **800/228-9290** or 912/233-7722. Fax 912/233-3765. www.marriott.com. 397 units. $179–$259 double; from $239 suite. Children 12 and under stay free in parent's room. AE, DC, DISC, MC, V. Parking $18 per day. **Amenities:** 4 restaurants; 2 bars; exercise room; Jacuzzi; 2 pools (1 indoor); room service; spa. *In room:* A/C, TV, hair dryer, Wi-Fi ($13 per day).

The Westin Savannah Harbor Golf Resort & Spa ★ Savannah's largest hotel is in a 16-story blockbuster that rises somewhat jarringly from what were until the late 1990s sandy, scrub-covered flatlands on the swampy far side of the river. Deriving the bulk of its business from corporate groups who arrive for large conventions throughout the year, it's the largest of the four large-scale hotels that dominate the city's convention business. Yet despite a worthy collection of contemporary art that accents the labyrinth of high-ceilinged public rooms here, there's something just a bit sterile, even lifeless, about this relatively anonymous hotel. It's also quite isolated, but free cross-river shuttle ferries deposit guests into the center of the River Street bar-and-restaurant frenzy. The most elaborate guest rooms are on the two top floors and contain extras and comforts designated as Club Level. Otherwise, rooms are comfortable but bland.

1 Resort Dr. (PO Box 427), Savannah, GA 31421. © **800/WESTIN-1** (800/937-8461) or 912/201-2000. Fax 912/201-2001. www.westinsavannah.com. 403 units. $249–$419 double; from $450 suite. AE, DC, DISC, MC, V. From I-95 and Savannah International Airport, take exit 17A to I-16 toward Savannah. Follow sign for Rte. 17–Talmadge Bridge. Take the Hutchinson Island exit onto Resort Dr. Resort fee of $20 covers parking and the Internet. **Amenities:** 4 restaurants; 3 bars; babysitting; exercise room; 18-hole golf course; Internet (included in resort fee; see above); Jacuzzi; outdoor pool; room service; sauna. *In room:* A/C, TV, hair dryer, minibar.

MODERATE

Olde Harbour Inn ★ The interior of this place is well furnished and the neighborhood has been gentrified, but you still get a whiff of riverfront seediness as you approach from Factors Walk. The building was constructed in 1892 as a warehouse for oil, and its masonry bulk is camouflaged with shutters, awnings, and touches of wrought iron. Inside, a labyrinth of passages leads to small but comfortable suites, many of which reveal the building's massive timbers and structural iron brackets and offer views of the river. Some decors feature the original brick, painted white. Each unit contains a well-maintained bathroom along with its own kitchen—useful for an extended stay.

Family-Friendly Hotels

Hampton Inn Historic District (p. 49)   One of the most appealing of the city's middle-bracket hotels, this family favorite rises on historic Bay Street. Rooms are spacious, and there's a pool and sun deck on the roof.

The Mulberry Inn (p. 47)   In the heart of the Historic District, this family hotel lets kids 17 and under stay free if they share a room with their parents. Children enjoy the pool, and cribs are provided for free.

The River Street Inn (below)   The best bet along the riverfront for families with children is this converted cotton warehouse from 1817. Large rooms make family life easier, and children 12 and under stay free. The inn also has a game room, and there are many casual restaurants just outside the front door.

Despite the overlay of chintz, you'll have a constant sense of the building's thick-walled bulk. Breakfast is the only meal served.

508 E. Factors Walk, Savannah, GA 31401. ℂ **800/553-6533** or 912/234-4100. Fax 912/233-5979. www.oldeharbourinn.com. 24 units. $129–$269 suite. Rates include continental breakfast. AE, DC, DISC, MC, V. **Amenities:** Breakfast room. *In room:* A/C, TV, hair dryer, Internet (free), kitchenette (in some).

The River Street Inn ★★ **Kids**   When Liverpool-based ships were moored on the nearby river, this building stored massive amounts of cotton produced by upriver plantations. After the boll weevil decimated the cotton industry, it functioned as an icehouse, a storage area for fresh vegetables, and the headquarters of an insurance company. Its two lowest floors, built in 1817, were made of ballast stones carried in the holds of ships from faraway England. The building was later converted into some of the most comfortable and well-managed hotel rooms in town. In 2007, the owners poured nearly $2.5 million into renovations, as part of an ongoing effort to keep this charming, well-located inn a viable competitor. If night crawls among the bars and restaurants of River Street are a priority, no other hotel is better positioned than this one.

124 E. Bay St., Savannah, GA 31401. ℂ **800/253-4229** or 912/234-6400. Fax 912/234-1478. www.riverstreetinn.com. 86 units. $139–$189 double. Children 13 and under stay free in parent's room. AE, DC, DISC, MC, V. Parking $8. **Amenities:** 2 restaurants; exercise room. *In room:* A/C, TV, hair dryer, Wi-Fi (free).

VERY EXPENSIVE

Ballastone Inn ★★   This glamorous inner-city B&B occupies a dignified 1838 building separated from the Juliette Gordon Low Birthplace (home of the founder of the Girl Scouts of America) by a well-tended formal garden; it's richly decorated with all the hardwoods, elaborate draperies, and antique furniture you'd expect. For a brief period (only long enough to add a hint of spiciness), the place functioned as a bordello *and* a branch office for the Girl Scouts (now next door). It has an elevator, unusual for Savannah B&Bs, but no closets (supposedly because they were taxed as extra rooms in the old days). It also has truly unusual furnishings—including cachepots filled with scented potpourri and art objects that would thrill the heart of any decorator. A full-service bar is tucked into a corner of what was originally a double parlor. Each suite has a Jacuzzi tub as well as a private dressing area.

14 E. Oglethorpe Ave., Savannah, GA 31401. ✆ **800/822-4553** or 912/236-1484. Fax 912/236-4626. www.ballastone.com. 16 units. $179–$335 double; $335 suite. Rates include full breakfast, afternoon tea, and evening hors d'oeuvres. AE, MC, V. Free parking. No children 15 and under. **Amenities:** Breakfast room; Jacuzzi; spa. *In room:* A/C, TV, hair dryer, Wi-Fi (free).

Four Points by Sheraton Historic Savannah ★   In the midst of Savannah's Historic District, near shop-flanked Ellis Square, this five-story, brick-fronted building is the city's most amenity-filled hotel. Featuring panoramic views of the downtown area and the Talmadge Bridge in the distance, rooms are airy and spacious. Accommodations are known for their special features such as microwave ovens, an iron and ironing board, fluffy bathrobes, hypoallergenic pillows, coffee makers, express checkouts by video, free national newspapers, deluxe bathroom amenities, rollaway beds, full-length mirrors, and cordless phones. Room choices come in three categories: standard, suite, and king-size. You can work up a sweat in the fitness center, then cool down in the pool on the roof. At night, the restaurant serves first-class American cuisine and guests often gather in the piano bar.

520 W. Bryan St., Savannah, GA 31401. ✆ **912/790-1000.** Fax 912/721-1270. www.fourpoints.com/historicsavannah. 127 units. $95–$210 double; $175–$285 suite. AE, DC, DISC, MC, V. **Amenities:** Restaurant; piano bar; exercise room; rooftop pool. *In room:* A/C, TV, fridge (in some), Wi-Fi (free).

The Gastonian ★★   One of the two or three posh B&Bs in Savannah, the Gastonian incorporates a pair of Italianate Regency buildings constructed in 1868 by the same unknown architect. Hard times began with the 1929 stock market crash—the buildings were divided into apartments for the payment of back taxes. In 1984, the Lineberger family, who were visiting from California, saw the place and fell in love with it. They poured $2 million into restoring it. Today everything is a testimonial to Victorian charm, except for a skillfully crafted serpentine bridge connecting the two buildings curving above a semitropical garden. The guest rooms are plush, comfortable, cozy, and beautifully furnished. The Gastonian has repeatedly received the AAA Four Diamond Award for excellence.

220 E. Gaston St., Savannah, GA 31401. (C) **800/322-6603** or 912/232-2869. Fax 912/232-0710. www.gastonian.com. 17 units. $179–$285 double; $295–$375 suite. Rates include full breakfast. AE, DISC, MC, V. No children 11 and under. **Amenities:** Breakfast room; lounge. In room: A/C, TV, hair dryer, Wi-Fi (free).

Hamilton-Turner Inn ★★   This is one of the most noteworthy B&Bs in Savannah, boasting a unique (and sometimes bizarre) pedigree that's unlike any other in town. It was built in 1873 for the then-astronomical price of $100,000 by a local power broker, Samuel Hamilton. Mayor of Savannah, president of the Shriners, a reputed blockade runner during the Civil War, and owner of the local electrical company, the waterworks, the icehouse, and the town's biggest "fancy goods store," Hamilton was one of the inspirations for Margaret Mitchell's character of Rhett Butler in *Gone With the Wind*. His four-story French Empire house was almost obscenely ostentatious at the time. Today, with more than 10,000 square feet, it's the largest upscale B&B (in terms of sheer square footage) in Savannah.

Most of the modern-day notoriety associated with this place comes from its portrayal, in John Berendt's *Midnight in the Garden of Good and Evil*, as the party house of Savannah's favorite rakish twosome, Joe and Mandy Odom. In 1997, the building was acquired by native Savannahians who poured money and a strong dose of respectability back into the place. Today owners Gay and Jim Dunlop, long-time innkeepers, continue to invest money in maintaining the property and continuing its legacy.

330 Abercorn St., Savannah, GA 31401. (C) **888/448-8849** or 912/233-1833. Fax 912/233-0291. www.hamilton-turnerinn.com. 17 units. $159–$279 double; $299–$369 suite. Rates include full breakfast and afternoon wine and cheese. AE, DC, DISC, MC, V. Free parking. **Amenities:** Breakfast room. In room: A/C, TV, Internet (free).

The Kehoe House ★★★   Want to spend the night in a haunted house? According to James Caskey, in *Haunted Savannah* (available in local bookstores), the Kehoe House is haunted. You can read all about it in his book, which claims that Kehoe is the only four-star haunted B&B in the South—and quite possibly all of America. For most of the 20th century, this building was a funeral parlor. In 1980, Joe Namath, a former New York Jets quarterback, purchased Kehoe and tried to turn it into a nightclub, but there was a massive outcry. On one edge of Columbia Square, the Queen Anne Mansion, built in 1892, is today a deluxe B&B filled with live bodies . . . and, allegedly, some ghosts.

123 Habersham St., Savannah, GA 31401. © **800/820-1020** or 912/232-1020. Fax 912/231-0208. www.kehoehouse.com. 13 units. $175–$215 double. Rates include full breakfast, evening tea, and hors d'oeuvres. AE, DC, DISC, MC, V. **Amenities:** Breakfast room. In room: A/C, TV, hair dryer, Wi-Fi (free).

EXPENSIVE

The Azalea Inn ★ (Finds The furnishings of this B&B are a little richer, its colors a bit more evocative, and its decor more appealingly cluttered than those of many of its nearby competitors. The setting is an Italianate house (ca. 1889) set less than 2 blocks east of Forsyth Park, within a "historically correct" garden laid out as a garden might have been in Victorian times, contrary to the modernity of its swimming pool. It was originally built for Captain Walter Coney, an army officer whose fortune derived from a then-flourishing maritime supply company. Rooms are furnished with period antiques, and each has its own distinctive Victorian-era decor. Especially appealing is the Gentleman's Parlor, a ground-floor guest room once dominated by men discussing manly things, which still carries a hint of bourbon and cigars. More frilly and feminine is the Magnolia Room, while the Cotton Exchange guest room features a massive four-poster bed and a deck overlooking the swimming pool.

217 E. Huntingdon St., Savannah, GA 31401. © **800/582-3823** or 912/236-6080. Fax 912/236-0127. www.azaleainn.com. 10 units. $199–$300 double; $275–$400 2-bedroom suite. Rates include full breakfast. AE, DISC, MC, V. **Amenities:** Outdoor pool. In room: A/C, TV, hair dryer, iron, Wi-Fi (free).

Catherine Ward House Inn ★ (Finds It isn't as spectacular or desirable as it was when it was newer, but the 2005 restoration of this house has won several civic awards, and it's so evocative of Savannah's "carpenter Gothic" Victorian revival that Clint Eastwood inserted a long, graceful shot of its exterior in *Midnight in the Garden of Good and Evil.* New paint, new wallpaper, and new floor coverings are applied every year on as-needed basis, so it maintains its original freshness and appeal. Built by a sea captain for his wife (Catherine Ward) in 1886, it's just a short walk from Forsyth Park. It also offers some of the most lavishly decorated interiors of any B&B in

Savannah, but at significantly lower prices than at better-known B&Bs a few blocks away. Leslie Larson, the owner and innkeeper, maintains a policy that discourages children 13 and under. A garden in back encourages languid sun-dappled dialogues. Each midsize guest room is richly decorated.

118 E. Waldburg St., Savannah, GA 31401. ℂ **800/327-4270** or 912/234-8564. Fax 912/231-8007. www.catherinewardhouseinn.com. 9 units. $139–$249 double. Rates include full breakfast. AE, DISC, MC, V. **Amenities:** Breakfast room. *In room:* A/C, TV, hair dryer, Wi-Fi (free).

Foley House Inn ★ In 2010, AAA granted this inn four diamonds, and year after year it receives accolades as one of the best B&Bs in the South. Decorated with all the care of a private home, this brick-sided building was constructed in 1896. Its owners doubled its size in the early 1990s by acquiring the simpler white-fronted house next door, whose pedigree predates its neighbors by half a century. All rooms are neatly furnished. The staff will regale you with tales of the original residents of both houses. Breakfast and afternoon hors d'oeuvres, tea, and cordials are served in the two houses' connected gardens. Enjoy home-baked sweets every afternoon in the parlor wing and homemade appetizers from 6 to 7pm.

14 W. Hull St., Savannah, GA 31401. ℂ **800/647-3708** or 912/232-6622. Fax 912/231-1218. www.foleyinn.com. 19 units. $199–$354 double. Rates include full breakfast, afternoon hors d'oeuvres, wine, and cordials. AE, MC, V. No children 11 and under. **Amenities:** Breakfast room. *In room:* A/C, TV, hair dryer, Wi-Fi (free).

Hilton Savannah DeSoto ★ The name of this well-managed commercial hotel still evokes a bit of glamour. Built in 1890, this hotel was for many generations the city's grandest. But after thousands of wedding receptions and debutante parties, the building was demolished in 1967 and rebuilt a year later in a bland, angular, modern format. A recent $12-million restoration included a massive overhaul of the public areas and the guest rooms, which, for the most part, are moderate in size. New beds were installed along with renewed furnishings and new plumbing fixtures. Local artwork by Savannah artists decorates the walls. Despite the absence of antique charm, many guests like this place for its polite efficiency and modernism.

15 E. Liberty St. (PO Box 8207), Savannah, GA 31401. ℂ **800/445-8667** or 912/232-9000. Fax 912/232-6018. www.desotohilton.com. 246 units. $109–$279 double; $209–$509 suite. AE, DC, DISC, MC, V. Valet parking $17; self-parking $13. **Amenities:** 2 restaurants; bar; babysitting; exercise room; room service. *In room:* A/C, TV, hair dryer Wi-Fi (free).

The Mulberry Inn ★ Kids Locals proudly point to the Mulberry as a sophisticated and surprisingly elegant hotel. Built in 1868 as a stable and cotton warehouse, the previously derelict building was converted in 1982 into a simple hotel, and in the 1990s it received a radical upgrade and a dash of decorator-inspired Chippendale glamour. Today its lobby looks like that of a grand hotel in London, and the rooms, though small, have a formal decor (think of an English country house with a Southern accent). The hotel's brick-covered patio, with fountains, trailing ivy, and wrought-iron furniture, evokes the best aspects of New Orleans.

601 E. Bay St., Savannah, GA 31401. ℂ **877/468-1200** or 912/238-1200. Fax 912/236-2184. www.savannahhotel.com. 145 units. $99–$309 double. Children 17 and under stay free in parent's room. AE, DC, DISC, MC, V. Parking $12. **Amenities:** Restaurant; exercise room; Jacuzzi; outdoor pool; room service; Wi-Fi (free). *In room:* A/C, TV, fridge, hair dryer.

The President's Quarters ★ This hotel combines the coziness of a B&B with the advantages of a small and elegant inn. Labyrinthine hallways wind through two interconnected 1850s-era brick-built town houses whose modern-day gazebo and walled garden jut out into Oglethorpe Square. Laid out in 1742, this square is not only historic, but arguably the city's most beautiful, peaceful oasis. This is the only B&B in Savannah with enough on-site parking for all of its guests, and with a working fireplace in every room. Each room is named after a U.S. president. Breakfast is a big deal here, served in a somewhat cramped dining room with old-fashioned accessories. Complimentary wine and hors d'oeuvres are presented every evening between 5:30 and 6:30pm.

225 E. President St., Savannah, GA 31401. ℂ **800/233-1776** or 912/233-1600. Fax 912/238-0849. www.presidentsquarters.com. 16 units. $189–$239 double; $329 suite. AE, DC, MC, V. Free parking. **Amenities:** Breakfast room. *In room:* A/C, TV, hair dryer, minibar (in suite), Wi-Fi (free).

Whitaker-Huntingdon Inn ★ This historic house was built in 1883 for a member of the eight-man Confederate delegation that surrendered the city of Savannah to General Sherman in December 1864. Later, a local cotton merchant who served a 4-year term as the city's mayor owned it. In 1923, the doctor who was using the house as the base for his medical practice added an all-brick addition onto its backside. Today, the restored interior boasts 12-foot ceilings, period antiques, Oriental carpets, and pine floors—all gracefully arranged in a look that's faithful to the original decorative theme but much more comfortable than it was in the building's original days.

Book early if you want to stay here: There are just two two-bedroom suites available, one with one bathroom and the other with two; both have kitchenettes. There's also allegedly a resident ghost on site.

601 Whitaker St., Savannah, GA 31401. © **877/232-8911** or 912/232-8911. Fax 912/772-6292. www.whinn.com. 2 units. $130–$175 double. Rates include continental breakfast. AE, DISC, MC, V. **Amenities:** Breakfast room. *In room:* TV, kitchenette, Wi-Fi (free).

MODERATE

Dresser Palmer House To create this building, two separate houses sharing an Italianate facade were lavishly restored and reunified in 1997. It continues to be exceptionally well maintained. Notably, this place now has the city's longest and most stately front porch (called a gallery in Savannah) and inner ceilings that are almost dizzyingly high. Each guest room is beautifully furnished, and most are equipped with a well-maintained bathroom containing a tub/shower combination. The breakfasts are social events, each featuring a different dish, like curried eggs or Southern grits casserole. Wine and cheese are served daily from 5:30 to 7pm.

211 E. Gaston St., Savannah, GA 31401. © **800/671-0716** or 912/238-3294. www.dresserpalmerhouse.com. 16 units. $169–$319 double. AE, DISC, MC, V. **Amenities:** Breakfast room. *In room:* A/C, TV, Wi-Fi (free).

East Bay Inn Though the views from its windows might be uninspired, the East Bay Inn is near the bars and attractions of the riverfront. It was built in 1853 as a cotton warehouse, but green awnings and potted geraniums now disguise the building's once-utilitarian design. A cozy lobby contains Chippendale furnishings and elaborate moldings. The guest rooms have queen-size four-poster beds and reproductions of antiques. The inn frequently houses tour groups from Europe and South America, and its midafternoon tea, wine, and cheese offerings are a highly visible social ritual. In the cellar is **Skyler's** (© **912/232-3955**), an independently managed restaurant specializing in European and Asian cuisine. The entire building is strictly nonsmoking.

225 E. Bay St., Savannah, GA 31401. © **800/500-1225** or 912/238-1225. Fax 912/232-2709. www.eastbayinn.com. 28 units. $159–$259 double. Rates include continental breakfast. AE, DC, DISC, MC, V. **Amenities:** Breakfast room. *In room:* A/C, TV, hair dryer, Wi-Fi (free).

Eliza Thompson House ★★ Many newer and less well-funded B&Bs attempt to re-create this inn's patina of historicity (ca. 1847), often with less success. It's set on a distinguished tree-lined street whose weather-beaten cobblestones demonstrate their long-ago craftsmanship. The wrought-iron accents and meticulously maintained details of its shutter-accented facade imply enormous care on the part of its owners. And inside, high ceilings, elaborate cove moldings, and well-chosen antiques imply a mixture of genteel propriety and discrete romance. Historical references abound within rich but understated interiors, and decorator wannabes often salivate at the ideas they garner for historical projects of their own. About half the rooms in this stately looking inn are within the main house; the other half lie within a much-restored and very tasteful building in back that was originally conceived as a stable and carriage house. Linking the two buildings is one of the largest and most lavishly landscaped courtyards in the city's historic core. In the words of a writer from *Georgia Magazine*, "Like its namesake, the Eliza Thompson House is a hospitable hostess."

5 W. Jones St., Savannah, GA 31401. (℗ **800/348-9378** or 912/236-3620. Fax 912/238-1920. www.elizathompsonhouse.com. 25 units. $139–$200 double. Rates include continental breakfast. AE, DC, DISC, MC, V. **Amenities:** Breakfast room; lounge. *In room:* A/C, TV, hair dryer.

Forsyth Park Inn ★ One of the grandest buildings on the western flank of Forsyth Park is this frame house built in the 1890s by a sea captain (Aaron Flynt, also known as Rudder Churchill). A richly detailed staircase winds upstairs from a paneled vestibule, and the Queen Anne decor of the formal salon extends through the rest of the place. Guest rooms have oak paneling and oversize doors that are testimonials to turn-of-the-20th-century craftsmanship. The more expensive guest rooms, including one in what used to be the dining room, are among the largest in town. Home-baked breads and pastries are staples at breakfast.

102 W. Hall St., Savannah, GA 31401. (℗ **866/670-6800** or 912/233-6800. Fax 912/233-6804. www.forsythparkinn.com. 11 units, 1 cottage with kitchenette. $195–$295 double; $245 cottage. Rates include full breakfast. AE, DISC, MC, V. **Amenities:** Breakfast room. *In room:* A/C, TV, Internet (free).

Hampton Inn Historic District (Kids) This is one of the most appealing of the city's middle-bracket large-scale hotels. Opened in 1997, it rises seven redbrick stories above the busy traffic of historic Bay Street, across from Savannah's Riverwalk and some of the city's most animated nightclubs. Its big-windowed lobby was designed to mimic an 18th-century Savannah salon, thanks to the recycling of heart pine flooring from an old sawmill in central Georgia and the use of antique Savannah bricks. Comfortably formal seating arrangements, a blazing fireplace, and an antique bar add cozy touches. The guest rooms are simple and comfortable, with wall-to-wall carpeting, midsize tiled bathrooms, and flowered upholstery. On the roof are a small pool and a sun deck supplemented by an exercise room on the seventh floor. There's no restaurant, but many eateries are a short walk away.

201 E. Bay St., Savannah, GA 31401. © **800/426-7866** or 912/721-1600. Fax 912/721-1610. www.hampton-inn.com. 154 units. $107–$249 double. AE, DC, DISC, MC, V. Parking $8. **Amenities:** Breakfast room; rooftop pool; Wi-Fi (free). *In room:* A/C, TV, hair dryer.

The Marshall House Some aspects of this hotel—especially the second-story cast-iron veranda—might remind you of a 19th-century hotel in the French Quarter of New Orleans. It originally opened in 1851 as the then-finest hotel in Savannah. In 1864 and 1865, it functioned as a Union army hospital before housing such luminaries as Conrad Aiken and Joel Chandler Harris, author of *Stories of Uncle Remus*. After a ratty-looking decline, it closed—some people thought permanently—in 1957. In 1999, it reopened as a "boutique-style" inn. Much attention and detail have gone into the bedrooms. Room size varies depending on the accommodations, but all have king-size beds (or twins), updated plumbing, flatscreen LCD TVs, in-room safes, dual-line phones, custom-designed nightstands, a writing desk, tea- and coffee-making service, and luxurious bathrooms. Seven of the largest and most historically evocative rooms in the hotel are on the second floor, overlooking noisy Broughton Street, and feature wrought-iron verandas with wrought-iron furniture. The bar has exposed brick, a very Southern clientele, and green leather upholstery. **45 Bistro,** (© **912/234-3111**), set beneath the glassed-in roof of what used to be the hotel's rear stable yard, serves Southern and international cuisine.

123 E. Broughton St., Savannah, GA 31401. © **800/589-6304** or 912/644-7896. Fax 912/234-3334. www.marshallhouse.com. 68 units. $109–$219 double; $249–$279 suite. Rates include continental breakfast. AE, DC, DISC, MC, V. **Amenities:** Restaurant; bar. *In room:* A/C, TV, hair dryer, Wi-Fi (free).

Planters Inn This small European-style inn is more businesslike than the average Savannah B&B. Built adjacent to Reynolds Square in 1912 as a seven-story brown brick tower, it boasts a lobby with elaborate millwork and a scattering of Chippendale reproductions. The guest rooms are comfortably outfitted with four-poster beds and flowery fabrics; they're rather dignified and formal. Each contains a neatly kept bathroom with a tub/shower combination. The Planters Inn isn't associated with the highly recommended Planters Tavern, which stands next door.

29 Abercorn St., Savannah, GA 31401. © **800/554-1187** or 912/232-5678. Fax 912/232-8893. www.plantersinnsavannah.com. 59 units. $119–$239 double. Rates include continental breakfast and evening wine reception. AE, DC, MC, V. Parking $14. **Amenities:** Breakfast room. *In room:* A/C, TV, hair dryer, Wi-Fi (free).

Staybridge Suites ★★ The five-story antique brick walls of this hotel originally housed a pickle factory and cannery in the 19th century; later it was an auto repair shop. Today it boasts one of the city's most striking fireplaces, deep sofas, and lots of exposed wood, evoking the lobby of a ski lodge in Vermont. Rooms are medium size but well furnished, nicely upholstered, and quite appealing, outfitted with formal, Queen Anne–inspired reproductions and thick carpeting. Each room has a writing table built into one corner and a full kitchen with stovetop, microwave, and refrigerator. It's the kind of setup where a traveling salesman could establish a headquarters during an extended business trip. Frankly, if you have even a hint of claustrophobia, you'll be happiest in a room with a bona fide window, rather than one that overlooks a narrow interior atrium (about a third of the rooms are set up this way). But then again, if you appreciate calm and quiet, artificial lighting, and a sense of hermetically sealed, climate-controlled regularity, you might like one of the interior units just fine.

301 E. Bay St., Savannah, GA 31401. ℭ **800/225-1237** or 912/721-9000. Fax 912/721-9019. www.ichotelsgroup.com. 104 units. $139–$349 double. Rates include continental breakfast. AE, DC, MC, V. **Amenities:** TV lounge. *In room:* A/C, TV, kitchen, Wi-Fi (free).

INEXPENSIVE

Bed & Breakfast Inn ★ Value Adjacent to Chatham Square, in the oldest part of historic Savannah, this dignified stone-fronted town house was built in 1853. You climb a gracefully curved front stoop to reach the cool, high-ceilinged interior, outfitted with a combination of antique furniture and reproductions. The good-size bedrooms inside are up to date and tastefully furnished. For more privacy, guests can opt for a few choice rooms in one of the old carriage houses, which have been converted into romantic cottages. They're decorated in plantation style, with four-poster beds and 19th-century ceramics and artwork. All the private bathrooms contain new plumbing, and there's access to peaceful gardens and courtyard areas. Thoughtful extras include warm chocolate chip cookies and cold milk in the evening.

117 W. Gordon St. (at Chatham Sq.), Savannah, GA 31401. ℭ **888/238-0518** or 912/238-0518. Fax 912/233-2537. www.savannahbnb.com. 18 units. $99–$209 double. Rates include full breakfast. AE, DISC, MC, V. **Amenities:** Breakfast room. *In room:* A/C, TV, hair dryer, Wi-Fi (in some; free).

Fairfield Inn by Marriott This reliable budget hotel offers basic but comfortable guest rooms with large desks and well-kept bathrooms. Health-club privileges are available nearby, as are several good, moderately priced restaurants.

2 Lee Blvd. (at Abercorn Rd.), Savannah, GA 31405. ☎ **800/228-2800** or 912/353-7100. Fax 912/355-5290. www.marriott.com. 135 units. $99–$129 double. Rates include continental breakfast. Children 17 and under stay free in parent's room. AE, DC, DISC, MC, V. Free parking. **Amenities:** Breakfast room; outdoor pool; smoke-free rooms. *In room:* A/C, TV, hair dryer, Wi-Fi (free).

Thunderbird Inn (Value) Although it's within a 5-minute walk from the edge of Savannah's Historic District, the Sputnik-era architecture of this hip hotel makes it seem a world away. Originally built in 1964, it had degenerated into a sun-beaten relic—like something you'd expect to find along a dusty stretch of Route 66—until a radical overhaul turned its former seediness into something more campy cool. Expect bright, geometric patterns in primary colors, an indulgent staff of Australian and European hipsters at the reception desk, and a punk-rock vibe that's refreshing when compared to other hotels in Savannah's Historic District. It's also pet friendly.

611 W. Oglethorpe Ave., Savannah, GA 31401. ☎ **866/324-2661** or 912/232-2661. www.thethunderbirdinn.com. 42 units. $79–$339 double. Rates include continental breakfast. AE, DC, DISC, MC, V. **Amenities:** Breakfast room; Wi-Fi (free). *In room:* A/C, TV, fridge.

3 NEARBY HOTELS & INNS

MODERATE

Baymont Inn & Suites This motor lodge, one of the best in the Savannah area, has a prime location on Main Street. It's also convenient for making day trips to Hilton Head, which is just 18 miles to the north. The inn offers attractively furnished and good-size guest rooms. Each room features such extras as ergonomic chairs and free bottled water. Many families visiting relatives at Hunter Army Airfield lodge here. Several affordable restaurants are nearby, but the hotel fills you up with complimentary morning treats such as waffles and French toast before you head out for the day. The hotel also has a senior discount program, interior-corridor room entrances, free local calls, and a 24-hour staffed front desk and switchboard.

357 Main St., Savannah, GA 31418. ☎ **877/229-6668** or 912/964-8669. Fax 912/964-7770. www.baymontinns.com. 57 units. $68–$80 double. Rates include continental breakfast. Children 17 and under stay free in parent's room. AE, DC, DISC, MC, V. **Amenities:** Outdoor pool. *In room:* A/C, TV, hair dryer, Internet (free).

Homewood Suites by Hilton Built in 1990, about a 6-mile drive south of Savannah's historic core, this is a bland member of a nationwide chain. But each room is a suite with one or two bedrooms, so the hotel tends to be favored by business travelers who want larger-than-usual quarters on extended business trips. It occupies a commercial neighborhood with suburban-style traffic and plenty of nearby restaurants and shopping malls. An evening cocktail party, hosted by the manager, takes the edge off the sense of anonymity that sometimes prevails here. If you're looking for space to move around within a modern, uncontroversial setting, this place might be fine for you. Each room has a fully equipped kitchen with a microwave, full-size refrigerator, and cooking utensils.

5820 White Bluff Rd., Savannah, GA 31405. © **800/225-5466** or 912/353-8500. Fax 912/354-3821. www.homewoodsuitessavannah.com. 106 units. $129–$169 double; $249–$259 suite. AE, DC, DISC, MC, V. **Amenities:** Restaurant; exercise room; outdoor pool. *In room:* A/C, TV, hair dryer, Internet (free).

Wingate Inn   This is one of the newer and more comfortable hotels in the shopping-mall zone south of Savannah. Although the distance to the city's historic core is about 8 miles, part of the transit is via interstate highways, so the drive can take under 20 minutes (if traffic is light). Built in a four-story brick-and-stucco format in 1999, with a bit of architectural flair, the inn offers comfortable, family-friendly rooms outfitted with modern furniture that carries no pretensions of Southern Colonial plantation life. (This might be a relief after a heavy dose of that style in other modern hotels nearby.)

11 Gateway Blvd. E., Savannah, GA 31419. © **800/228-1000** or 912/925-2525. Fax 912/925-7904. www.wingatehotels.com. 101 units. $99–$139 double. Rates include continental breakfast. AE, DC, DISC, MC, V. **Amenities:** Exercise room; outdoor pool. *In room:* A/C, TV, Internet (free), kitchenette.

Where to Eat in Savannah

Savannah is known for an abundance of excellent sea-food restaurants. They're among the top spots in Georgia, rivaled only by those in Atlanta. The best dining is generally in the Historic District, along River Street, bordering the water. But locals also like to escape the city and head for favorites on Tybee and other offshore islands.

Some of Savannah's restaurants, like **Elizabeth on 37th,** are ranked among the finest in the South. Others, like **Mrs. Wilkes' Dining Room,** are places to go for real Southern fare—from collard greens and fried okra to fried chicken, cornbread, and hot biscuits.

1 ALONG OR NEAR THE RIVERFRONT

EXPENSIVE

Chart House ★ STEAK/SEAFOOD   Overlooking the Savannah River and Riverfront Plaza, "the home of the mud pie" is part of a nationwide chain—and one of the better ones. Here in Savannah, it's housed in a building that predates 1790, reputed to be the oldest masonry structure in Georgia and once a sugar-and-cotton warehouse. You can enjoy a view of passing ships from the outside deck, perhaps enjoying an appetizer and a drink there before dinner. The bar is one of the most atmospheric along the riverfront. As in all Chart Houses, the prime rib is slow roasted and served au jus. The steaks from corn-fed beef are aged and hand cut on the premises before being chargrilled. You may prefer one of the fresh catches of the day, which can be grilled to your specifications.

202 W. Bay St. ✆ **912/234-6686.** www.chart-house.com. Reservations recommended. Main courses $18–$44. AE, DC, DISC, MC, V. Mon–Fri 5–10pm; Sat 11am–10:30pm; Sun 11am–9pm.

Alligator Soul **12**

Back in the Day **23**

Barnes Restaurant **23**

Belford's **10**

Broughton & Bull **14**

Casbah **15**

Cha Bella **17**

Chart House **1**

Clary's Café **21**

Elizabeth on 37th **23**

Garibaldi's **11**

Johnny Harris Restaurant **23**

The Lady & Sons **9**

Moon River Brewing Company **2**

Mrs. Wilkes' Dining Room **20**

The Olde Pink House Restaurant **7**

Outback Steakhouse **3**

The Pirates' House **6**

Ruan Thai **13**

Sapphire Grill **8**

700 Drayton Restaurant **22**

17 Hundred 90 **16**

Shrimp Factory **5**

Six Pence Pub **19**

Tubby's Tank House **4**

Wall's **18**

MODERATE

Garibaldi's SEAFOOD/ITALIAN   Designed as a fire station in 1871, this Italian cafe still boasts the original pressed-tin ceiling. But its walls have since been updated with fanciful murals painted by the owner's daughter. Their theme is "the jungles of Italy," and they've made the place popular among the city's art crowd. If you're looking for a quiet, contemplative evening, you might want to go elsewhere—the setting is loud and convivial during the early evening and even louder later at night.

Menu items include roasted red peppers with goat-cheese croutons on a bed of wild lettuces, crispy flounder with an apricot-shallot sauce, artichoke hearts with aioli, about a dozen kinds of pasta, and a repertoire of Italian-inspired chicken, veal, and seafood dishes. Daily specials change frequently but may include duck, king-crab fettuccine, and a choice of lusciously fattening desserts.

315 W. Congress St. ✆ **912/232-7118.** www.garabaldisavannah.com. Reservations recommended. Main courses $13–$40. AE, MC, V. Mon–Thurs 5–10:30pm; Fri–Sat 5pm–midnight; Sun 5–10:30pm.

INEXPENSIVE

The Lady & Sons ★★ (Finds) SOUTHERN   Paula Deen opened this restaurant in 1990 after creating a successful catering business with just $200 and the help of her sons. Her first cookbook, *The Lady & Sons Savannah Country Cookbook,* is still a bestseller, and she hosts three shows on the Food Network, including "Paula's Home Cooking." One bite of her food and you'll understand why she gets so much attention. Lunches at the restaurant are busy with a loyal following; dinners are casual and inventive. Menu items like crab cakes (one Maryland visitor claimed they were the best he'd ever eaten), crab burgers, and several creative varieties of shrimp best exhibit Paula's style. The locals love her buffets, which are Southern to the bone and feature fried chicken, meatloaf, collard greens, beef stew, "creamed" potatoes, and macaroni and cheese. The most aphrodisiac dish has to be the raw oyster shooters, each served in a shot glass. Paula's signature dish is chicken potpie topped with puff pastry. Be careful not to fill up on the cheese biscuits and hoecakes that constantly land on your table. If for some reason you don't want a glorious glass of syrup-sweet tea, you'd better ask for it unsweetened. In 2007, Paula Deen and Co. established a cookware store (p. 107) in a space adjacent to the restaurant.

102 W. Congress St. ✆ **912/233-2600.** www.ladyandsons.com. Reservations recommended for dinner. Main courses $7–$14 lunch, $19–$28 dinner; all-you-can-eat buffet $14 lunch, $18 dinner; Sun buffet $16. AE, DISC, MC, V. Mon–Thurs 11am–3pm and 5–9pm; Fri–Sat 11am–3pm and 5–10pm; Sun 11am–5pm (buffet only).

Shrimp Factory (Value) SEAFOOD   Yes, this place is touristy (often attracting tour buses), but its exposed old brick and wooden plank floors form a nice setting for harborside dining in a cotton warehouse (ca. 1850). Lots of folks drop in before dinner to watch the boats pass by, perhaps enjoying a Chatham Artillery punch in a souvenir snifter. A salad bar rests next to a miniature shrimp boat, and fresh seafood comes from local waters. A specialty, pine bark stew, is served in a little iron pot with a bottle of sherry on the side; it's a potage of five kinds of seafood simmered with fresh herbs but minus the pine bark. Other dishes include peeled shrimp, shucked oysters, Maine lobsters, sirloin steaks, and various fish filets.

313 E. River St. (2 blocks east of the Hyatt). (C) **912/236-4229.** www.theshrimp factory.com. Reservations not accepted. Main courses $7–$15 lunch, $21–$35 dinner. AE, DC, DISC, MC, V. Mon–Thurs 11am–10pm; Fri–Sat 11am–11pm; Sun noon–10pm.

Tubby's Tank House SEAFOOD   Hungry diners flock here for the fresh fish. This old-brick building has a nautical decor, a casual atmosphere, and an outdoor deck with river views. The menu is corny—appetizers, for example, are called "Tubby's Teasers"—but the food is affordable and hearty. Oysters Savannah is a favorite starter, baked with andouille sausage and Parmesan cheese. Lemon garlic shrimp is another savory opening. The chefs make the best crab stew along River Street. When we drop in, we generally opt for the fresh fish of the day. It's grilled to perfection over an open flame and served with fresh steamed vegetables and your choice of a starch such as fettuccine alfredo. Families like to order the seafood baskets, or else one of the steam pots served with hush puppies. The most savory kettle of fish is the Low Country platter with steamed oysters, rock shrimp, steamed shrimp, snow crab, deviled crab, sausage, and corn on the cob. A limited number of steak and chicken dishes are offered, including a 14-ounce rib-eye and a charbroiled chicken breast.

115 E. River St. (C) **912/233-0770.** http://liveoakrestaurants.net. Main courses $17–$30. AE, MC, V. Daily 11am–2am. Closed Thanksgiving and Christmas.

2 IN THE HISTORIC DISTRICT

VERY EXPENSIVE

Broughton & Bull SOUTHERN   In this open space with big windows looking out onto the street and high ceilings, diners enjoy Southern favorites. Live music is featured Thursday to Saturday nights. The food is freshly prepared and full of flavor. Unique starters include braised veal cheeks flavored with apple cider and roasted shallots or pumpkin soup with toasted pumpkin seeds and truffle oil. For your main course, try the huge jumbo lump crab cake or the monster pork chop stuffed with bacon and apple, served with spaghetti squash. More traditional favorites such as country fried steak and pan-roasted chicken also appear on the menu.

2 E. Broughton St. (℃) **912/231-8888.** www.broughtonandbull.com. Reservations recommended. Main courses $17–$26. AE, DC, DISC, MC, V. Mon–Thurs 4–10pm; Fri–Sat 4–11:30pm; Sun 4–9:30pm.

Sapphire Grill ★ AMERICAN/LOW COUNTRY   One of the city's hippest restaurants, this place evokes a low-key, counterculture bistro, but its cuisine is grander and more cutting edge than its industrial-looking decor suggests. The Pennsylvania-born chef, Christopher J. Nason, continues to garner national and regional attention for his "coastal cuisine," based on seafood hauled in, usually on the day of its preparation, from nearby waters. In 2010, Nason was featured on the Food Network's "Best of Dining" program and on the Discovery Channel's "Great Country Inns." If you opt for a table here, you won't be alone: Scads of media and cinematic personalities will have preceded you. Launch your repast with endive, rocket, and baby field lettuce with sesame cream sauce and confit of tomato and Stilton cheese, or barbecued wild halibut with sweet corn broth. Each day, the chef offers a tasting menu that features such main dishes as seared Muscovy duck breast in a caramelized shallot vinaigrette, or pork belly braised in apple juice.

110 W. Congress St. (℃) **912/443-9962.** www.sapphiregrill.com. Reservations recommended. Main courses $19–$36; 6-course tasting menu $100, with wine $145. AE, DC, MC, V. Sun–Thurs 6–10:30pm; Fri–Sat 5:30–11:30pm.

700 Drayton Restaurant ★★★ INTERNATIONAL   This is the culinary showplace of Savannah's most plush and sybaritic hotel—the Mansion on Forsyth Park (see p. 40). It occupies the oldest section of the hotel—a brick-built mansion from 1888—and inside, scattered over two floors of the echoing, high-ceilinged interior, are 150 seats and six dining rooms. Each contains remnants and reminders (including the working fireplaces) of the building's original role as a private home. The well-chosen menu is market inspired and one of the most seductive in Savannah, as evoked by the fried green tomatoes served with baked goat cheese, grilled pork chops stuffed with tomatoes and thyme, pecan-crusted rack of New Zealand lamb in a balsamic syrup, pan-roasted Gulf Coast grouper with a shrimp fricassee, and the most upscale version of tuna tartare we've seen. The New York strip steak came as an imaginative and delightful surprise; it was Gorgonzola crusted with caramelized shallots and a blackberry compote. Skewered shrimp with grits are served in a saffron-flavored shellfish sauce. Even if you're famished, we recommend a before-dinner drink at **Casimir's Bar,** which lies on the building's second floor.

In the Mansion on Forsyth Park, 700 Drayton St. ✆ **912/721-5002.** www. 700drayton.com. Reservations recommended. Main courses $9–$15 breakfast, $8–$16 lunch, $24–$35 dinner. AE, DC, DISC, MC, V. Daily 7–11am, 11:30am–2pm, and 5–9:30pm.

EXPENSIVE

The Olde Pink House Restaurant ★★ SEAFOOD/SOUTHERN

Built in 1771 and sheathed with a layer of pink stucco, this house has functioned as a private home, a bank, a tearoom, and military head-quarters during the Civil War. Today its interior is rather formal, spartan, and dignified, with stiff-backed chairs, bare wooden floors, and an 18th-century aura similar to what you'd find in Williamsburg, Virginia. Richly steeped in the traditions of the Low Country, the restaurant's cuisine includes sautéed local shrimp with country ham and a grits cake, crispy scored flounder with apricot sauce, steak au poivre, black grouper stuffed with blue crab and drenched in white onion and butter sauce, and grilled tenderloin of pork served with collard greens and yams. You can enjoy your meal in a candlelit din-ing room here or at the more casual Planters Tavern. Added during renovations in 2008, the tavern is set in an antique cellar room outfit-ted with a generously proportioned bar.

23 Abercorn St. ✆ **912/232-4286.** Reservations recommended. Main courses $18–$35. AE, MC, V. Daily 5–10pm.

17 Hundred 90 INTERNATIONAL In the brick-lined, low-ceilinged cellar of Savannah's oldest inn (which seems to be showing its age a bit these days), this restaurant evokes a seafaring tavern along the coast of New England. Many visitors opt for a drink at the woodsy-looking bar in a separate back room before heading down the slightly claustrophobic corridor to the nautically inspired dining room. Students of paranormal psychology remain alert to the ghost rumored to wander through this place, site of Savannah's most-famous 18th-century suicide. Lunch might include the quiche of the day, Southern-style crab cakes, and a choice of salads and sandwiches. Dinners are more formal, featuring crab bisque, snapper, steaks, and bourbon-flavored chicken. The chef is not an imaginative navigator in the kitchen, but that's not a put-down. The cooking is much the same as it's been over the decades—familiar, well prepared, and flavor-ful fare based on market-fresh ingredients and time-tested recipes.

307 E. President St. ✆ **912/236-7122.** www.17hundred90.com. Reservations recommended. Main courses $23–$38. AE, DISC, MC, V. Mon–Fri 11:30am–3pm and 6–10pm; Sat–Sun 6–10pm.

MODERATE

Casbah MOROCCAN   With its North African theme, this restaurant offers a lush and sensual atmosphere. Brocade tapestries on the walls and tented velvet ceilings create the aura; fortunetellers predict your future and belly dancers entertain you. It has all that faux "Come with me to the Casbah" allure. We like to start with a festival of Moroccan salads; ask your server about the day's selection. One other tantalizing appetizer is the cornish hen bastila—served boneless and baked in a pastry along with onions, parsley, spiced eggs, and toasted almonds, then garnished with cinnamon and powdered sugar. Your most economical option is to order the three-course Moroccan Diaffa dinner, in which you select your appetizer, main course, and dessert, finishing off with hot mint tea. For main courses, we like the chicken and caramelized apricots dipped in a honey-nutmeg sauce. But our favorite is the spicy roast lamb, oven roasted with saffron rice and a choice of vegetables. If you like kabobs, you can opt for the Sultan's Feast, an assortment of chicken, beef, and lamb.

118 E. Broughton St. ✆ **912/234-6168.** www.casbahrestaurant.com. Reservations recommended. Main courses $17–$25; 3-course menu $30. AE, DC, DISC, MC, V. Daily 5:30–10:30pm.

Cha Bella ★ ORGANIC MEDITERRANEAN   Overlooking East Broad Street, this restaurant is hip and trendy, occupying a brick industrial structure with high ceilings, a popular bar, and a series of modern paintings on the wall. The owners promise—and deliver—delectable, market-fresh food, with plenty of local seafood and fusions of Italian and Mediterranean tastes. Appealing starters include a peppery baby arugula salad with spiced pecans, Gorgonzola cheese, and fresh raspberries, all bound together in a raspberry vinaigrette dressing. You could also try a salad of goat cheese, eggplant, and plum tomatoes flavored with fresh sweet basil. For a main course, you might select an 8-ounce filet of beef with a mushroom demi-glace, or else black grouper, freshly caught, and seared with a succotash of peas, sweet corn, and lump crabmeat. For dessert, you can sample such temptations as "Chocolate Fourways"—a chocolate hazelnut truffle, a chocolate mouse, a chocolate almond brownie, and a pair of chewy chocolate cookies.

102 E. Broad St. ✆ **912/790-7888.** www.cha-bella.com. Reservations recommended. Main courses $17–$32. AE, DC, MC, V. Sun–Thurs 5:30–9pm, Fri–Sat 5:30–10pm.

★ **Outback Steakhouse** STEAKS/SEAFOOD This woodsy look-ing, comfortable, and well-run restaurant serves food that's tasty, well prepared, and a lot better than what's offered at some competing chains. In truth, much of the food is all-American fare marketed with an Australian accent. For instance, the "Alice Springs chicken"—slathered with cheese, sliced ham, mushrooms, and honey-mustard sauce—is delicious, but Australians may wonder about the dish's name, given that Alice Springs is a desert and doesn't produce chicken. The restaurant's focal point is the large, rectangular bar area where you can wait until your table becomes available. There's a sense of bustling popularity, high turnover, and charm in this place that has nothing to do with historic Savannah, but the food is affordable and good, with a menu that includes filets, prime rib, burgers, sirloins, pasta, chicken, shrimp, and lobster tail.

7 Drayton St. ✆ **912/232-1611.** www.outback.com. Reservations recommended for dinner. Lunch sandwiches, salads, and platters $7–$14; dinner main courses $12–$25. AE, MC, V. Mon–Thurs 11:30am–10pm; Fri 11:30am–11pm; Sat 3–11pm; Sun noon–9pm.

Pearl's Saltwater Grille SEAFOOD/AMERICAN "Let's not cook tonight; let's go to Pearl's," is the nightly refrain often heard in local homes. Customers know they'll get good food and plenty of it, everything from fresh seafood to perfectly grilled steaks. Dress is casual, and service is good except when the waitstaff is overwhelmed by a packed house. "This is where I take my guests from the north to show them how we eat in Savannah," one patron informed us. The crowd is varied. Many diners arrive early for more than one drink at the bar before proceeding to a table. And on our last visit, we noticed many families dining here.

The cuisine may not be inspired, but it's tasty and filling, begin-ning with fresh hush puppies with sweetened butter. Southern-style vegetables—referred to as "sides" by the locals—accompany the main courses. Favorite dishes include shrimp and crab au gratin with a rich white sauce, and a shrimp trio—fried shrimp, garlic shrimp, and shrimp wrapped in bacon. Other good-tasting dishes include barbe-cued pork chops and pepper steak.

7000 La Roche Ave. ✆ **912/352-8221.** http://savannahmenu.com/pearls. Reser-vations not accepted. Main courses $15–$25. AE, DC, DISC, MC, V. Sun–Thurs 5–10pm; Fri–Sat 5–10:30pm.

The Pirates' House AMERICAN/SOUTHERN Positioned a few blocks east of Savannah's commercial bustle, this is the most his-toric and atmospheric restaurant in town, complete with alleged ghost sightings. It's also the most touristy place to eat in Savannah. The

Pirates' House incorporates a half-dozen antique houses and a relatively modern section, all conjoined into a labyrinth. You'll dine in a confusing but distinctive warren of 15 dining rooms, each sheathed in dark paneling and each with a low ceiling. The floors and walls are a bit creaky and out of alignment. The spot that receives the highest number of ghost sightings (and the highest number of eerily overexposed photographs) is the Herb House. Dating from 1733, it was built for the caretaker of a state-sponsored experimental garden that used to grow here. Don't be surprised if, during the course of your drink or meal here, a tourist or two arrives, gawking in a kind of voyeuristic horror at the brick tunnels that honeycomb beneath this place, reacting to the statue of a (faux) prisoner's skeleton positioned at the bottom of a spooky-looking subterranean vault, or listening to the commentary about how Robert Louis Stevenson, who rented one of the rooms upstairs from time to time, was inspired by the place during his authorship of the world's most famous pirate epic, *Treasure Island.*

The food is closely linked to Low Country traditions, featuring crab cakes, meal-size salads, various she-crab and shellfish gumbos and chowders, slow-cooked baby back ribs, steaks, and seafood. The Plantation Buffet, which includes the kind of traditional Southern food that might have been laid out in 1925 by the owner of a farmhouse to feed the field hands on a hot summer day, is the most popular choice here.

20 E. Broad St. ✆ **912/233-5757.** www.thepirateshouse.com. Reservations recommended for dinner. Lunch sandwiches, salads, and platters $10–$12; Low Country buffet lunch $14; dinner main courses $20–$25; Low Country buffet dinner $17. AE, DC, DISC, MC, V. Daily 11am–9:30pm (Fri–Sat till 10pm).

INEXPENSIVE

Back in the Day ★ (Finds) BAKED GOODS This bakery is beloved by locals, and it's a great spot for lunch—with some of the best sandwiches in town. All its products are made from scratch, including homemade desserts and hearth breads using quality ingredients. Some favorites are the "Hum Bee" sandwich, featuring a house-made butterbean hummus, and the Madras curry chicken on ciabatta. Sweet treats worth tasting include the blackberry pie bar and orange coconut scones.

2403 Bull St. ✆ **912/495-9292.** www.backinthedaybakery.com. Sandwiches $7–$10. AE, MC, V. Tues–Fri 7:30am–4pm; Sat–Sun 8am–3pm.

Barnes Restaurant ★ (Kids) BARBECUE/LOW COUNTRY This casual, family-style restaurant is very affordable. Local hotels and B&Bs often refer their budget-minded guests to this joint for its

Family-Friendly Restaurants

Barnes Restaurant (p. 62)   This informal restaurant feeds families well with large servings. The cooks are known for such offerings as fried onion rings and deviled crab, seared in a pan. The sandwiches are well stuffed and made with fresh ingredients, and a kids' menu is also offered.

Mrs. Wilkes' Dining Room (p. 64)   Since your kid didn't grow up in the era of the boardinghouse, here's a chance to experience a long-faded American dining custom. This is an all-you-can-eat, family-style place. Children might balk at the okra and collards, but they'll probably go for the corn on the cob and barbecued chicken.

Wall's (p. 65)   If your child is from the North and has never tasted Southern barbecue, come here. Complete with bibs and plastic booths, there's no finer introduction. Spareribs and barbecue sandwiches are the hearty fare, but there's also a vegetable plate for the nonmeat eater in the family.

generous helpings and good food. A tradition since 1975, it's typical of many eateries in the South, serving barbecue dinners, oyster po'boys, and fried catfish. "These dishes are popular," a waiter confided, "because it's what the customers want to eat day after day." Favorite appetizers include spicy chicken wings with a blue cheese dressing, hand-cut freshly battered onion rings, and zesty Jalapeno peppers stuffed with cream cheese. The sandwiches are among the best in the area, including fish sandwiches, chicken sandwiches, and crab burgers. The spareribs are slowly smoked over oak or hickory wood, and the chicken is crispy and tasty outside, tender and moist inside, as it emerges from the rotisserie. A children's menu is also offered.

5320 Waters Ave. (at 68th St.). ℭ **912/354-8745.** http://savannahmenu.com/barnes. Main courses $7–$13. AE, DC, DISC, MC, V. Sun–Thurs 10:30am–10pm; Fri–Sat 10:30am–10:30pm. Closed Easter, Thanksgiving, and Christmas.

Clary's Café ★ Ⓥⓐⓛⓤⓔ AMERICAN   Owner Jan Wilson is one of Savannah's best-known restaurateurs, enjoying a loyal clientele and the subject of many newspaper articles. Starting out as the cashier, she worked her way to the top, eventually buying this landmark cafe. "We

WHERE TO EAT IN SAVANNAH

5

IN THE HISTORIC DISTRICT

fed your great-grandfather, your grandfather, your father—and now you," she tells a new generation of diners flocking to her cafe. The place was famous long before it was featured in *Midnight in the Garden of Good and Evil* in its former role as Clary's drugstore, where regulars like eccentric flea-collar inventor Luther Driggers breakfasted and lunched. John Berendt is still a frequent patron, as is the fabled Lady Chablis. Begin your day with the classic Hoppel Poppel (scrambled eggs with chunks of kosher salami, potatoes, onions, and green peppers) and go on from there. Fresh salads, New York–style sandwiches, and stir-fries, along with Grandmother's homemade chicken soup and flame-broiled burgers, are served throughout the day, giving way in the evening to chicken potpie, stuffed pork loin, or planked fish (a fresh filet of red snapper—broiled, grilled, or blackened).

404 Abercorn St. (at Jones St.). ℂ **912/233-0402.** Breakfast $5–$13; main courses $6–$12. AE, DC, DISC, MC, V. Mon–Fri 7am–4pm; Sat–Sun 8am–4pm.

Masada Café ★ **Finds** SOUTHERN If you're looking for some of the best down-home Southern cooking in Savannah, in-the-know foodies will point you to a buffet at the United House of Prayer for All People. The South has a long tradition of church and food going together. Head straight out Bay Street to discover this cafe in the back of the church, part of a group founded by Charles ("Sweet Daddy") Grace. In the tiled-floor cafeteria, you can enjoy a filling lunch or an early supper. The fried chicken with a peppery bite is a must. Alongside it, try the tender pole beans, stewed squash, or heavenly macaroni and cheese, which is crusty and cheesy but not too rich. On any day, expect soul-food classics. And on some days, you might hear shouts of "Hallelujah" coming from the front as you're enjoying your meal. Amen to that.

2301 W. Bay St. ℂ **912/236-9499.** Reservations not necessary. Main courses $9–$10. No credit cards. Tues-Sat 11am-3pm; Sun 11am-6pm.

Mrs. Wilkes' Dining Room ★ **Kids** SOUTHERN Remember the days of the boardinghouse, when everybody sat together and belly-busting food was served in big dishes in the center of the table? Before her death in late 2002 at the age of 95, Sema Wilkes had served breakfast and lunch to locals and travelers in just that manner since the 1940s. Bruce Willis, Demi Moore, and Clint Eastwood are on the long list of celebrities who've dined here. The tradition continues. Expect to find a line of people patiently waiting for a seat at one of the long tables in the basement dining room of this 1870 brick house with curving steps and cast-iron trim.

Mrs. Wilkes believed in freshness and planned her daily menu around the seasons. Your food will be a reflection of the cuisine

Savannah residents have enjoyed for generations—fried or barbecued chicken, red rice and sausage, black-eyed peas, corn on the cob, squash and yams, okra, cornbread, and collard greens.

107 W. Jones St. (west of Bull St.). ② 912/232-5997. www.mrswilkes.com. Lunch $16. No credit cards. Mon–Fri 11am–2pm.

Ruan Thai (Value) This is the Savannah branch of a three-member chain that does a roaring business in other parts of coastal South Carolina and Georgia. It occupies a high-ceilinged former storefront along Savannah's main downtown shopping corridor—a welcome alternative to a constant dose of regional cuisine. An ongoing favorite here is lemon-grass chicken topped with peanut sauce and served with rice. Other dishes to try include spring rolls; satay skewers with peanut sauce; and your choice of chicken, pork, beef, shrimp, tofu, or vegetables prepared with ginger sauce, garlic sauce, or various curries. Menu items come in whatever degree of spiciness you specify.

17 W. Broadway St. ② 912/231-6667. Reservations not necessary. Main courses $8–$25. AE, MC, V. Mon–Fri 11am–3pm and 4:30–10pm; Sat–Sun noon–11pm.

Six Pence Pub AMERICAN/BRITISH This is the most authentic English pub in Georgia, originally founded by two expats from Manchester. Today the watering hole is run by two gents who have expanded the beer, wine, and liquor selection and added a full menu of traditional English and American comfort foods. Every day a homemade soup is prepared. Other tasty starters include smoked salmon, nachos, and baked brie with fresh fruit. Sandwiches are a lunchtime favorite, with burgers being the most popular selection. English specialties include shepherd's pie with ground beef and vegetables, even a beef Guinness marinated in stout. The bourbon pecan pie is a sure pick for dessert.

245 Bull St. ② 912/233-3151. www.sixpencepub.com. Reservations not necessary. Salads, sandwiches, and platters $7–$15. AE, MC, V. Daily 11:30am–1am. Bar daily 11:30am–2am.

Wall's (Kids) BARBECUE Southern barbecue aficionados have built-in radar to find a place like this, which arguably offers the best barbecue in Savannah. Once they see the plastic booths, bibs, Styrofoam cartons, and canned drinks from a fridge, they'll know they've found home. Like all barbecue joints, the place is aggressively casual and great for kids. Spareribs and barbecue sandwiches star on the menu. Deviled crabs are the only nonbarbecue item, and a vegetable plate is served for nonmeat eaters.

515 E. York Lane (btw. York St. and Oglethorpe Ave.). ② 912/232-9754. Main courses $7–$11. No credit cards. Thurs–Sat 11am–9pm. Closed mid-July to mid-Aug.

EXPENSIVE

Alligator Soul ★ NEW SOUTHERN We've had readers who adore this place, sinking right into its agreeable bar area and cozy dining room. Others view it as a heavy-handed, theme-ridden, and overpriced bastion of Southern redneckism appealing shamelessly to local chauvinism and a yearning for the Old South. The best way to choose is to drop in for a cocktail at its bar. Meals mingle local ingredients with updated versions of time-tested recipes. Examples include fried green tomatoes with chipotle mayonnaise and bacon-flavored macaroni and cheese with shrimp. Main courses include oversize grilled steaks as well as "a big 'ol" grilled pork chop stuffed with apricot sausage and garnished with bourbon-braised Georgia peaches. A particularly scrumptious dessert is the house version of banana beignets served with roasted banana ice cream and candied pecans.

114 Barnard St. ✆ **912/232-7899.** www.alligatorsoul.com. Reservations recommended. Main courses $23–$32. AE, DC, DISC, MC, V. Daily 5:30–10pm.

Belford's ★ LOW COUNTRY This local favorite near the old city market features a rich, flavorful cuisine with local ingredients. This is one of the best places to introduce yourself to regional dishes, as long as you're prepared to dig into some fried food. The setting is nostalgic, with hardwood floors, brick walls, high ceilings, and a patio. The cooks prepare a daily crab stew that is excellent, along with such other favorites as fried green tomatoes, fried calamari, and crab cakes, the latter served with a spicy tomato jam and lemon aioli. A trio of pastas is featured daily, our favorite being the lobster and wild mushroom ravioli served with a spicy calamari salad and a balsamic brown butter sauce. Delightful main courses often include potato-wrapped grouper with a prosciutto-enhanced beurre blanc sauce. The hazelnut red snapper is another temptation, served with prawns and lump crabmeat in a hazelnut-liqueur sauce and a side of apple chutney. Shrimp, greens, and grits is a sure winner, complete with smoked bacon, green onions, and a chardonnay butter sauce.

315 W. St. Julian St. ✆ **912/233-2626.** www.belfordssavannah.com. Reservations recommended. Breakfast buffet $8; lunch $8–$19; dinner $14–$34; Sun brunch $6–$17. AE, DC, DISC, MC, V. Mon–Sat 8–11am, 11:30am–3pm, and 5:30–10pm; Sun 11:30am–3pm and 5:30–10pm. Closed Thanksgiving, Christmas Eve (night), and Christmas Day.

Moon River Brewing Company AMERICAN/LOW COUNTRY

This welcoming place, a local favorite, successfully combines a restaurant and a bar with a brewpub. You get a *Cheers*-like atmosphere as well as good food, affordable prices, and fresh ingredients. A local critic called the kitchen a "boiling pot of diversity," and so it is, offering a wide range of dishes. The atmosphere is pubby; the brewing company's dark wood and huge brewing tanks behind glass walls can be viewed by customers while they're eating or sampling the suds.

The restaurant is in the former City Hotel Building, where such notables as General Winfield Scott, the Marquis de Lafayette, and John James Audubon have stayed. Audubon stayed here for 6 months after a gale marooned his boat, and it was at this site that he worked on his book, *Ornithological Biographies.*

The kitchen is big on crab, with appetizers including fried crab and crab cakes. There is always a delectable array of soups, sandwiches, and salads made fresh daily. A perfectly seasoned, 16-ounce grilled rib-eye is served, as well as local favorites: platters of fried catfish, shrimp 'n' grits, or chicken and sausage Creole. One reliable bet is the catch of the day. Ask the waiter what's on the grill, and tell him or her how you'd like it cooked.

21 W. Bay St. ✆ **912/447-0943.** www.moonriverbrewing.com. Reservations not required. Main courses $15–$21. AE, DC, DISC, MC, V. Sun–Thurs 11am–11pm; Fri–Sat 11am–midnight.

4 IN THE VICTORIAN DISTRICT

VERY EXPENSIVE

Elizabeth on 37th ★★ MODERN SOUTHERN   This restaurant is frequently cited as the most glamorous and upscale in town. It's housed in a palatial neoclassical-style 1900 villa ringed with semitropical landscaping and cascades of Spanish moss. The menu items change with the seasons and manage to retain their gutsy originality despite an elegant presentation. They may include roast quail with mustard-and-pepper sauce and apricot-pecan chutney, herb-seasoned rack of lamb, broiled salmon with mustard-garlic glaze, and a grilled-eggplant soup to start. There's also an impressive wine list. The desserts are the best in Savannah.

105 E. 37th St. ✆ **912/236-5547.** www.elizabethon37th.net. Reservations required. Main courses $20–$38, 7-course fixed-price menu $90. AE, DC, DISC, MC, V. Daily 6–9pm.

MODERATE

Johnny Harris Restaurant AMERICAN   Started as a roadside diner in 1924, Johnny Harris is Savannah's oldest continuously operated restaurant. The place has a lingering aura of the 1950s and features all that great food so beloved back in the days of Elvis and Marilyn: barbecue, charbroiled steaks, and seafood. The barbecue pork is especially savory, and the prime rib is tender. Colonel Sanders never came anywhere close to equaling the fried chicken here. Guests can eat in the "kitchen" (an area with a view into the slow-cooking barbecue pits) or in the main dining room, where you can dance under the star-lit ceiling. The place will make you nostalgic.

1651 E. Victory Dr. (Hwy. 80). ✆ **912/354-7810.** www.johnnyharris.com. Reservations recommended. Main courses $7–$12 lunch, $12–$23 dinner. AE, DC, DISC, MC, V. Mon–Thurs 11:30am–9:30pm; Fri–Sat 11:30am–10:30pm.

6

Exploring Savannah

The very name evokes a romantic antebellum aura.
Savannah is the city that General William Tecumseh Sherman gave
President Abraham Lincoln as a Christmas present. Crowds flock here
to search for Forrest Gump's bench and other monuments, as well as
to visit Juliette Gordon Low's Birthplace, now the National Center of
the Girl Scouts of the U.S.A.

The city, founded in 1733 by James Oglethorpe as Georgia's first
settlement, is 18 miles inland from the Atlantic on the Savannah
River at the South Carolina border. A deep channel connects Savannah to the ocean, attracting massive freighters to the terminals at the
Georgia Ports Authority. Lined with classy nightspots and upscale
restaurants, as well as a few pubs, galleries, and artsy boutiques, cobblestone River Street has become a hub for visitors.

Many things in Savannah never change. It remains one of America's loveliest old cities, organized around a grid of 21 squares. But that
doesn't mean there's nothing new to offer. Restoration continues to be
on the minds of locals, as reflected by what's happening in Ellis
Square. Once dominated by a parking lot, the area is now being
restored to its antebellum glory. The art scene, highlighted by a major
expansion of the Telfair Museum, continues to flourish. The city's
creative energy is further enhanced by students at the Savannah College of Art and Design.

SIGHTSEEING SUGGESTIONS

If You Have 1 Day

Don't set foot outside the Historic District—even there, you won't
see it all. Go to the Savannah Visitor Information Center for a general orientation and a 15-minute video presentation. Pick up a free
map before going to an adjacent building to see the Savannah History Museum. Then set out on our walking tour of Savannah's Historic Squares (see chapter 7, "Savannah Strolls"). You'll see sites like
the Mercer Williams House Museum, which is featured in *Midnight*

in the Garden of Good and Evil. Later, dine along River Street and relax at one of the riverfront pubs or take a harbor cruise.

IF YOU HAVE 2 DAYS

Spend day 2 exploring historic River Street, a 9-block plaza facing the Savannah River with shops, restaurants, galleries, and pubs. Take the Riverwalk tour in chapter 7.

IF YOU HAVE 3 DAYS

Spend days 1 and 2 as suggested above. On your third day, stroll the Bull Street corridor with its shops, galleries, museums, and beautiful squares, and pay a visit to some of the elegant historic inns, perhaps considering where you'd like to stay on your next visit to Savannah. After that, sit back and enjoy a leisurely horse-and-carriage ride to see the city in a different light. You'll especially enjoy this tour in the evening as the lights come on in the houses. Or you could opt for an evening ghost tour.

IF YOU HAVE 4 DAYS

Spend days 1, 2, and 3 as recommended above. On your fourth day, start off at the Telfair Museum of Art, the oldest public art museum in the South, and check out the newer adjoining Jepson Center. If you have time, walk about 6 blocks and also see the historic Owens-Thomas House and Museum, where Lafayette spent the night in 1825. In the afternoon, venture about 2 miles out of town to see Old Fort Jackson, Georgia's oldest standing fort. To top off your day, return to the city and enjoy a martini in Bonaventure Cemetery (take note—it closes at 5pm).

IF YOU HAVE 5 DAYS

Spend days 1, 2, 3, and 4 as recommended above. On your fifth day, get going early and travel 41 miles northeast of Savannah. Here you can visit an array of beaches or enjoy other outdoor activities at the nature preserves, especially the Pinckney Island National Wildlife Refuge with 115 prehistoric and historic sites, some dating back to when the island was inhabited by French and Spanish settlers in the 16th century. You can also work in a visit to the historic little town of Bluffton (see p. 131).

1 HISTORIC HOMES

Andrew Low House After her marriage, Juliette Gordon Low lived in this 1848 house and actually founded the Girl Scouts here. She died on the premises in 1927. The classic mid-19th-century

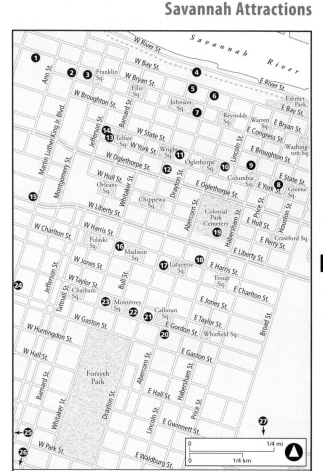

Andrew Low House **17**
Cathedral of St. John the Baptist **18**
Chamber of Commerce **6**
Christ Episcopal Church **7**
Colonial Park Cemetery **19**
Customs House **5**
Davenport House Museum **9**
Factors Walk **4**
First African Baptist Church **3**
First Bryan Baptist Church **1**
Green-Meldrim Home **16**
Juliette Gordon Low's Birthplace **12**
Laurel Grove-South Cemetery **26**
Lutheran Church of the Ascension **11**
Massie Heritage Interpretation Center **20**

Mercer-Williams House **23**
Nicholsonboro Baptist Church **27**
Owen-Thomas House and Museum **10**
Ralph Mark Gilbert Civil Rights
  Museum **24**
St. Phillip Monumental A.M.E. Church **25**
Savannah History Museum **15**
Savannah Visitor Center **15**
Second African Baptist Church **8**
Ships of the Sea Maritime Museum **2**
Telfair Museum of Art **14**
Temple Mickve Israel **22**
Trinity United Methodist Church **13**
Wesley Monumental
  United Methodist Church **21**

house facing Lafayette Square is made of stucco over brick with elaborate ironwork, shuttered piazzas, carved woodwork, and crystal chandeliers. William Makepeace Thackeray visited here twice (the desk at which he worked is in one bedroom), and Robert E. Lee was entertained at a gala reception in the double parlors in 1870.

329 Abercorn St. (✆ **912/233-6854.** www.andrewlowhouse.com. Admission $8 adults; $4.50 students, children 6–12, and Girl Scouts; free for children 5 and under. Mon–Wed and Fri–Sat 10am–4:30pm; Sun noon–4:30pm. Closed major holidays.

Davenport House Museum   Constructed between 1815 and 1820 by master builder Isaiah Davenport, this is one of the truly great Federal-style houses in the United States, with delicate ironwork and a handsome elliptical stairway. The building is also noteworthy because it was here that seven determined women started the Savannah restoration movement in 1954. They raised $22,500, an impressive sum back then, and purchased the house, saving it from demolition and a future as a parking lot. That was the start of the Historic Savannah Foundation.

324 E. State St. (✆ **912/236-8097.** www.davenporthousemuseum.org. Admission $8 adults, $5 children 6–18, free for children 5 and under. Mon–Sat 10am–4pm; Sun 1–4pm. Closed major holidays.

Green-Meldrim House   This impressive house was built on Madison Square for cotton merchant Charleston Green, but its moment in history arrived when it became the Savannah headquarters of General William Tecumseh Sherman at the end of his 1864 March to the Sea. It was from this Gothic-style house that Sherman sent his now infamous (in Savannah, at least) Christmas telegram to President Lincoln, offering him the city as a Christmas gift. Now the Parish House for St. John's Episcopal Church, the building is open to the public. The former kitchen, servants' quarters, and stable are used as a rectory for the church.

14 W. Macon St. (✆ **912/233-3845.** Admission $8 adults, $2 children. Tues and Thurs–Fri 10am–4pm; Sat 10am–1pm.

Juliette Gordon Low's Birthplace   Juliette Gordon Low—the founder of the Girl Scouts—lived in this Regency-style house as a child. Today it's maintained both as a memorial to her and as a national program center for the Girl Scouts. The Victorian additions to the 1818–21 house were made in 1886, just before Ms. Gordon married William Mackay Low.

10 E. Oglethorpe Ave. (✆ **912/233-4501.** www.julietgordonlowbirthplace.org. Admission $8 adults, $7 children 6–18, free for children 5 and under. Mon–Sat 10am–4pm; Sun 11am–4pm. Closed major holidays and some Sun Dec–Jan.

A Visit to the U.S. Custom House

The U.S. Custom House is a Greek Revival building, designed by John Norris and completed in 1852. The oldest federal building in Georgia, it's an austere granite temple with a "Tower-of-the-Winds" portico. It also lies on historic ground: James Edward Oglethorpe lived in the area, and John Wesley delivered his first sermon in Savannah on this site. Today, if you look across Bay Street near Savannah City Hall, you'll see cannons that were presented to the Chatham Artillery in 1791 by George Washington.

A one-story frame house originally stood on the site in 1733 and was rented by Oglethorpe. All the granite in the present building was brought down from New England by sea and rail. The granite columns out front weighed 15 to 20 tons each; it took 30 days to transport each column up the 30-foot bluff from the river to the site of the Customs House. Once there, it took yet another month to move the mammoth pillars into place. The carved capitals were modeled from the pattern of a tobacco leaf.

The U.S. Custom House stands at 1 E. Bay St. (📞 **912/652-4264**), and can be viewed at any time.

2 MUSEUMS

Owens-Thomas House and Museum ★ Famed as a place where Marquis de Lafayette, a French aristocrat and military officer who served under George Washington, spent the night in 1825, this house evokes the heyday of Savannah's golden age. It was designed in 1816 by English architect William Jay, who captured the grace of Georgian Bath in England and the splendor of Regency London. The place has been called a "jewel box." You can visit not only the bedchambers and kitchen, but also the garden and the drawing and dining rooms. Adapted from the original slave quarters and stable, the Carriage House Visitors' Center opened in 1995.

124 Abercorn St. 📞 **912/233-9743.** Admission $15 adults, $5 students, $3 children 6–12, free for children 5 and under. Tues–Sat 10am–5pm; Sun 1–5pm; Mon noon–5pm.

Savannah History Museum   Housed in the restored train shed of the old Central Georgia Railway station, this museum is a good introduction to the city. *The Siege of Savannah* plays in the theater, and an exhibition hall displays memorabilia from every era of Savannah's history.

303 Martin Luther King Jr. Blvd. ℂ **912/651-6825.** www.chsgeorgia.org/shm. Admission $5 adults, $4.50 seniors and children 7–11, free for children 6 and under. Mon–Fri 8:30am–5pm; Sat–Sun 9am–5pm.

Ships of the Sea Maritime Museum   This museum has intricately constructed models of seagoing vessels, from Viking warships to nuclear-powered ships. In models ranging from the size of your fist to 8 feet in length, you can see such famous ships as the *Mayflower* and the *Savannah,* the first steamship to cross the Atlantic. More than 75 ships are in the museum's ship-in-a-bottle collection, most of them constructed by Peter Barlow, a retired British Royal Navy commander.

41 Martin Luther King Jr. Blvd. ℂ **912/232-1511.** www.shipsofthesea.org. Admission $8 adults, $6 children 8–12, free for children 7 and under. Tues–Sun 10am–5pm. Closed major holidays.

Telfair Museum of Art ★   This is the oldest public art museum in the South, housing a collection of both American and European paintings. The building was designed and built by William Jay in 1818 as a home for Alexander Telfair, son of Edward Telfair, the governor of Georgia. Jay was a young English architect noted for introducing the Regency style to America. A sculpture gallery and rotunda were added in 1883, and Jefferson Davis attended the formal opening in 1886. William Jay's period rooms have been restored, and the Octagon Room and Dining Room are particularly outstanding.

In 2006, the adjoining **Jepson Center for the Arts** opened at 207 W. York St. (ℂ **912/790-8800**). This light-filled building features more than 7,500 square feet of gallery space reserved for major contemporary traveling exhibitions of art. There is also a permanent collection with some of the biggest 20th-century names in art, including Jasper Johns, Roy Lichtenstein, Jeff Koons, and Robert Rauschenberg. Also on display are works by some of the most notable artists in Georgia, including James Brooks, Helen Levitt, and William Christenberry.

121 Bernard St. ℂ **912/232-1177.** www.telfair.org. Admission $20 adults, $5 students, $4 children 5–12, free for children 4 and under. Mon noon–5pm; Tues–Sat 10am–5pm (Jepson Center is closed Tues); Sun 1–5pm.

3 HISTORIC CHURCHES & SYNAGOGUES

For other historic churches, see "Black History Sights," later in this chapter.

Cathedral of St. John the Baptist This is the oldest Catholic Church in Georgia and the seat of the Diocese of Savannah. Organized in 1799, it was the first house of worship built on Liberty Square. In 1876, the first rendition of this current Victorian Gothic cathedral was constructed but it was destroyed by fire in 1898. Based on original designs, the cathedral was rebuilt. Over the past several years, the cathedral has undergone massive renovations. A new altar and baptismal font has been fashioned out of Carrara marble, with designs taken from the old high altar. A new pulpit features engravings of four evangelists. Its twin spires and chiming bells make it one of Savannah's most notable landmarks. Inside, you'll see marble railings, murals, Persian rugs, stained-glass windows from Austria, large carved wooden Stations of the Cross, and a 2,081-pipe Noack tracker organ.

222 E. Harris St. ✆ **912/233-4709.** www.savannahcathedral.org. Self-guided tours Mon–Fri 9–11:30am and 12:30–5pm.

Christ Episcopal Church Savannah was founded as a Church of England settlement, and its center of religious life was this church—the first one established in the colony. It was known as the "Mother Church of Georgia." The present building on this site is in the style of an early Greek Revival public building, having been designed by James H. Cooper in 1838. The church was nearly destroyed by fire in 1898, but was rebuilt within its original walls. Famous clergy in the history of this church include John Wesley and George Whitehead. The first Sunday school conducted in Georgia was held here, and the first hymnal in English was published here. Its 1819 Revere Bell is one of the rarest in the country. The bell bears this ominous engraving: "THE LIVING TO THE CHURCH I CALL, AND TO THE GRAVE I SUMMON ALL."

28 Bull St. ✆ **912/238-0434.** www.christchurchsavannah.org. Most Fri–Sat 10:30am–3pm.

Lutheran Church of the Ascension Few churches in Georgia have had the bizarre history of this landmark. Its origins are in 1734, when Austrians emigrating from Salzburg founded the church. They came to settle in Savannah a year after James Oglethorpe landed. Although most of the Salzburgers settled in a community called

Ebenezer outside Savannah, not all of them did. The Reverend Johann Bolzius, who had created the Ebenezer New Jerusalem Lutheran Church, came back to Savannah in 1741 to create this church for the Salzburgers who had settled in the historic core. A wooden structure originally stood on this site, until a Greek Revival church replaced it in 1844. Thirty-five years later, architect George B. Clarke added the second floor and the medieval-style turrets. Today it's a fine example of the Grecian-Doric style that swept eastern America.

When General Sherman invaded Savannah in 1864, the church pew cushions were used as beds by his soldiers, and the pews themselves were used as firewood. The church was turned into a hospital for the sick and wounded. Although the building was damaged, it was not destroyed. Today it's known for its spectacular "Ascension Window" inside the sanctuary behind the pulpit, and for its rose window featuring Martin Luther and his coat of arms in front of the building.

120 Bull St. on Wright Sq. ✆ **912/232-4151.** www.elcota.org. Mon–Fri 9am–1pm.

Temple Mickve Israel At Monterey Square, this temple is home to Georgia's oldest Jewish congregation, the third-oldest congregation in the U.S. Designed by architect Henry G. Harrison, who had previously designed only Christian churches, this is the nation's only Gothic synagogue (ca. 1878). Its founding members were Spanish, Portuguese, and German Jews who came to Savannah in 1733 to escape persecution in their homelands. With them, the group carried a precious relic, the Sepah Torah, the oldest Torah in America. The temple today houses a museum with more than 1,800 historical artifacts on view, including portraits, religious objects, documents, and letters to the congregation from presidents George Washington, Thomas Jefferson, and James Madison.

20 E. Gordon St. (on Monterey Sq.). ✆ **912/233-1547.** www.mickveisrael.org. $5 donation suggested. Tours and museum Mon–Fri 10am–1pm and 2–4pm. Closed major Jewish holidays.

Trinity United Methodist Church This church, dedicated in 1848, is known as the "Mother Church of Savannah Methodism." It is hardly the most opulent church in Savannah, but it holds a fascination for students of architecture. It is known for its hand-hewn pine on its interior. It was constructed of stucco over Savannah gray brick, and its interior design is evocative of the Wesley Chapel in London. The formula for the Savannah gray brick is no longer in existence, having died with its inventor.

225 W. President St. ✆ **912/233-4766.** Mon–Fri 9am–3pm.

Gateway to Historic Savannah

On a bluff above the river, **Factors Walk** and **Factors Row** are arrays of redbrick structures named for the men who graded cotton in these buildings in the heyday of the 19th-century King Cotton economy. They were called "Factors." The structures themselves were built by skilled architects who had to contend with a bluff rising sharply from the river. On this bluff, they designed a series of multitiered buildings that were made from ballast stone and brick, hauled across the Atlantic.

Rice and cotton were the main crops held in the warehouses along Factors Walk, both flourishing industries at the time. During Savannah's peak as a seaport, ships from all over the world docked adjacent to the row of warehouses so their exports could be directly loaded into their holds.

The rows of warehouses were made accessible by a network of iron bridgeways over cobblestone ramps. Today this section, lying between Bull and East Broad streets, is filled with shops and restaurants. Ramps lead from the Bay Street level down the bluff to River Street, which you can explore after checking out Factors Row and Factors Walk.

Wesley Monumental United Methodist Church Built between 1876 and 1890, this Gothic Revival church is a memorial to John and Charles Wesley, the founders of Methodism. It is based on designs for Queen's Kirk in Amsterdam and holds 1,000 parishioners surrounded by stained-glass windows dedicated to the historic figures of Methodism. (Queen's Kirk is the popular name for Nieuwe Kerk, the best known and most visited church in Amsterdam, standing next to the Royal Palace on Dam Square. For some 2 centuries, Nieuwe Kerk has been the inaugural church for Holland's kings and queens.) Wesley Monumental took a long time to erect because of financial problems in the Reconstruction era and a catastrophic outbreak of yellow fever in Savannah.

429 Abercorn St. © **912/232-0191.** www.wesleymonumental.org. Mon–Fri 9am–5pm.

4 THE FORTS: CIVIL WAR MEMORIES

Old Fort Jackson   About 2½ miles east of the center of Savannah via the Islands Expressway is Georgia's oldest standing fort, with a 9-foot-deep tidal moat around its brick walls. In 1775, an earthen battery was built here. The original brick fort was begun in 1808 and manned during the War of 1812. It was enlarged and strengthened between 1845 and 1860 and saw its greatest use as headquarters for the Confederate river defenses during the Civil War. Its arched rooms, designed to support the weight of heavy cannons mounted above, hold 13 exhibit areas.

1 Fort Jackson Rd. (*) **912/232-3945.** Admission $6 adults, $5.50 seniors and children 6–18, free for children 5 and under. Daily 9am–5pm.

Fort McAllister   Lying 10 miles southwest on U.S. 17, on the banks of the Great Ogeechee River, is a restored Confederate earthwork fortification. Constructed in 1861–62, it withstood nearly 2 years of bombardments before it finally fell on December 13, 1864, in a bayonet charge that ended General Sherman's infamous March to the Sea. There's a visitor center with historic exhibits and also walking trails and campsites.

Richmond Hill. (*) **912/727-2339.** Admission $5 adults, $3.50 seniors, $2.50 children 6-18, free for 5 and under. Tues–Sat 8am–5pm.

Fort Pulaski   This national monument is 15 miles east of Savannah off U.S. 80 on Cockspur and McQueen islands at the very mouth of the Savannah River. It cost $1 million to build, and took 25 tons of brick plus 18 years of toil to finish. Then it was captured in just 30 hours by Union forces. Completed in 1847 with walls 7½ feet thick, it was occupied by Confederate forces at the beginning of the war. However, on April 11, 1862, defense strategy changed worldwide when Union cannons, firing from more than a mile away on Tybee Island, overcame the masonry fortification. The effectiveness of rifled cannon (firing a heavier, bullet-shaped projectile with great accuracy at longer range) was clearly demonstrated. The new Union weapon marked the end of the era of masonry fortifications. The fort was pentagonally shaped, with galleries and drawbridges crossing the moat. You can still find shells from 1862 embedded in the walls. There are exhibits of the fort's history in the visitor center.

Cockspur and McQueen islands. (*) 912/786-5787. www.nps.gov/fopu. Admission $3 adults, free for children 16 and under. Daily 9am–7pm. Closed Christmas.

Colonial Park Cemetery The oldest burial ground (ca. 1750) in Savannah is filled with magnolia trees and is such a beautiful setting that the city turned it into a park in 1986. Many distinguished Georgians are buried here, none more famous than the two duelers who fought one of the most famous battles of insults in the state.

Button Gwinnett, one of the signers of the Declaration of Independence, is buried here. He died of wounds suffered in a duel with General Lachlan McIntosh, another Georgia hero.

The feud between the two men stemmed from insults McIntosh leveled against Gwinnett after the abortive Georgia invasion of Florida in 1777. Infuriated, Gwinnett challenged McIntosh to a duel on what is now the cemetery grounds. Both men were shot in the thigh, at which point their seconds stopped the duel. McIntosh, though injured, had only sustained a flesh wound. Gwinnett's injury was far more serious, and he died 3 days after being taken to a hospital. McIntosh was tried for murder but acquitted. Mrs. Gwinnett refused to condemn McIntosh for the death of her husband.

Nonetheless, other members of the Savannah colony turned on McIntosh, who left the city to take a command under George Washington. In time, he redeemed himself by leading troops successfully at the Battle of Savannah in 1779. He became an esteemed citizen of Savannah in his later years. Those two enemies, Gwinnett and McIntosh, are buried very near each other.

201 E. Oglethorpe Ave. ✆ **912/651-6843.** www.savannahga.gov. Free admission. Daily 9am–5pm.

Laurel Grove South Cemetery Many of the city's most prominent African Americans are buried in this cemetery, one of the oldest black cemeteries in America. Both antebellum plantation slaves and free blacks during the Reconstruction era were buried here, including Andrew Bryan (1716–1812), a pioneer Baptist preacher in the area.

802 W. Anderson St. ✆ **912/651-6772.** www.savannahga.gov. Free admission. Daily 8am–5pm.

6 BLACK HISTORY SIGHTS

For a preview of a famous cemetery of African Americans, see "Cemeteries," above.

First African Baptist Church This was the first African Baptist church built in America. It was established by George Leile, a slave whose master allowed him to preach to other slaves when they made visits to plantations along the Savannah River. Leile was granted his freedom in 1777 and later raised some $1,500 to purchase the present church from a white congregation. The black congregation rebuilt the church brick by brick, and it became the first brick building in Georgia to be owned by African Americans. The pews on either side of the organ are the work of African slaves.

23 Montgomery St., Franklin Sq. © **912/233-6597.** http://theoldestblackchurch. org. Sun worship 8:30am and 11:30am.

First Bryan Baptist Church A congregation of slaves purchased a lot on Bryan Street to build this place of worship. The land is the

ⓂMoments   Martinis in the Cemetery

Fans of *Midnight in the Garden of Good and Evil* must pay a visit to the now world-famous **Bonaventure Cemetery,** 330 Bonaventure Rd. (© **912/651-6843**), on the low-lying eastern edge of the city. Filled with obelisks and columns and dense shrubbery and moss-draped trees, it's open every day from 8am to 5pm. You get here by taking Wheaton Street east out of downtown to Skidaway to Bonaventure Road.

This cemetery lies on the grounds of what was once a great oak-shaded plantation, built by Colonel John Mulryne. In the late 1700s, the mansion caught fire during a formal dinner party; reportedly, the host quite calmly led his guests from the dining room and into the garden, where they settled in to finish eating while the house burned to the ground in front of them. At the end, the host and the guests threw their crystal glasses against the trunk of an old oak tree. It's said that on still nights you can hear laughter and the sounds of crashing crystal. In The Book, Mary Harty calls these ruins the "scene of the Eternal Party. What better place, in Savannah, to rest in peace for all time—where the party goes on and on."

oldest parcel of real estate in America to be owned by blacks. As such, it has figured greatly over the years into the history of Savannah. In 1788, Reverend Andrew Bryan, a slave, was ordained as minister. With his preaching, Bryan aroused the fear of plantation owners, who tried to prevent him from holding meetings. Somehow, Bryan managed to hold his devout group of followers together.

A slave insurrection in Haiti set off fears in Low Country plantations. Bryan and his brother, Sampson, were beaten savagely and imprisoned, and their meetinghouse was taken away. Sympathetic white preachers intervened and secured their release. After Bryan's owner, Jonathan Bryan, died, Andrew Bryan was able to purchase his freedom for 50 pounds sterling. He and his brother restored their church for African Americans. The former slave lived until 1812. In

At this cemetery, John Berendt has martinis in silver goblets with Miss Harty, while they sit on the bench-gravestone of poet **Conrad Aiken.** She points out to the writer the double gravestone bearing the names of Dr. William F. Aiken and his wife, Anna, parents of Conrad. They both died on February 27, 1901, when Dr. Aiken killed his wife and then himself. The Aikens are buried in Lot #78H. Songwriter **Johnny Mercer** is buried in Lot #49H.

But not **Danny Hansford,** the blond hustler of The Book. You can find his grave at Lot #6, Block G-8 in the Greenwich Cemetery, next to Bonaventure. After entering Bonaventure, turn left immediately and take the straight path to Greenwich. Eventually, you'll see a small granite tile which says:

DANNY LEWIS HANSFORD

MARCH 1, 1960

MAY 2, 1981

Incidentally, **Jim Williams** is buried in Gordon, Georgia, a 3½-hour drive northwest of Savannah.

The "Bird Girl" statue, made famous by its appearance on the cover of The Book, now resides at the Telfair Museum of Art.

1873, his church was torn down, and John Hogg designed a new church for the site.

559 W. Bryan St. ☏ **912/232-5526.** Free tours by appointment only.

Nicholsonboro Baptist Church   This church serves as a monument to an African-American community founded during the Reconstruction days by 200 former slaves who relocated to Nicholsonboro from St. Catherine's Island. Eighteen settlers signed a $5,000 mortgage for 200 acres of land, paying it off in 5 years and receiving title. For a time, they thrived as a fishing and farming community before falling on hard times. Eventually, their economic base all but disappeared. Now this small clapboard church serves as a memorial to those early settlers. Some of the original pews and a porcelain doorknob remain from the original church, which had no electricity but was warmed by a wood-burning stove. In 1978, the church was placed on the National Register of Historic Places. The current Nicholsonboro Baptist Church (ca. 1890) is adjacent to the original structure and holds weekly services.

13319 White Bluff Rd. ☏ **912/921-0566.** Tours available by appointment only. Take Bull St. south until it runs into White Bluff Rd.

Ralph Mark Gilbert Civil Rights Museum   Close to the Savannah Visitor Information Center, this pioneer museum opened in 1996. It's dedicated to the life and service of African Americans and their contributions to the civil rights movement in Savannah. Dr. Gilbert died in 1956, but during his lifetime he was a leader in early efforts to gain educational, social, and political equity for African Americans in Savannah.

460 Martin Luther King Jr. Blvd. ☏ **912/231-8900.** www.savcivilrights.com. Admission $8 adults, $6 seniors, $4 children. Tues–Sat 9am–5pm.

Second African Baptist Church   This early African-American church (ca. 1802) was known for training more ministers—black or white—than any other church in the country. Two historic events took place here. First, General William Tecumseh Sherman read the Emancipation Proclamation to Savannah citizens at this church in 1864, promising the newly freed slaves 40 acres and a mule. Second, Dr. Martin Luther King, Jr., proclaimed his "I have a dream" sermon here before the famous march on Washington in 1963.

123 Houston St. ☏ **912/233-6163.** www.secondafrican.org. Mon–Fri 10am–2pm.

St. Phillip Monumental A.M.E. Church   This was the first African Methodist Episcopal Church to be established in Savannah. It was organized by Reverend A. L. Stanford in June 1865, the year the Civil War ended. The original church was destroyed by a storm in 1896, but was rebuilt into the church standing today.

1112 Jefferson St. ℂ **912/233-8547.** Mon–Fri 9am–5pm.

7 LITERARY LANDMARKS

Long before John Berendt's *Midnight in the Garden of Good and Evil,* there were other writers associated with Savannah. Chief among them is **Flannery O'Connor** (1925–64), one of the South's greatest writers, author of *Wise Blood* (1952) and *The Violent Bear It Away* (1960). She is also known for her short stories, including the collection *A Good Man Is Hard to Find* (1955). She won the O. Henry Award three times. You can visit the **Flannery O'Connor Childhood Home,** 207 E. Charlton St. (ℂ **912/233-6014**). It's only open on Saturday and Sunday from 1 to 4pm. Admission is free.

Conrad Aiken (1889–1973)—the American poet, critic, writer, and Pulitzer Prize winner—was born in Savannah. He lived at 228 (for the first 11 years of his life) and at 230 E. Oglethorpe Ave. (for the last 11 years of his life). In *Midnight in the Garden of Good and Evil,* Mary Harty and author John Berendt sip martinis at the bench-shaped tombstone of Aiken in Bonaventure Cemetery (see "Martinis in the Cemetery," above).

8 ESPECIALLY FOR KIDS

Most of Savannah is kid friendly, and your little ones will probably enjoy just walking along the waterfront and across the cobblestones of the Historic District. Kids will also have fun at the **Ships of the Sea Maritime Museum** and the **Civil War forts** on the outskirts of the city. For a fun day trip, don't miss the beaches at Tybee Island; see chapter 10. Here's one more sight of interest.

Massie Heritage Interpretation Center (Kids) Geared toward school-age children, this center features various exhibits about Savannah, including such subjects as the city's Greek, Roman, and Gothic architecture; the Victorian era; and a history of public education. Other exhibits include a period costume room and a 19th-century classroom, where children can experience a classroom environment from days gone by.

207 E. Gordon St. ℂ **912/201-5070.** www.massieschool.com. Admission $5 adults, $3 children under 12. Mon–Fri 9am–4pm.

6

A Visit to the Murder House

The Mercer Williams House, paid for by General Hugh W. Mercer, great-grandfather of Johnny Mercer, was completed around 1868. It became known as "the envy of Savannah." Decades later, there were rumors that Jacqueline Onassis wanted to purchase it for use as a private home.

Mostly its fame was promulgated by the John Berendt book *Midnight in the Garden of Good and Evil*. It was here, in May 1981, as related in the book, that the wealthy homosexual antiques dealer Jim Williams fatally shot his lover, that blond "walking streak of sex," Danny Hansford, age 21. The house was also the setting where Williams gave his legendary Christmas parties each year. In January 1991, Williams died of a heart attack at the age of 59 in the same room where he'd shot Hansford.

For years, heirs to Williams's estate have downplayed its prurience and emphasized, with much justification, Williams's role as a bon vivant and the savior of at least 60 historic houses in and around Savannah.

The Mercer Williams House is open for tours. Buy your ticket in the carriage house behind the Mercer Williams House, inside a gift shop loaded with objects of which Jim, the decorator, might have approved, and a few that he might have found sappy and sentimental. You'll be ushered into one of an ongoing series of tours, each lasting about 30 or 35 minutes. Tours depart from the Carriage House Shop, at the compound's back entrance (430 Whitaker St.).

Don't think for a second that questions about Williams's sexuality, his promiscuity, or his murder will be engaged.

9 ORGANIZED TOURS

If you're looking for a *Midnight in the Garden of Good and Evil* tour, you've obviously come to the right place. Virtually every tour group in town offers visits to the *Midnight* sites, many of which are included on their regular agenda. If you don't see them listed, just ask. ***Note:*** Some tour outfits will accommodate only groups, so if you're traveling alone or as a pair, be sure to make that known when you make your tour reservations.

Guides firmly advise before tours even begin that these are AAA tours (including only questions about art, architecture, and antiques). Photos are rigidly forbidden, and a strong-willed guide will emphatically urge you "not to touch, drool on, dribble on, or engage the furniture or art objects in any way."

You'll learn that the Mercer family commissioned the design of the house but no member ever actually lived here; that a dry moat surrounds the house, allowing for light and air to enter the lower floors; that there's a ballroom on the second floor, but because of fire codes, no one is allowed upstairs.

The house has been used as the setting for movies, including Clint Eastwood's film of The Book, *Swamp Thing,* and *Return of Swamp Thing.* It is gorgeously furnished in a style that befits a sophisticated millionaire. It is not an authentic re-creation of a Federal or mid-Victorian home, thanks to the presence of comfortable 20th-century sofas, personalized photos, and art objects, and the eclectic vision of its style setter.

The tour makes you realize that Jim Williams was a helluva benefactor to Savannah, and the city has richly profited from his efforts ever since.

The Mercer Williams House Museum is at 429 Bull St. (© **912/236-6352;** www.mercerhouse.com). Admission is $13 for adults and seniors and $8 for students with ID (both college and grad school). Tours run every 40 minutes daily from 10:30am to 4:10pm.

One of the latest tours offered in Savannah is the Paula Deen Tour (© **800/517-9007** or 912/234-8128), and you'll need to book it 48 hours in advance. The tour relates Paula's "Rags to Riches" story and includes a gift bag full of culinary goodies as well as lunch at Uncle Bubba's Oyster House. It costs $56 for adults and $34 for children under 12 (kids under 5 are free), and you can arrange to be picked up at your hotel.

A delightful way to see Savannah is by horse-drawn carriage. An authentic antique carriage carries you over cobblestone streets as the coachman spins a tale of the town's history. A 1-hour tour ($20 for adults, $10 for children 5–11) covers 15 of the 20 squares. Reservations are required, so contact **Carriage Tours of Savannah** at ℂ **912/236-6756** or www.carriagetoursofsavannah.com.

Old Town Trolley Tours (ℂ **912/233-0083;** www.trolleytours.com) operates tours of the Historic District, with pickups at most downtown inns and hotels ($25 for adults, $10 for children 4–12), as well as a 1-hour **Haunted History** tour detailing Savannah's ghostly past (and present). Call to reserve for all tours.

Savannah Walks, Inc., from its headquarters at Abercorn Street just south of Reynolds Square (ℂ **912/238-9255;** www.savannah walks.com), offers three well-orchestrated walking tours. The most mainstream one is the *Savannah Stroll,* a well-articulated ramble through the city's most central parks and thoroughfares—an anecdotal introduction to the city's history, lore, and legend. There's also a tour focusing on Savannah's triumphs, torments, and despair during the War Between the States. Both of these tours last 90 minutes, and are offered twice daily, at 10am and 1pm. After dark, the venue gets more mystical and spookier, with the *Savannah Ghost Tour,* a 90-minute exposure to the city's flair for the macabre, with departures at 7:30pm and 9:30pm. When business warrants, there is a tour at 5:30pm as well. Each of the above-mentioned tours requires an advance reservation, and costs $16 for adults, and $7 for children 6 to 14. Your guide might be a part-time student at Savannah College of Art and Design (SCAD) or an older, long-term resident of the city, but the likelihood is high that he or she will have some dramatic flair and a gift for oratory as well.

Gray Line Savannah Tours (ℂ **866/374-8687**) has joined forces with **Historic Savannah Foundation Tours** to feature narrated bus tours of museums, squares, parks, and homes. Reservations must be made for all tours, and most have starting points at the visitor center and pickup points at various hotels. Tours cost $15 per person.

Riverboat cruises are offered aboard the *Savannah River Queen,* operated by the River Street Riverboat Co., 9 E. River St. (ℂ **800/786-6404** or 912/232-6404; www.savannah-riverboat.com). You get a glimpse of Savannah as Oglethorpe saw it back in 1733. You'll see the historic cotton warehouses lining River Street and the statue of *Savannah's Waving Girl* as the huge modern freighters see it when they arrive daily at Savannah. The fare is $19 for adults and $11 for children 12 and under.

Ghost Talk Ghost Walk takes you through Colonial Savannah on a journey filled with stories and legends based on Margaret Debolt's book *Savannah Spectres and Other Strange Tales.* If you're not a believer at the beginning of the guided tour, you may be by the end. The tour

Hours for tour departures can vary. The cost is $10 for adults and $5 for children 12 and under.

Low Country River Excursions offers narrated nature cruises, departing from the Bull River Marina, 8005 Old Tybee Rd. (U.S. 80 E.). Call © **912/898-9222** for more information. Passengers are taken on a 40-foot pontoon boat, *Natures Way,* for an encounter with friendly bottle-nosed dolphins. Both scenery and wildlife are on view during the 90-minute cruise down the Bull River. Trips are offered daily at noon, 2pm, and sunset—spring through fall, weather-permitting. The fare is $15 for adults, $12 for seniors, and $10 for children 11 and under. There's a 30-passenger limit.

---

10 SPORTS & OUTDOOR ACTIVITIES

Recreational opportunities abound in Savannah, and many outfitters in the area stand ready to hook you up with the action.

BIKING The city doesn't usually have a lot of heavy traffic except during rush hours, so you can bicycle up and down the streets of the Historic District, visiting as many of the green squares as you wish. (***Note:*** You must *walk* your bike across the squares). There's no greater city bicycle ride in all of Georgia. The best outfitter is **Bicycle Link,** at 408 Martin Luther King Jr. Blvd. (© **912/233-9401;** www.bicycle linksav.com), which rents bikes for $15 per half-day, or $20 per full day. The shop is open Monday to Saturday 10am to 6pm. Many inns and hotels also provide bikes for their guests.

CAMPING The **Savannah Oak RV Resort,** 805 Fort Argyle Rd. (© **912/748-4000;** www.savannahoaks.net), is 2½ miles west of I-95, 4½ miles west of U.S. 17, and 12 miles from the Savannah Historic District on the banks of the Ogeechee River. Facilities include full hookups, LP gas service, a store, self-service gas and diesel fuel, a dump station, hot showers, laundry facilities, and a pool. The rate is $39 for an RV hookup.

Open year-round, **Skidaway Island State Park** (© **912/598-2300;** www.gastateparks.org/info/skidaway) offers 88 camping sites with hookups, costing $28. On arrival, you'll purchase a $5 parking pass valid for your entire stay. The grounds include 1- and 3-mile nature trails, grills, picnic tables, a pool, a bathhouse, and laundry facilities. Also open year-round, the **River's End Campground and RV Park,** Polk Street, Tybee Island (© **912/786-5518;**

Exploring the Savannah National Wildlife Refuge

A 10-minute drive across the river from downtown Savannah takes you into the wild, even though you can see the city's industrial and port complexes in the background. The **Savannah National Wildlife Refuge ★** (*(*)* **912/652-4415;** www.fws.gov/savannah), which overflows into South Carolina, was the site of rice plantations in the 1800s and is now a wide expanse of woodland and marsh—ideal for a scenic drive, a canoe ride, a picnic, and most definitely a look at a variety of animals.

From Savannah, get on U.S. Hwy. 17A, crossing the Talmadge Bridge. It's about 8 miles to the intersection of highways 17 and 17A, where you turn left toward the airport. You'll see the refuge entrance, marked LAUREL HILL WILDLIFE DRIVE, after going some 2 miles. Inside the gate to the refuge is a visitor center that distributes maps and leaflets.

Laurel Hill Wildlife Drive goes on for 4 miles or so. It's possible to bike along this trail. People come here mainly to spy on the alligators, and sightings are almost guaranteed. However, other creatures in the wild abound, including bald eagles and otters. Hikers can veer off the drive and go along Cistern Trail, leading to Recess Island. Because the trail is marked, there's little danger of getting lost.

Nearly 40 miles of dikes are open to birders and backpackers. Canoeists float along tidal creeks, which are fingers of the Savannah River. Fishing and hunting are allowed under special conditions and in certain seasons. Deer and squirrels are commonplace; rarer is the feral hog known along coastal Georgia and South Carolina.

You can visit the refuge daily from sunrise to sunset. For more information, go to **www.fws.gov/savannah** or write to the Savannah National Wildlife Refuge, U.S. Fish & Wildlife Service, Savannah Coastal Refuges, PO Box 8487, Savannah, GA 31412.

www.riversendcampgroundga.com), consists of 128 sites featuring full hookups, with groceries and a beach nearby. Tent sites cost $34 to $39 per day and RV sites are $45 to $55 per day.

DIVING The **Diving Locker-Ski Chalet,** 74 W. Montgomery Cross Rd. (✆ **912/927-6603;** www.divinglockerskichalet.com), offers a wide selection of equipment and services for various watersports. Scuba classes cost $225 for a series of weekday evening lessons and $240 for a series of lessons beginning on Friday evening. A full scuba-gear package, including a buoyancy-control device, tank, and wet suit, is included. It's open Monday to Friday 10am to 6pm and Saturday 10am to 5pm.

FISHING **Amick's Deep Sea Fishing,** 6902 Sand Nettles Dr. (✆ **912/897-6759;** www.amicksdeepseafishing.com), offers daily charters featuring a 41-foot 1993 custom-built boat. The rate is $120 per person and includes your rod, reel, bait, and tackle. Bring your own lunch, but beer and soda are sold onboard. Reservations are recommended, though if you show up 30 minutes before the scheduled departure, there may be space available. The boat departs at 7am and returns at 5pm.

GOLF **Bacon Park,** Shorty Cooper Drive (✆ **912/354-2625;** www.baconparkgolf.com), is a 27-hole course with greens fees of $21 to $23 for an 18-hole round, including carts. Golf facilities include a lighted driving range, putting greens, and a pro shop. It's open daily from dawn to dusk.

Henderson Golf Club, 1 Henderson Dr. (✆ **912/920-4653;** www.hendersongolfclub.com), includes an 18-hole championship course, a lighted driving range, a PGA professional staff, and a golf school that offers lessons. The greens fees are $39 Monday to Friday and $48 Saturday and Sunday. It's open daily 7am to 10pm.

At the 9-hole **Mary Calder,** 1201 West Lathrop Ave. (✆ **912/238-7100**), greens fees, including cart, are $28 per day Monday to Friday and $30 per day Saturday and Sunday. It's open daily 7am to 8pm (to 5:30pm in winter).

JOGGING "The most beautiful city to jog in"—that's how the president of the Savannah Striders Club characterizes Savannah. He's correct. The historic avenues provide an exceptional setting for your run. The Convention & Visitors Bureau can provide you with a map outlining three of the Striders Club's routes: Heart of Savannah YMCA Course, 3 miles; Symphony Race Course, 5 miles; and Children's Run Course, 5 miles.

NATURE WATCHES Explore the wetlands with **Palmetto Coast Charters,** 1 Billy Susser Rd. (✆ **912/786-5403;** www.boatcharters savannah.com). Charters include trips to the Barrier Islands for shell collecting and watching for otter, mink, birds, and other wildlife. The captain is a naturalist and a professor, so he can answer your questions.

Palmetto also features a dolphin watch usually conducted daily from 4:30pm to 6:30pm, when the shrimp boats come in with dolphins following behind. The cost is $170 for up to six people for a minimum of 4 hours, plus $50 for each extra hour.

RECREATIONAL PARKS **Bacon Park** (see "Golf," above, and "Tennis," below) includes 1,021 acres, with archery, golf, tennis, and baseball fields. **Daffin Park,** 1001 E. Victory Dr. (© **912/351-3851**), features playgrounds, tennis, basketball, baseball, a pool, a lake pavilion, and picnic grounds. Both parks are open daily May to September 8am to 11pm and October to April 8am to 10pm.

Located at Montgomery Cross Road and Sallie Mood Drive, **Lake Mayer Park** (© **912/652-6780**) consists of 75 acres featuring a multitude of activities, such as public fishing and boating, lighted jogging and bicycle trails, a playground, and pedal-boat rentals.

SAILING **Sail Harbor,** 606 Wilmington Island Rd. (© **912/897-2896;** www.sailharbormarina.com), features the Catalina 25, a fiberglass monohull, sloop-rigged sailboat known for its sun deck as well as a taller mast and shorter boom than most yachts. A journey costs $150 per full day, with an extra day costing $125. It's open Tuesday to Saturday 10am to 6pm and Sunday 12:30pm to 5:30pm.

TENNIS **Bacon Park** (see "Golf," above; © **912/351-3850**) offers 16 lighted courts open Monday to Friday 8:30am to 9pm, Friday 9am to 4pm, and Saturday 9am to 1pm. **Forsyth Park,** at Drayton and Gaston streets (© **912/351-3850**), has four courts open daily 7am to 9pm. Both parks charge $5 per hour. The use of the eight lighted hard courts at **Lake Mayer Park,** Montgomery Cross Road, costs nothing. They're open daily from 8am to 11pm.

Savannah Strolls

The best way to discover Savannah is in your walking shoes. Just be sure to wear sturdy ones along the often-cobbled streets.

WALKING TOUR 1	SAVANNAH'S HISTORIC SQUARES

START:	City Hall.
FINISH:	Whitefield Square.
TIME:	2½ hours.
BEST TIMES:	Any day from 9am to 5pm, when there's less traffic.
WORST TIMES:	Between 5 and 6:30pm, when stores are closing and traffic is heavier. Also after dark.

Much of Savannah's charm is found in the layout of its historic squares, mapped out by Oglethorpe in the early 18th century. This tour exposes you to the allure of at least a dozen squares, with notable highlights en route.

Begin at the corner of Bay Street and Bull Street, directly at:

❶ City Hall

Completed in 1906, City Hall is one of the grandest civic buildings in the country. Its gilt-clad copper dome is designed in the neo-Renaissance style. The building's two floors open onto the spot where, on May 22, 1819, the SS *Savannah* set sail, becoming the first steamship to cross the Atlantic.

After you've looked around, turn your back to City Hall and walk along Bull Street. Within 2 short blocks, you'll be at **Johnson Square,** the center of which is marked with a soaring obelisk commemorating Nathanael Greene, and the edges of which are almost entirely lined with banks and insurance companies.

A noteworthy exception is on the square's eastern edge, where you'll find:

❷ Christ Episcopal Church

Established in 1733, this church is described under "Historic Churches & Synagogues." See p. 75.

Cross over Broughton Street, downtown Savannah's main shopping street, and continue walking south on Bull Street.

After Bull Street's intersection with State Street, you'll enter:

❸ Wright Square

The square is named for Sir James Wright, the third and last colonial governor of Georgia. A large boulder marks the grave of Tomochichi, the Yamacraw Indian chief who befriended Oglethorpe's colonists. A monument here honors William Washington Gordon I, early Georgia financier and founder of the Central Georgia Railway.

The glistening neo-Renaissance bulk that rises from the western edge of Wright Square is:

❹ The Chatham County Courthouse

Much modified from its original design, the courthouse is evocative of the civic pride that Savannah exhibited around the turn of the 19th century.

From Wright Square, walk west along State Street for 2 blocks to:

❺ Telfair Square

In distinct contrast to the stately grandeur of Wright Square and Johnson Square, Telfair Square is relatively unadorned. It's basically a patch of manicured greenery, inhabited by squirrels and a distinct sense of residential, rather than "official," neighborhood life.

Located between York and State streets, the square was originally called St. James's Square but was renamed for the Telfair family in 1883. Modern federal buildings are located on two sides of the square. It's also home to the **Telfair Museum of Art** (see p. 74).

Exit from Telfair Square by walking for 2 blocks east along West York Street until you return once again to Wright Square. At Wright Square, turn south on Bull Street and walk for 2 blocks until you reach Oglethorpe Street, a street you'll recognize by the strip of greenery running down its middle.

Turn left on Oglethorpe and walk for a half block until you reach:

❻ Juliette Gordon Low's Birthplace

Many informed locals describe this elegant stone mansion at 10 E. Oglethorpe St. as one of the two or three best-furnished historic houses in Savannah. See p. 72 for more information.

Retrace your steps along Oglethorpe Street to Bull Street and continue walking south.

Within a few steps, on your left, you'll see the classical white bulk of the:

❼ Independent Presbyterian Church

This church's New England–born organist and music director, Lowell Mason (1792–1872), wrote at least three hymns that are among the best known of any Christian liturgy, including "My Faith Looks Up to Thee" and "Nearer, My God to Thee," the melody that was played

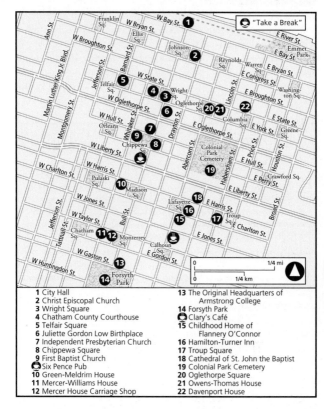

1 City Hall
2 Christ Episcopal Church
3 Wright Square
4 Chatham County Courthouse
5 Telfair Square
6 Juliette Gordon Low Birthplace
7 Independent Presbyterian Church
8 Chippewa Square
9 First Baptist Church
🍴 Six Pence Pub
10 Green-Meldrim House
11 Mercer-Williams House
12 Mercer House Carriage Shop

13 The Original Headquarters of
    Armstrong College
14 Forsyth Park
🍴 Clary's Café
15 Childhood Home of
    Flannery O'Connor
16 Hamilton-Turner Inn
17 Troup Square
18 Cathedral of St. John the Baptist
19 Colonial Park Cemetery
20 Oglethorpe Square
21 Owens-Thomas House
22 Davenport House

by the *Titanic's* orchestra as the ship sank into the depths of the North Atlantic.

Continue walking south along Bull Street to:

8 Chippewa Square

Set along Bull Street, between Perry and Hull streets, this square holds a bronze figure immortalizing General Oglethorpe, done by Daniel Chester French, dean of American sculptors. The square is visited today by hordes wanting to see not Georgia's founder but the bench where Tom Hanks sat in *Forrest Gump*. Unfortunately, the movie bench isn't here—it was only a prop—but plop yourself down somewhere on the square anyway and have a few minutes of rest.

On the west side of Chippewa Square stands:

⑨ First Baptist Church

This church was established in 1800, although the limestone facade you see today dates from 1922. This was one of the few churches to remain open throughout the course of the Civil War.

After passing through Chippewa Square, continue walking south along Bull Street. On the right, at 245 Bull St., immediately adjacent to an old-fashioned, red-painted replica of a London phone booth, you'll find your first place to:

> **TAKE A BREAK**
> Cozy, pine-paneled, and (mercifully) air-conditioned against the sometimes staggering heat, the **Six Pence Pub**, at 245 Bull St. (📞 **912/233-3151**), is a fine choice for salads, sandwiches, hot or iced tea, pastries, shepherd's pie, and bangers and mash. In its quirky way, the pub is famous in Savannah for its role as a movie location. It is here that the character played by Julia Roberts confronts her husband, the philandering character played by Dennis Quaid, in *Something to Talk About*. For more on this cheerful pub, see p. 65.

After your refueling, continue walking south along Bull Street 'til you reach Madison Square, site of:

⑩ Green-Meldrim House

This house functioned as General Sherman's headquarters during the Civil War. Originally built in the early 1850s for an English-born merchant—for the total cost of $93,000—this Gothic Revival–style building was, at the time of construction, one of the most expensive houses ever built in Georgia. See p. 72 for more information.

At Madison Square, turn right onto West Harris Street for 2 blocks until you reach Pulaski Square. Walk to its southernmost edge (Charlton St.), heading east along Charlton Street 'till you find yourself once again in Madison Square. From here, turn right (southward) onto Bull Street, walking for 4 blocks to Monterey Square. There, on the west side of the square is the:

⑪ Mercer Williams House Museum

This splendid Italianate redbrick mansion at 429 Bull St. was built around 1860. It was here in May 1981 that wealthy antiques dealer Jim Williams, about 50, fatally shot his lover-assistant, blond "walking streak of sex" Danny Hansford, age 21. Williams claimed that he'd shot Hansford in self-defense because Hansford was waving a gun around and taking shots. Williams was tried three times in Savannah. He was found guilty twice, though each conviction was overturned; the third time was declared a mistrial because of a hung jury. He finally was acquitted at a fourth trial, held in Augusta, far removed from the intrigues of the Savannah swamps. As a result, Jim Williams became the first person in Georgia to be tried four times for murder.

Mercer Williams House is also where each year Williams gave his legendary Christmas parties: Friday night for the cream of society and Saturday night "for gentlemen only." Note the lavender interior shutters on the second story's right-hand window. They shield from the sun what Williams called his "playroom," site of *trompe l'oeil* baroque-style frescoes and one of Savannah's most valuable pipe organs. The shooting occurred (as you face the house) in Williams's study, illuminated by the ground floor's right-hand window.

In January 1990, Jim Williams died of a heart attack at 59. As recounted in the book *Midnight in the Garden of Good and Evil,* a strange coincidence occurred at this time: Williams died in the room where he'd killed Hansford, and his body was found behind his desk in the exact spot where his body would have been found in 1981 if Hansford had shot at him and not missed.

Though Jacqueline Kennedy Onassis reportedly once offered Williams $2 million for the house, it's today inhabited by Williams's sister, Dorothy Williams Kingery, who allowed Clint Eastwood's film crew complete access—all for a price, mind you, despite her condemnation of the "circus atmosphere" surrounding her brother's trials and the publication of The Book. Johnny Mercer never lived in this house, though his great-grandfather built it.

Monterey Square itself is one of the most beautiful in Savannah. The statue in this square represents Lady Liberty atop a stone plinth, and is dedicated to Casimir Pulaski, the gallant Polish military officer of Revolutionary War fame. He looks back archly over his shoulder at Mercer Williams House. During production of The Film, the statue was removed for restoration, so Clint Eastwood had a copy constructed of plywood, Styrofoam, and plastic.

In the back of the Mercer Williams House still stands:

⑫ The Carriage House Shop

It was here, in Mercer Williams House's detached carriage house at 430 Whitaker St., that Williams offered for sale some of the South's finest antiques, lovely pieces that he'd discovered and restored. He even managed to run this business while he was in jail after his second trial. The property is now a gift shop where you can buy souvenirs related to The Book and Savannah, as well as tickets to tour Mercer Williams House Museum.

From Monterey Square, continue your southbound trajectory on Bull Street. Within 2 short blocks, at the corner of Gaston Street, on the west side of the street stands:

⓭ The Original Headquarters of Armstrong College

From its inception as a small junior college, Armstrong grew into a university, increasing its initial enrollment of 175 students to 7,000 today, 86% of whom come from Georgia. When it occupied this original site, it was a liberal arts college and an integral part of downtown Savannah, offering plays, concerts, art exhibits, and lectures.

Bull Street's run through the Historic District comes to an end at:

⓮ Forsyth Park

This park is the largest swath of greenery in historic Savannah. From your perspective at the southern terminus of Bull Street, you can see, in the middle distance, the sprays of what is the most-photographed fountain in the South.

Now, turn left (eastward) along East Gaston Street to the corner of Abercorn Street, and then turn left (northward), and walk for 2 short blocks 'til you reach Calhoun Square. The sprawling brownish-pink building that dominates its southern edge is the **Massie Community School House.** Also on this square is the cathedral-like **Wesley Monumental United Methodist Church** (p. 77). Continue walking north on Abercorn Street. On the right-hand side of the street is **Clary's Café,** one of the most famous luncheonettes in the South. See p. 63 for a full review.

Time to:

> ### TAKE A BREAK
> Savannah has been enjoying great food and conversation at **Clary's Café,** 404 Abercorn St., at Jones Street (② **912/233-0402**), since 1903. Today, along with flame-broiled burgers, the store carries souvenirs of The Book, including T-shirts and postcards of Lady Chablis. Both Chablis ("my mama took my name from a wine bottle") and author John Berendt have frequented the place for its good-tasting food. When we last encountered her ladyship here, she informed us that all this "fuss about The Book is helping [her] save up the big ones for [her] retirement one day."

After your refueling, continue walking north on Abercorn Street until you reach Lafayette Square. When you get here, turn right onto Charlton Street 'til you reach the square's southeast corner. At 207 E. Charlton St. is the:

⓯ Childhood Home of Flannery O'Connor

The author of such classics as *Wise Blood* and *The Violent Bear It Away*, Flannery O'Connor is one of the South's greatest writers. When in Savannah, she lived at this address; for more details, see p. 83.

⓰ Hamilton-Turner Inn

Built in the 1870s for the then-astronomical sum of $100,000, almost obscenely ostentatious at the time, this building is featured as the notorious home of two characters (Joe and Mandy Odum) in John Berendt's *Midnight in the Garden of Good and Evil.* Since 1997, it has been operated as a respectable and very elegant B&B. It's recommended in chapter 4, "Where to Stay in Savannah."

Now, turn right (eastward) on Charlton Street (it's the one that separates the Flannery O'Connor home from the Hamilton-Turner Inn) and walk for 2 blocks to:

⓱ Troup Square

Entirely surrounded by historic private homes, this is considered by many aficionados to be the most beautiful and architecturally perfect square in Savannah. An astrolabe rises from its center.

Walk to the north end of Troup Square, then turn left (westward) onto Harris Street, which will bring you back to the northern edge of the previously visited Lafayette Square. Immediately on your right are the soaring twin Victorian Gothic needles of the oldest Catholic Church in Georgia.

⓲ Cathedral of St. John the Baptist

Organized in 1799, this is the seat of the Diocese of Savannah. See p. 75 for more information.

Turn right (northward) onto Abercorn Street, and walk for a few blocks until, on your right, behind an iron fence, you'll see:

⓳ Colonial Park Cemetery

This green space functioned as Savannah's burial ground from 1750 to 1853, and as such, it's loaded with the graves of and memorials to many heroes of the American Revolution. In 1896, it was designated a city park. See p. 79.

Cross over the double traffic lanes of East Oglethorpe Avenue, and continue walking north along Abercorn Street until you reach:

⓴ Oglethorpe Square

Mapped out in 1742, the square between State and York streets honors, of course, General James Oglethorpe, founder of Georgia.

Rising on the northeastern edge of the square is the:

㉑ Owens-Thomas House

This is one of the most intriguing, lavish, and authentically furnished historic homes in Savannah, with strong links to the 18th-century aristocracy of England and to the Marquis de Lafayette (p. 73). From here, walk 2 blocks east along East State Street or East President's Street. Within 2 short blocks, you'll find yourself in Columbia Square.

SAVANNAH STROLLS

7

SAVANNAH'S HISTORIC SQUARES

From its northwest edge rises the elegant outline of:

㉒ Davenport House

This is the building that caused so much ruckus back in the days when historic Savannah risked being torn down. It's more famous for its exterior, whose proportions are believed to be "perfect," than for the quality of its interior furnishings. (It has a worthy collection of porcelain, but the furniture doesn't compare with that in the Owens-Thomas House.) See p. 72. Your visit to Davenport House marks the end of this walking tour.

WALKING TOUR 2   THE RIVERWALK

START:	Bull Street.
FINISH:	The Riverfront.
TIME:	2 hours.
BEST TIMES:	Any day from 9am to 5pm.
WORST TIMES:	Between 5 and 6:30pm.

Begin your tour at the northernmost terminus of Bull Street, at the corner of Bay Street, at:

❶ City Hall

Built between 1903 and 1906, City Hall is capped with a soaring cupola in the Renaissance Revival style. You can enter the lobby of this monument Monday to Friday, from 8am to 5pm, for a view of its elaborate mosaics and a three-tiered row of circular balconies that extend upward to an elaborate circular stained-glass skylight at the top. In the lobby is a small-scale exhibit of the role that the building has played in the region's history. Between 1986 and 1987, an anonymous philanthropist paid $200,000 to have the copper-clad cupola of the building clad in gold leaf. Films that have been shot in or around the building include the 1962 version of *Cape Fear,* with Gregory Peck and Robert Mitchum, as well as *The Gingerbread Man* (1998) and *The Legend of Bagger Vance* (2000).

After you exit City Hall, take a short detour to the west to a point directly in front of the Hyatt Regency Savannah Hotel.

A large bronze plaque lies very close to both a granite marker and a marble bench from around 1906 that commemorate:

❷ Yamacraw Bluff

In 1733, Oglethorpe pitched his tent here after his long sea-and-land voyage from England. Today, it's credited as the site where the fledgling colony of Georgia began. Now, retrace your steps back to the entrance to City Hall, and continue walking left (eastward).

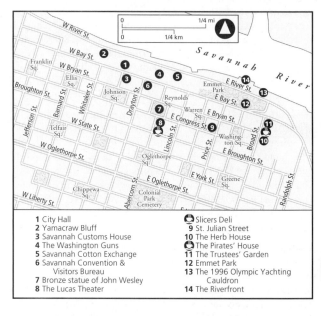

1 City Hall
2 Yamacraw Bluff
3 Savannah Customs House
4 The Washington Guns
5 Savannah Cotton Exchange
6 Savannah Convention & Visitors Bureau
7 Bronze statue of John Wesley
8 The Lucas Theater
🍴 Slicers Deli
9 St. Julian Street
10 The Herb House
🍴 The Pirates' House
11 The Trustees' Garden
12 Emmet Park
13 The 1996 Olympic Yachting Cauldron
14 The Riverfront

Immediately across Bay Street, on the southeast corner of Bull Street, rises the granite, Grecian-style portico of the:

❸ U.S. Custom House

The six soaring columns at this building have "Temple of the Winds" capitals, a style that's rare in Savannah and worth a look. But you can't visit the interior, so remain on the same side of Bay Street as City Hall, and continue walking eastward.

Within about 30 paces, you'll see a covered, open-air pavilion containing:

❹ The Washington Guns

Captured by George Washington during the Revolutionary War's Battle of Yorktown, he donated these guns to the Savannah militia after they feted him lavishly during his visit to Savannah several years after the end of the American Revolution. Since then, they've been fired as a welcome gesture to VIPs including James Monroe, the Marquis de Lafayette, James Polk, Millard Fillmore, Chester A. Arthur, Jefferson Davis, Grover Cleveland, William McKinley, William H. Taft, and FDR. Interestingly, one of the two guns bears the insignia of the English king George III, and the other features the coat of arms of the French king Louis XIV.

Now, continue walking eastward along the north side of Bay Street.

Within about 30 more paces, you'll see a fountain spewing water from the mouth of a terra-cotta gryphon (a lion with wings), marking the rust-colored brick facade of the:

❺ Savannah Cotton Exchange

The former exchange building now houses Solomon's Lodge Number 1 of the Free Masons. Originally, when it was built in 1887, it was a major center for cotton trading. An example of the Romantic Revival period, it became one of the first buildings in the United States to use "air rights" and was erected completely over a public street. Its wrought-iron railing honors famous writers and politicians.

Immediately across the roaring traffic of Bay Street rises the dignified Doric portico of the:

❻ Savannah Convention & Visitors Bureau

This building's soaring and stately looking interior was originally conceived in the 20th century as a bank. Today, at 101 E. Bay St., you'll find the most complete and comprehensive array of printed information in town. After perusing the brochures, enjoy some shade under the live oak trees that rise above you on Bay Street and then turn right onto Abercorn Street.

Within 2 very short blocks, you'll reach Reynolds Square, which is dominated by a:

❼ Bronze Statue of John Wesley

This monument honors Methodism's founder, who was pivotal to Savannah's history. Wesley is dressed in the vestments of his former role as a minister of the Church of England. On the western edge of the square, notice the Planters Inn and the Olde Pink House Restaurant, separately recommended in chapters 4 and 5, respectively.

On the south side of Reynolds Square is:

❽ The Lucas Theater

This Art Deco movie palace is now used as a performance-art showcase by the Savannah College of Art and Design, among others.

A few paces to the south, if you're hungry, consider a stop to:

> **TAKE A BREAK**
> **Slicers Deli,** at 42 Abercorn St. (📞 **912/236-1458**), is open Monday to Friday 7:30am to 2pm and Saturday and Sunday 10:30am to 3pm. It's the most recent incarnation of Beth Bolton's locally popular deli. Its predecessor, established in 1984 in a location a few blocks away, is cited as one of downtown Savannah's first New York–style delis. Don't expect anything fancy: You'll place your order for breakfast or lunchtime salads and sandwiches directly at the counter. But the service is cheerful and the prices are relatively affordable.

Now, return to the Lucas theater and turn east onto East Congress Street. Within 2   **101**
short blocks, you'll find yourself in Warren Square. Built in 1790, this is one of the most
historic parts of Savannah. Today, it's filled with homes that were saved from demolition and restored. After a visit to the square, head toward the eastern (most distant)
end from where you entered, and exit from:

❾ St. Julian Street

The short length of houses, about 2 blocks, lining St. Julian Street
between Warren and Washington squares is particularly rich in Federal and mid-19th-century architecture. Much of it was restored in
the early 1980s after the neighborhood had devolved into a virtual
slum. Don't be shy about wandering through the surrounding streets,
now one of downtown Savannah's loveliest and most elegantly understated neighborhoods. Also note the pavement along this stretch of St.
Julian Street: It's one of the few remaining oyster-shell pavements left
in a city where many equivalent sections have been covered with more
modern building materials.

Continue your eastbound walk through Washington Square,
which competes with Troup Square (visited in Walking Tour 1) as the
most beautiful square in Savannah. Wander through, admiring the
architecture, until you come to the wide asphalt thoroughfare of East
Broad Street, where you turn left.

**At 25 E. Broad St. is the crazed and skewed facade of what's believed to be the oldest
house in Georgia:**

❿ The Herb House

This small building adjoins the most famous restaurant in Savannah,
the Pirates' House (see p. 61). Erected in 1734, it's said to be the oldest standing house in Georgia. It originally housed a gardener for the
estate that stood here. The bricks used in the construction of this
house were manufactured only a short block away under the bluff by
the Savannah River where brick making was begun by the colonists as
early as 1733.

> **☕ TAKE A BREAK**
> The **Pirates' House,** at 20 E. Broad St. (**©** **912/233-5757**),
> contains a bar that doubles as a cafe. Its labyrinthine interior,
> almost like a maze, connects 15 dining rooms in at least six different
> antique buildings, some of which many Savannahians believe to be
> haunted. For more on the rich and sometimes bizarre history of this
> place, which often functions as a tourist attraction in its own right, see
> p. 61. If you're in the mood for a drink, the house specialties include a
> "Skullcrusher," composed of three different kinds of rum and three differ-
> ent fruit juices, and a "Chatham Artillery Runner," made with gin, brandy,
> rum, Benedictine, and fruit juices. You can keep your glass as a souvenir.

In the parking lot that flanks the Pirates' House are a bronze plaque and the ruins of a low redbrick wall. They are all that remain of:

⓫ The Trustees' Garden

This site was the first public agricultural experimental garden in America, modeled after the Chelsea Physic Garden in London. From here were sown the upland cotton and peach trees that later became indelibly associated with Georgia. Queen Caroline sometimes dressed in silk derived from this garden as a gesture of public support for the entrepreneurial efforts of its researchers. Alas, the experiments in the manufacture of both silk and wine failed, and the garden's patrons in faraway London, not realizing the benefits that might have come from experimentation with other crops, ended all funding for the garden in 1755. More recently, the historic 10-acre garden was paved over for parking and building sites.

After your refreshment, turn northward on East Broad Street, then cross Bay Street. (There's a crosswalk directly in front of the Mulberry Inn, a few paces to the west.) You'll find yourself on the verdant lawns of:

⓬ Emmet Park

You can pass quickly through this park (we suggest that you descend the curved iron-railed stone steps at the park's most easterly end, close to the point where you initially entered the park). Or you can stop and admire the park's individual monuments. Moving from east to west (about 50 paces apart from one another), they include **Harbor Light,** an ornate cast-iron Victorian column at the tip of which perches a light that once guided ships in and out of Savannah Harbor. It's flanked with five antique iron anchors. The **Vietnam War Veterans Memorial** contains the names of local soldiers killed during that conflict, with a reflecting pool and a replica of a rifle, boots, and helmet. A stone replica of a **Celtic Cross** was erected in honor of Savannah's Irish community, as represented by the park's 19th-century namesake (Mr. Emmet). A small-scale **obelisk** is engraved with the names of soldiers from Savannah's 10th Infantry Division during the Korean War.

At the bottom of the curved stone stairs, clutch the railing carefully. It, like all of the stairs leading from Emmet Park down to the Savannah riverfront, is steep and narrow.

Directly in front of you, you'll see two nearly side-by-side bronze memorials:

⓭ The 1996 Olympic Yachting Cauldron

A bronze replica of the eternal Olympic flame is perched atop four bronze columns. It commemorates the yachting competitions that were conducted here in 1996 as part of the Atlanta-based Olympics. A few steps to the west, in a miniplaza surrounded by evergreen

shrubs, stands the statue, **Savannah's Waving Girl.** It honors Flor-
ence Martus (1869–1943), who rushed to the riverbank waving a
white cloth countless times to welcome sailors into Savannah. Cynics
(and some bona fide historians) cite her as a symbol of the hordes of
prostitutes who welcomed sailors, one way or another, into Savannah's
Riverfront District during its heyday as a maritime center.

**In any event, the statue is an appropriate symbol for the final phase of your walking
tour, an east-to-west ramble along:**

⑭ The Riverfront

It's the single most-visited neighborhood in Savannah, the subject of
thousands of tales of euphoria and sorrow. In the 19th century, slaves
toiled and sweated, loading bales of cotton onto ships and barges
bound for Liverpool and Boston, and merchants made and lost for-
tunes erecting the brick-and-stone warehouses that line the river's
banks. Today, the Riverfront is the closest thing to a New Orleans
series of honky-tonk bars, seafood and steak restaurants, and souvenir
shops—some of them tacky, all of them colorful. Meander along the
riverfront for as long as you'd like, perhaps grabbing a quick drink or
finding a place to return later for cocktail hour.

Shopping in Savannah

While you may not be in Savannah solely for the shopping, you'll discover some unique places to browse (especially if you're looking for antiques) and several excellent galleries. Of course, the popular chains and several department stores are represented at the major malls, and outlet shopping is available as well.

River Street is a shopper's delight, with some 9 blocks (including Riverfront Plaza) of interesting stores, offering everything from crafts to clothing to souvenirs. The **City Market**—between Ellis and Franklin squares on West Saint Julian Street—is home to art galleries, boutiques, and sidewalk cafes; it's also a picturesque area for a horse-and-carriage ride. Additional boutiques, bookstores, and antiques shops are between Wright Square and Forsyth Park.

Oglethorpe Mall, at 7804 Abercorn St., has more than 100 specialty shops, four major department stores, a Barnes & Noble, and a selection of restaurants and fast-food outlets. The **Savannah Mall,** 14045 Abercorn St., is the city's newest shopping center, offering two floors of shopping. Included on the premises is a food court with its own carousel. The anchor stores are Dillard's, Target, and Bass Pro Shops Outdoor World.

Some 30 manufacturer-owned "factory direct" stores offer savings up to 70% at the **Savannah Festival Factory Stores,** Abercorn Street at I-95 (© **912/925-3089;** www.savannahfestival.com). Shops feature name brands of shoes, luggage, gifts, cosmetics, household items, toys, and clothing. Stores include the Bass Outlet, Carter's, Dress Barn, and Samsonite. Most are open Monday to Saturday, from 9am to 9pm. Only a few are also open on Sunday, mainly from 11am to 6pm.

1 SHOPPING A TO Z

ANTIQUES

Abercorn Antique Village This "shabby chic" shopping area features some 50 dealers and designers—set up in a historic house, a cottage, and an adjacent carriage house. The "village" is strong on vintage silver, crystal, furniture, linens, clocks, and paintings from the 18th to the 20th centuries. 201 E. 37th St. ℂ 912/233-0064. www. 37aad.com.

Alex Raskin Antiques   This shop offers a wide array of antiques from various time periods. The selection includes everything from accessories to furniture, rugs, and paintings. 441 Bull St. (in the Noble Hardee Mansion), Monterey Sq. ℂ **912/232-8205.**

Clipper Trading Company   This store imports antique furnishings and decorative accent pieces from Southeast Asia, including China, Myanmar (Burma), and Thailand. To make it easier for you, the collection is arranged by country. Vendors sell rare pieces such as Han dynasty burial urns (206 B.C.–A.D. 220), Song dynasty bowls (A.D. 960–1279), and Ming and early Qing dynasty furniture. Other items of interest are woodcarvings, alabaster Buddha statues, ancestral paintings, and temple objects. 201 W. Broughton St. ℂ **912/238-3660.** www.clippertrading.com.

J.D. Weed & Co.   This shop prides itself on providing that wonderful treasure that combines history and personal satisfaction with rarity and value. If you're looking for a particular item, let the staff know and they'll try to find it for you. 102 W. Victory Dr. ℂ **912/234-8540.** www. jdweedco.com.

ART & SCULPTURE

Compass Prints, Inc./Ray Ellis Gallery   From 1998 to 2000, Ray Ellis was the artist chosen to paint the official White House Christmas card. Three of his original paintings are part of the permanent White House collection of art. This gallery features Ellis's original watercolors, oils, and bronzes, as well as limited-edition prints, reproductions, art books, and other gift items. 205 W. Congress St. ℂ **800/752-4865** or 912/234-3537. www.rayellis.com.

Desotorow Gallery   A nonprofit organization, this is a gallery operated by art students who stage the most avant-garde exhibitions in town. The studio lies in an up-and-coming section of Savannah, called "Starland," and is filled with galleries and studios. Exhibitions are forever changing—one, for example, featured painted big box radios. 2427 De Soto Ave. ℂ **912/220-0939.** www.desotorow.org

Gallery 209   Housed in an 1820s cotton warehouse, this two-story gallery displays original paintings by local artists, sculpture, woodworking, fiber art, gold and silver jewelry, enamels, photography, batiks, pottery, and stained glass. You'll also find a wide selection of limited-edition reproductions and notecards of local scenes. 209 E. River St. ℂ **912/236-4583.** www.gallery209savannah.com.

John Tucker Fine Arts ★ This gallery offers museum-quality pieces by local and international artists, including Haitian and Mexican craftspeople. The restored 1800s home features 19th- and 20th-century landscapes, marine-art paintings, portraits, folk art, and still lifes. 5 W. Charlton St. ✆ **912/231-8161.** www.johntuckerfinearts.com.

Morning Star Gallery This gallery features the works of more than 80 artists. Pieces include handthrown pottery, metalwork, paintings, prints, woodworks, jewelry, and glass (handblown and leaded). 8 E. Liberty St. ✆ **912/233-4307.**

Village Craftsmen This collective of artisans offers a wide array of handmade crafts, including handblown glass, needlework, folk art, limited-edition prints, restored photographs, and handthrown pottery. 223 W. River St. ✆ **912/236-7280.** www.thevillagecraftsmen.com.

BAKED GOODS

Baker's Pride Bakery If it's baked, it's here: a wide range of pastries, rich-tasting cookies, and the town's most delectable and aromatic muffins fresh from the oven. The leading family bakery in Savannah since 1982, the establishment has been expanded to include a dining section for those who want to consume their baked goods on-site. Gathering the makings for a party, we loaded up on such desserts as cream puffs, both Key lime and pecan squares, coconut tarts, date bars, assorted rugelach, éclairs, strawberry tarts, and strudel. Kids love the store's gingerbread men, and there's nothing to fault in the superb macaroons. 840 E. DeRenne Ave. ✆ **912/355-1155.** www.savannahbakery.com.

BOOKS

Barnes & Noble This superstore is located in the Oglethorpe Mall. It hosts many events, including a regular open mic night for poetry readings. 7804 Abercorn St. ✆ **912/353-7757.** www.barnesandnoble.com.

Books-a-Million This enormous store is located in the Abercorn Plaza. 8108 Abercorn St. ✆ **800/201-3350.** www.booksamillion.com.

Book Warehouse This place offers more than 75,000 titles, including fiction, cookbooks, children's books, computer manuals, and religious tomes. Prices begin at less than a dollar, and all proceeds are donated to Emory University for cancer research. 11 Gateway Blvd. ✆ **912/927-0824.**

E. Shaver, Bookseller Housed on the ground floor of a Greek Revival mansion, E. Shaver features 12 rooms of tomes. Specialties include architecture, decorative arts, regional history, and children's

books as well as 17th-, 18th-, and 19th-century maps. 326 Bull St. **107**
© **912/234-7257.**

CANDY & OTHER FOODS

Byrd Cookie Company Located 6 miles from the historic center, this store started as a small, family-run local bakery in 1924. Today it's one of Georgia's leading manufacturers in the gourmet industry. Its retail store and showplace—the mammoth Gourmet Market-place—has it all, including a complete floral design department, daily in-store sampling displays, custom designs such as gift baskets, nautically themed merchandise and, of course, the entire Byrd Cookie line of products. They include cookies and candy, along with relishes, jams, preserves, salsas, salad dressings, and other specialty items. 6700 Waters Ave. © **800/291-2973** or 912/355-1716. www.byrdcookie company.com.

Plantation Sweets Vidalia Onions Outside Savannah, check out the Vidalia onion specialties offered by the Collins family for more than 50 years. The shop sells gift baskets, cookbooks, salad dressings, barbecue sauce, pickles, relish, and peach salsa. Call for directions. Rte. 2, Cobbtown. © **800/541-2272** or 912/684-2272. www. plantationsweets.com.

River Street Sweets Begun more than 20 years ago as part of the River Street restoration project, this store offers a wide selection of candies, including pralines, bear claws, fudge, and chocolates. Included among the specialties are more than 30 flavors of taffy made on a machine from the early 1900s. 13 E. River St. © **800/793-3876** or 912/234-4608. www.riverstreetsweets.com.

Savannah's Candy Kitchen Chocolate-dipped Oreos, glazed pecans, pralines, and fudge are only a few of the delectables at this confectionery. Staff members are so sure you'll be delighted with their offerings that they offer a full money-back guarantee if you're not satisfied. 225 E. River St. © **800/443-7884** or 912/233-8411. www.savannahcandy.com.

COOKWARE

The Paula Deen Store In 2007, the Paula Deen group took over what had previously functioned as a pub and transformed it into a retail outlet selling the cookbooks and gadgets you'll need to cook like a pro and emulate the award-winning TV technique of Savannah's most famous chef. It's adjacent to Ms. Deen's also-recommended restaurant (see Chapter 5, "Where to Eat in Savannah"), within tempting view of the lines that form prior to mealtimes. 108 W. Congress St. © **866/957-2852** or 912/233-2600.

GIFTS & COLLECTIBLES

8

The Book Gift Shop   At Calhoun Square, this store is the official memorabilia headquarters for *Midnight in the Garden of Good and Evil.* Just about anything you can think of that has to do with The Book can be found here, including The Book itself (of course), coasters, T-shirts, charms, earrings, golf towels, statues, cookies, bookmarks, music, and DVDs. 127 E. Gordon St. ✆ **912/233-3867.** www.midnightinsavannah.com.

Charlotte's Corner   Featuring local items, this shop offers a wide array of gifts and souvenirs. The selection encompasses children's clothing, a few food items, collectibles including Sheila Houses, and Savannah-related books, including guidebooks and Southern cookbooks. 1 W. Liberty St. (at Bull St.). ✆ **912/233-8061.**

The Christmas Shop   This local shop keeps the Christmas spirit alive all year with a large selection of ornaments, Santas, nutcrackers, and collectibles. Collectors will appreciate the various featured lines, including Department 56, Polonaise, Christina's World, and Patricia Breen. 307 Bull St. ✆ **912/234-5343.** www.thechristmasshop.homestead.com.

A Fine Choice   This is one of the best places for high-quality gifts in Savannah, with more than 20 different lines of merchandise. Among them are paperweights from Scotland and America, Polish hand-carved wooden boxes, Polish mouth-blown glass, Italian porcelains, Celtic pieces, lead glass "fairies" and angels, and art reproductions. 10 W. State St. ✆ **912/650-1845.**

ShopSCAD   Opened by the Savannah College of Art and Design's president in 2003, this raging success now has satellite shops at the college's other locations in Atlanta and Lacoste, France. Amy Zurcher, the gallery's managing director, frequently displays works made by students and alumni, who create gift-worthy pieces. Some of the most innovative and unique art and design work in the city is on display here, including handmade jewelry, paintings, sculpture, and pottery, in addition to photography, handbags, and clothing. 340 Bull St. ✆ **912/525-5180.** www.shopscadonline.com.

True Grits   Located along River Street, this outlet welcomes you aggressively to the land of cotton. Civil War books, a display of Civil War swords, even authentic Civil War artifacts keep alive the memory of "the War of Northern Aggression." Naturally, there are Confederate T-shirts and such "fun" items as 10-gauge blank-firing cannons. The shop is strong on nautical accessories, including ship bells and models. It also features Southern gourmet food items. 107 E. River St. ✆ **912/234-8006.**

Levy Jewelers   Located downtown, this boutique deals mainly in antique jewelry. It offers a large selection of gold, silver, gems, and watches. Among its other items are crystal, china, and gift items. 101 E. Broughton St. ℂ **800/237-5389.** www.levyjewelers.com.

Simply Silver   The specialty here is sterling flatware, ranging from today's designs to discontinued items of yesteryear. The inventory includes new and estate pieces along with a wide array of gift items. 236 Bull St. ℂ **912/238-3652.**

9

Savannah After Dark

River Street, along the Savannah River, is the city's main after-dark attraction. Night owls stroll the waterfront until they hear the sound of music they like, then follow their ears inside.

In summer, concerts of jazz, Big Band, and Dixieland music fill downtown **Johnson Square** with foot-tapping sounds that thrill both locals and visitors. Some of Savannah's finest musicians perform regularly at this historic site.

1 THE PERFORMING ARTS

The **Savannah Symphony Orchestra,** one of two fully professional orchestras in the state of Georgia, presents its regular nine-concert masterworks series in the Savannah Civic Center's **Johnny Mercer Theatre,** Orleans Square (© **912/651-6556;** www.savannahcivic. com), which is also home to ballet performances, musicals, and Broadway shows. Call to find out what's on stage at the time of your visit. Tickets range from $15 to $100.

Savannah Theatre, Chippewa Square (© **912/233-7764;** www. savannahtheatre.com), presents contemporary plays. Tickets are usually $33 for regular admission, $31 for seniors and students, and $16 for those 17 and under.

Late September brings the 5-day **Savannah Jazz Festival** (www. savannahjazzfestival.org), with nationally known musicians appearing around the city.

2 LIVE MUSIC CLUBS

American Legion Post ★ (Finds)   One of the most unusual bars to visit in Savannah is at the American Legion Post, south of Forsyth Park, in a historic Gothic-revival facade featuring fortress-like elements. In 1942, this was the local home of the Eighth Air Force. Today, not just war veterans, but clients of various ages patronize this place. Thursday is ladies night, from 4pm to midnight, featuring $1 beers. On Fridays, men get the same deal: $1 beers from 6 to 8pm. Open Monday to Saturday 4pm to midnight. 1108 Bull St. ☏ 912/233-9277. www.americanlegionpost.com.

Deja Groove   The setting is a severe-looking 19th-century warehouse perched on soaring bulwarks on the sloping embankment between Riverwalk and the busy traffic of Bay Street. Inside, you'll find an intriguing blend of exposed brick and timber, psychedelic artwork, and a hip crowd (under 35-ish). There's a dance floor featuring music from the '70s and '80s, at least two sprawling bar areas, video games, and about a dozen pool tables, priced at $1 per game. Entrance is usually free, but sometimes a $3 cover charge is levied after 10pm. Hours are Tuesday through Thursday 8:30pm to 3am and Friday and Saturday 8pm to 3am. 301 Williamson St. ☏ 912/644-4566.

The Jinx ★   A punk-rock haven to hundreds of local fans, this is Savannah's number-one venue for live music and dancing. When we asked the owner about his patrons, he called them, "party freaks, krunk bots, metal heads, hot bitches, witch doctors, glamites, scad bees, zombies, rastas, vampires, hipsters, and wild turkeys of all shapes and sizes." On the nights when there's not live music, DJs spin tunes as patrons bump and grind. Hours are Monday through Saturday from 5pm to 3am. 127 W. Congress St. ☏ 912/236-2281. www.thejinx.net/home.php. Cover for live music $4–$10, depending on the band.

3 BAR HOPPIN' & PUB-CRAWLIN'

Bernie's River Street   This bar and grill, conveniently located on the riverfront, lies in one of the city's pre–Civil War cotton warehouses and has the ambience of an old portside pub. The bar offers live music, televised sports, and extended late weekend hours. The bartenders claim their bloody mary, which is presented in a Mason jar and topped with pickled okra, is the best on River Street. If you're hungry, a light menu features seafood, burgers, and sandwiches. It's open Monday to Thursday 11am to midnight, Friday to Saturday 11am to 3am, and Sunday noon to midnight. 115 E. River St. ☏ 912/236-1827. www.berniesriverstreet.com.

Churchill's Pub & Restaurant   If you like a cigar with your martini (the pub has a large selection), this is the place for you. Once the oldest bar in Savannah, it was originally built in England in 1860, dismantled, and shipped to Savannah in the 1920s. But a fire in 2003 forced it to move to this new location. On tap are such imported beers as John Courage, Guinness, Dry Blackthorn, and Bass Ale. You can also order pub grub like fish and chips, homemade bangers (English sausage), and shepherd's pie. The pub is open Sunday to Friday 5pm to 2am and Saturday noon to 2am. 13–17 W. Bay St. ✆ **912/232-8501.** www.thebritishpub.com.

Gallery Espresso   Facing Chippewa Square, occupying the site of what used to be a Victorian storefront, this is an artsy, New Age, bohemian enclave evoking the hippie heyday of the 1960s. If you can find an available seat on any of the battered, artfully mismatched sofas and armchairs, you might be tempted to remain in place a long, leisurely time. There's no waiter service—you'll order your espresso, salads, desserts, pastries, and ice cream directly from the countertop and display cases in back. Some of the macramé, weavings, and ceramics are for sale, and throughout are scattered free copies of the city's various student magazines and culture guides. The only alcohol served is wine, priced at $7 to $13 per glass. Open Monday to Friday 7:30am to 10pm and Saturday and Sunday 8am to 11pm. 234 Bull St. ✆ **912/233-5348.** www.galleryespresso.com.

Jazz'd Tapas Bar ★   It's hip, it's cool, and it's happening here, in City Market, at the bottom of an unlikely looking cement staircase that descends from the sidewalk into a venue that looks a bit spooky until you actually enter. Inside, you'll find low-slung leather sofas and bar stools; a stage where singers croon melodies that emulate latter-day versions of Frank Sinatra and Tony Bennett; and wild, large-scale paintings in tones of deep green and maroon. Choose from a wide selection of cocktails and tapas, small platters inspired by the traditions of Spain—or, in this instance, the cuisines of the world. As the menu says, "to eat tapas style is to eat by whim, free from rules and schedules," and that's exactly what the staff here encourages you to do. Select from an extensive menu that includes asparagus wrapped in prosciutto baked with béarnaise sauce and served on a bed of braised leeks; grilled baby lamb chops garnished with garlic and rosemary; Asian-style ahi tuna, encrusted with sesame coriander, poppy seed, and lime zest; or a potato-leek frittata with fig chutney. Tapas cost from $6.50 to $14, and hours are Sunday to Thursday 4:30pm to midnight and Friday and Saturday 4:30pm to 2am. 52 Barnard St. ✆ **912/236-7777.** www.jazzdsavannah.com.

Kevin Barry's Irish Pub   The place to be on St. Patrick's Day, this waterfront pub rocks all year. Irish folk music will entertain you as you choose from a menu featuring beef stew, shepherd's pie, and corned beef and cabbage. Many folks come here just to drink, often making a night of it in the convivial atmosphere. It's open Monday to Saturday 11am to 2am and Sunday noon to 1am. 117 W. River St. ✆ **912/233-9626.** www.kevinbarrys.com.

Mellow Mushroom   Don't expect grandeur here. A member of a Georgia-based restaurant chain, this spot appeals to a funky, irreverent, and sometimes raucous crowd of college students and faded counterculture aficionados from yesterday. Decor includes rambling murals painted with an individualized—and subjective—iconography that might require an explanation from a member of the cheerful waitstaff. There's the cut-off front end of a VW Beetle near the entrance; a limited menu that focuses almost exclusively on pizzas, salads, and calzones; and a die-hard emphasis on cheap beer, especially Pabst Blue Ribbon, which sells by the pitcher. Expect lots of SCAD (Savannah College of Art and Design) students, a battered and dimly lighted interior, recorded (not live) music, and a vague allegiance to the hard-rock, hard-drugs, and hard-sex fantasies of the early 1970s. Open daily 11am to 10pm. 11 W. Liberty St. ✆ **912/495-0705.** www.mellowmushroom.com.

Mercury Lounge   The venue is hip, counterculture, and artfully kitsch—almost more like a place you'd expect to find in Manhattan—with the added benefit of having the biggest martinis (10 oz.) in town. You'll find the most comfortable bar stools anywhere (they're covered in faux leopard and zebra prints), live music most nights, and, when a band is not performing, a jukebox. Everything is congenially battered, with enough rock music memorabilia to please the curators of a rock-'n'-roll hall of fame. It's open daily from 3pm to 3am. 125 W. Congress St. ✆ **912/447-6952.** www.mercury lounge.com.

Savannah Smiles   Near River Street and in back of the Quality Inn, this piano bar not only encourages audience participation, it requires it. A pair of talented musicians duels for the audience's attention as they play old-time favorites. Request a song, and the musicians will do the rest. There are several shows of the "dueling pianos" Wednesday to Saturday, and a karaoke night (featuring a live pianist) on Sunday. The bar is open Wednesday through Saturday 7pm to 3am. 314 Williamson St. ✆ **912/527-6453.** Cover varies from $5; free for ladies Wed.

17 Hundred 90 Lounge   This is Savannah's most haunted pub. The ghost of Anna Powers, who killed herself by jumping out of the third-floor window onto a brick courtyard, has been spotted wandering about at night. She committed suicide after falling in love with a married sea captain who sailed away. If you don't mind ghosts, you'll enjoy this cozy bar attached to one of Savannah's most acclaimed restaurants. It's open Monday through Friday noon to midnight, and Saturday and Sunday from 6 to 10pm. Happy hour with hors d'oeuvres lasts from 4:30 to 8:30pm Monday to Friday. 307 E. President St. ✆ **912/236-7122.** www.17hundred90.com.

Wet Willie's Few other nightspots in Savannah seem to revel so voluptuously in the effects produced by 190-proof grain alcohol. If you want to get falling-down drunk in a setting that evokes the more sociable aspects of a college fraternity/sorority bash, this is the place. When it's busy, it's loaded with the young, the nubile, and the sexually accessible—a worthy pickup joint if you're straight and not particularly squeamish. If you aren't sure what to order, consider such neon-colored head-spinners as Call-a-Cab, Polar Cappuccino, Monkey Shine, or Shock Treatment. Karaoke is the main attraction every Monday and Tuesday night; otherwise, it's something of a free-for-all with a Southern accent. Hours are Monday to Thursday 11am to 1am, Friday and Saturday 11am to 2am, and Sunday 12:30pm to 1am. 101 E. River St. ℂ **912/233-5650.** www.wetwillies.com.

4 GAY & LESBIAN BARS

Chuck's Bar Most of the bars along Savannah's River Street are mainstream affairs, attracting good numbers of tourists, some of whom drink staggering amounts of booze and who seem almost proud of how rowdy they can get. In deliberate contrast, Chuck's usually attracts local members of Savannah's counterculture, including lots of gay folk, who rub elbows in a tucked-away corner of a neighborhood rarely visited by locals. The setting is a dark and shadowy 19th-century warehouse, lined with bricks, just a few steps from the Jefferson Street ramp leading down to the riverfront. Hours are Monday to Wednesday 8pm to 3am and Thursday to Saturday 7pm to 3am. 305 Wet River St. ℂ **912/232-1005.**

Club One ★★ Club One—which defines itself as the premier gay bar in town—is one of the hottest and most amusing spots in town. Patrons include lesbians and gays from the coastal islands, visiting urbanites, and cast and crew of whatever film is being shot in Savannah at the time. (Demi Moore and Bruce Willis showed up here when they were still a couple.) There's also likely to be a healthy helping of voyeurs who've read *Midnight in the Garden of Good and Evil.*

You pay your admission at the door, showing ID if the attendant asks for it. Wander through the street-level dance bar, trek down to the basement-level video bar for a (less-noisy) change of venue, and (if your timing is right) climb one floor above street level for a view of the drag shows. There, a bevy of black and white *artistes* lip-sync the hits of Tina Turner, Gladys Knight, and Bette Midler. The bar is open daily from 5pm to 3am. Shows are nightly at 10:30pm and 12:30am. 1 Jefferson St. ℂ **912/232-0200.** www.clubone-online.com. Cover (after 9:30pm) $10 for those 18–20, $5 for those 21 and older.

The *Savannah River Queen,* a replica of the boats that once plied this waterway, is a 350-passenger vessel operated by the River Street Riverboat Co., 9 E. River St. (© **800/786-6404** or 912/232-6404; www.savannah-riverboat.com). It offers a 2-hour cruise with a prime rib or fish dinner and live entertainment. Reservations are necessary. The fare is $49 for adults and $28 for children 12 and under. Departures are usually daily at 7pm, but the schedule might be curtailed in the colder months.

Day Trips & Overnights from Savannah

You can use Savannah as a base for other journeys, returning to your lodging after local excursions, or embarking from the city to nearby points of interest, including South Carolina's Hilton Head and Daufuskie islands and the quaint Southern town of Beaufort.

We'll start off with a day trip and then move on to travel at greater distances, including a stop at one of Georgia's "Golden Isles."

1 TYBEE ISLAND ★★

14 miles E of Savannah

For more than 150 years, **Tybee Island** has lured travelers who enjoy swimming, sailing, fishing, and picnicking. Pronounced "*Tie*-bee," an Euchee Indian word for salt, the island offers 5 miles of unspoiled sandy beaches, just 14 miles east of Savannah. From Savannah, take U.S. 80 until you reach the ocean.

VISITOR INFORMATION

The **Tybee Island Visitors Information Center** (© 800/868-2322 or 912/786-5444; http://tybeevisit.com) provides complete information if you plan to spend more than a day on the island. It's open daily 9am to 5:30pm.

SEEING THE SIGHTS

Consisting of 5 square miles, Tybee was once called the "playground of the southeast," hosting millions of beach-loving visitors from across the country. In the early 1900s, Tybrisa Pavilion, on the island's south end, became one of the major summer entertainment pavilions in the South. Benny Goodman, Guy Lombardo, Tommy Dorsey, and Cab Calloway all played here. It burned down in 1967 and was rebuilt in 1996.

Over Tybee's salt marshes and sand dunes have flown the flags of pirates and Spaniards, the English and the French, and the Confederate

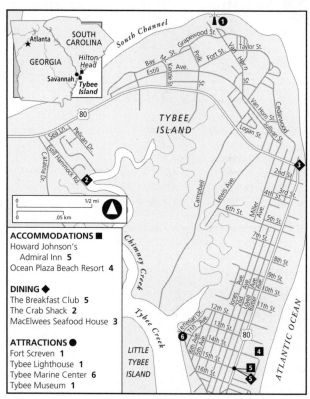

ACCOMMODATIONS ■
Howard Johnson's
Admiral Inn **5**
Ocean Plaza Beach Resort **4**

DINING ◆
The Breakfast Club **5**
The Crab Shack **2**
MacElwees Seafood House **3**

ATTRACTIONS ●
Fort Screven **1**
Tybee Lighthouse **1**
Tybee Marine Center **6**
Tybee Museum **1**

States of America. A path on the island leads to a clear pasture where John Wesley, founder of the Methodist Church, knelt and declared his faith in the new land.

Fort Screven, on the northern strip, began as a coastal artillery station and evolved into a training camp for countless troops in both world wars. Remnants of wartime installations can still be seen. Also in the area is the **Tybee Museum,** housed in what was one of the fort's batteries. Displayed is a collection of photographs, memorabilia, art, and dioramas depicting Tybee from the time the Native Americans inhabited the island through World War II. Across the street is the **Tybee Lighthouse** (www.tybeelighthouse.org), built in 1742 and the third-oldest lighthouse in America. It's 154 feet tall, and if you're fit,

(Finds) **Strolling Around Isle of Hope**

About 10 miles south of downtown Savannah is the charming community of **Isle of Hope ★**. First settled in the 1840s as a summer resort for the wealthy, it's now a showcase of rural antebellum life. To reach Parkersburg (as it was called in those days), citizens traveled by steamer down the Wilmington River or by a network of suburban trains. Today you can reach Isle of Hope by driving east from Savannah along Victory Drive to Skidaway Road. At Skidaway, go right and follow it to LaRoche Avenue. Take a left and follow LaRoche until it dead-ends on Bluff Drive.

This is the perfect place for a lazy afternoon stroll. The short path is home to authentically restored cottages and beautiful homes, most enshrouded with Spanish moss cascading from the majestic oaks lining the bluff. A favorite of many local landscape artists and Hollywood directors, Bluff Drive affords the best views of the Wilmington River.

As you head back toward Savannah, drive down Skidaway Road. On your left is **Wormsloe Plantation,** 7601 Skidaway Rd. (© **912/353-3023;** www.wormsloe.org). Wormsloe, the home of Noble Jones, is mostly in ruins now, but it's worth a look. After you enter the gates, you proceed down an unpaved oak-lined drive, and the ruins lie less than half a mile off the road. Dr. Jones was one of Georgia's leading colonial citizens and a representative to the continental Congress. Wormsloe was also home to forts and garrisons during the Civil War and the Spanish-American War. It's open Tuesday to Saturday 9am to 5pm and Sunday 2 to 5:30pm. Admission is $3.50 for adults and for students 6 to 18; children 5 and under are admitted free.

you can climb 178 steps to the top. From the panoramic deck you get a sense of the broad and beautiful marshes.

For information about the museum and lighthouse, call © **912/786-5801.** Both are open Wednesday to Monday 9am to 5:30pm. Admission is $6 for adults and $5 for seniors 62 and older and for children 6 to 17. Kids 5 and under enter free. The site has picnic tables, and access to the beach is easy.

Tybee Marine Center, in the 14th Street parking lot (© **912/786-5917;** http://tybeemarinescience.org), has aquariums with species indigenous to the coast of southern Georgia. Also on display is the usual cast of marine mammals, sharks, and other creatures. Hours are daily 9am to 5pm (closes at noon on Tues). Admission is $10 for ages 4 and over; free for children 3 and under.

WHERE TO STAY ON TYBEE ISLAND

If you're interested in daily or weekly rentals of a condo or beach house (one or two bedrooms), contact **Tybee Beach Rentals,** PO Box 2802, Tybee Island, GA 31328 (© **800/967-4433** or 912/786-0100; www.renttybee.com).

Howard Johnson's Admiral Inn (Kids)   Set within a mixed commercial and residential neighborhood, about a block from the beach, this is a clean, well-managed hotel. With only 41 units, the inn conveys a sense of intimacy. Guest rooms are chain-motel uncontroversial, with the kind of blandly international contemporary furniture you might expect in, say, Florida. The units are large enough to accommodate families. Some have microwaves and mini refrigerators. Some have whirlpool bathtubs. There's no restaurant, but lots of options lie within a short drive.

1501 Butler Ave. (U.S. 80 E.), Tybee Island, GA 31328. © **800/793-7716** or 912/786-0700. Fax 912/786-0399. www.tybeehowardjohnson.com. 41 units. $59–$170 double. Off-season discounts available. Children 16 and under stay free in parent's room. AE, DC, DISC, MC, V. **Amenities:** Babysitting; Jacuzzi; outdoor pool; room service. *In room:* A/C, TV, fridge (in some), hair dryer, Wi-Fi (free).

Ocean Plaza Beach Resort ★   This hotel has more direct exposure to the beach than any other hotel or motel on Tybee Island. As such, it considers itself among the island's upscale resorts, and it is certainly a bit plusher than the also-recommended Howard Johnson's Admiral Inn (above). Its bar-lounge and restaurant—added in 1999—boast big-windowed views of the sea. Guest rooms are a bit larger than those in some of the hotel's competitors, with bland furnishings and sliding glass doors that open onto private balconies. The hotel has a number of suites, each with a microwave and a refrigerator.

1401 Strand Ave., Tybee Island, GA 31328. © **912/786-7777.** Fax 912/786-4531. www.oceanplaza.com. 215 units. $99–$159 double. Off-season discounts available. Children 12 and under stay free in parent's room. AE, DC, DISC, MC, V. **Amenities:** Restaurant; bar; 2 outdoor pools; room service. *In room:* A/C, TV, fridge, hair dryer, Wi-Fi (free).

WHERE TO EAT ON TYBEE ISLAND

The Breakfast Club ★ (Value) AMERICAN   Established in 1976, this restaurant was selected to cater the wedding of the late John

Kennedy, Jr., on Cumberland Island. It's become so successful that lines form around the block daily, and it has won Savannah's "Best Place to Eat Breakfast" contest 11 times. What's the big attraction? The food and the affordable prices. The omelets are the best in the area, including a Philly steak omelet with top sirloin tips, sautéed onions, mushrooms, and cream cheese. The waffles are superb; most guests prefer the ones with pecans, although toppings are varied enough to include corned beef hash. If you drop in for lunch, know that the joint has consistently won "Best Burger in Savannah" awards. Expect a half pound of lean ground beef grilled to perfection and served on a freshly baked bun. Hot daily specials are also featured, including shrimp 'n' grits.

1500 Butler Ave. ℭ **912/786-5984.** Main courses $3–$9. DISC, MC, V. Daily 6:30am–12:30pm. Closed Christmas.

The Crab Shack ★ Kids SEAFOOD   This local joint advertises itself as the place "where the elite eat in their bare feet." Your lunch or dinner might have just arrived off the boat after swimming in the sea only an hour or so earlier. Crab is naturally the specialty. It's most often preferred in cakes or can be blended with cheese and seasonings. Boiled shrimp is another popular item. Kids delight in selecting their crabs from a tank. A Low Country boil (a medley of seafood) is a family favorite. The jukebox brings back the 1950s.

40 Estill Hammock Rd. ℭ **912/786-9857.** www.thecrabshack.com. Reservations not accepted. Main courses $16–$36. MC, V. Mon–Thurs 11:30am–10pm; Fri–Sun 11:30am–11pm.

MacElwee's Seafood House ★★ SEAFOOD   This restaurant was voted number one in Chatham County by *Food & Wine* magazine. Established in 1982, it is imbued with a nautical theme and opens onto ocean views from its location along Hwy. 80 at the big curve on Tybee Island. It is famous locally for its beer-battered shrimp and raw and steamed oysters. It's also known for grilling the best chicken and serving the best Angus beef on the island. The chef's special appetizer is oysters MacElwee on the half shell, topped with melted cheese, diced onions, bell peppers, and bacon. The crab soup is also an island favorite. The chef does a perfectly grilled filet mignon and rib-eye; his specialty is a 10-ounce steak Tybrisa, cooked to your specifications and smothered with fresh crabmeat, scallions, and mushrooms in a peppercorn demi-glace. The kitchen also turns out succulent pastas such as fettuccine Diane made with shrimp and scallops in a lobster brandy cream sauce.

101 Lovel Ave. ℭ **912/786-8888.** www.macelweesontybee.com. Main courses $5–$16. AE, MC, V. Mon–Fri 4–11pm; Sat–Sun noon–10pm. Closed Easter, Thanksgiving, and Christmas.

41 miles NE of Savannah

The largest sea island between New Jersey and Florida and one of America's great resort meccas, Hilton Head is surrounded by the Low Country, where much of the romance, beauty, and graciousness of the Old South survives. Broad white-sand beaches are warmed by the Gulf Stream and fringed with palm trees and rolling dunes. Palms mingle with live oaks, dogwood, and pines, and everything is draped in Spanish moss. Graceful sea oats, anchoring the beaches, wave in the wind. The subtropical climate makes all this beauty the ideal setting for golf and for some of the Southeast's finest saltwater fishing. Far more sophisticated and upscale than Myrtle Beach and the Grand Strand, Hilton Head's "plantations" (as most resort areas here call themselves) offer visitors something of the traditional leisurely life-style that's always held sway here.

Although it covers only 42 square miles (it's 12 miles long and 5 miles wide at its broadest point), Hilton Head feels spacious, thanks to judicious planning from the beginning of its development in 1952. And that's a blessing, because about 2.3 million resort guests visit annually (the permanent population is about 35,000). The expansive beaches on its ocean side; sea marshes on the sound; and natural wooded areas of live and water oak, pine, bay, and palmetto trees in between have all been carefully preserved amid commercial explosion. This lovely setting attracts artists, writers, musicians, theater groups, and craftspeople. The only city (of sorts) is Harbour Town, at Sea Pines Resort, a Mediterranean-style cluster of shops and restaurants.

ESSENTIALS
GETTING THERE

It's easy to fly into Savannah, rent a car, and drive to Hilton Head. From Savannah, take I-95 N. to U.S. 278 E., which leads directly into Hilton Head. If you're driving from other points south or north, exit I-95 to reach the island (exit 28 off I-95 S., exit 5 off I-95 N.). U.S. 278 leads over the bridge to the island. It's 52 miles northeast of Savannah and located directly on the Intracoastal Waterway.

VISITOR INFORMATION

The official **Welcome Center** of the Hilton Head Island–Bluffton Chamber of Commerce, 100 William Hilton Pkwy. (© **800/523-3373** or 843/785-3673; www.hiltonheadisland.org), is open daily from 8:30am until 5:30pm. You can pick up free vacation guides (or order them from the website) and free maps of the area. The staff can assist you in finding places of interest and activities, and the center also offers video tours in several languages.

GETTING AROUND

U.S. 278 is the divided highway that runs the length of the island.

Yellow Cab (© 843/686-6666; www.yellowcabhhi.com) has two-passenger flat fares determined by zone, with an extra $2 charge for each additional person.

SPECIAL EVENTS

Scattered cultural events in February, including basket-weaving classes, art exhibitions, and storytelling, showcase the island's mysterious Gullah heritage (see box, p. 123) as part of the annual **Gullah Celebration.** For more information, call © 843/689-9314 or visit www.gullahcelebration.com.

During the first week of March, the Hilton Head Hospitality Association sponsors **Winefest** (© 800/424-3387; www.hiltonhead hospitalityassociation.com), an annual outdoor wine tasting—the largest of its kind on the East Coast—that transforms even the most devoted beer drinkers into oenophiles and connoisseurs.

In mid-April, outstanding PGA golfers descend on the island for the **Verizon Heritage PGA Tour and Tournament** at the Harbour Town Golf Links at the Sea Island Resort (© 800/243-1107; www.verizonheritage.com).

To herald fall, the **Hilton Head Celebrity Golf Tournament** (© 843/842-7711; www.hhcelebritygolf.com) is held on Labor Day weekend at various island golf courses. For 3 days straddling Halloween, Hilton Head's Concours d'Elegance and Motoring Festival (© 843/785-7469; www.hhiconcours.com) provides a venue for some of the most sought-after antique automobiles in the world.

BEACHES & OTHER ACTIVE PURSUITS

You can have an active vacation here any time of year; Hilton Head's subtropical climate ranges in temperature from the 50s (teens Celsius) in winter to the mid-80s (around 30 Celsius) in the summer. And if you've had your fill of historic sights in Savannah or Charleston, don't worry—the attractions on Hilton Head mainly consist of nature preserves, beaches, and other places to play.

The **Coastal Discovery Museum,** at historic Honey Horn, 70 Honey Horn Dr. (© 843/689-6767; www.coastaldiscovery.org), provides a concentrated dose of information about the Low Country's ecology, history, and sociology. In 1990, the Town of Hilton Head bought 68 acres of landlocked flatlands (Honey Horn) historically

The Gullah Heritage of Hilton Head

Tours that take a journey back in time are offered through **Gullah Heritage Trail Tours** (www.gullaheritage.com). Arrangements can be made by calling ✆ **843/681-7066.** Gullah culture is a West African–based system of traditions, art forms, customs, and beliefs. A 2-hour narrated tour takes you through the hidden paths of Hilton Head, where you'll meet fourth-generation Gullah family members, relating firsthand stories of their traditions and even speaking Gullah for you. The tour also takes you to ruins or remnants of Hilton Head of yesterday, including a visit to a one-room schoolhouse, plantation tabby ruins, and a historic marker of the First Freedom Village. Tours depart at 10am and 2pm Wednesday to Saturday and at 2pm on Sunday, costing $25 for adults and $12 for children 11 and under. Tours depart from the Coastal Discovery Museum at 70 Honey Horn Dr.

used to grow cash crops such as rice and indigo, as a means of protecting it from development as a shopping center. The site contains about a dozen historic buildings, a few of them from before the Civil War. Today, the site is used for municipally sponsored events such as picnics, concerts, charity drives, and sporting events. It's administered by the Coastal Discovery Museum, whose mission involves teaching and celebrating the history and culture of Low Country South Carolina. A focal point for local volunteers, with adult and children's education programs and several ongoing lecture series, it sponsors guided tours focusing on the parcel's ecology and history. Tours go along island beaches and salt marshes or stop at Native American sites and the ruins of old forts or long-gone plantations. Children can search for sharks' teeth with an identification chart. The nature, beach, and history tours generally cost $12 for adults and $7 for children 4 to 12. The dolphin and nature cruise costs $19 per adult and $13 per child, and a kayak trip goes for $32 per adult and $28 per child. Hours are Monday to Saturday 9am to 4:30pm and Sunday 11am to 3pm. There is also an older and still active branch of the museum at 100 William Hilton Pkwy.

BEACHES

Travel + Leisure ranked Hilton Head's **beaches** ★★★ among the most beautiful in the world, and we concur. The sands are extremely firm, providing a sound surface for biking, hiking, jogging, and beach games. In the summer, watch for the endangered loggerhead turtles that lumber ashore at night to bury their eggs.

All beaches on Hilton Head are public, but the land bordering the beaches is private property. Most beaches are safe, although there's sometimes an undertow at the northern end of the island. At only the major beaches, lifeguards are posted, concessions are available, and you can rent beach chairs, umbrellas, and watersports equipment.

Most frequently used are **North** and **South Forest** beaches, adjacent to Coligny Circle (enter from Pope Ave. across from Lagoon Rd.). You can park in the lot opposite the Holiday Inn; the daily parking fee is $4. The adjacent beach park has toilets and a changing area, as well as showers, vending machines, and phones. It's a family favorite.

There are a number of public-access sites to popular beach areas. **Coligny Beach** at Coligny Circle at Pope Avenue and South Forest Beach Drive is the island's busiest strip of sand with toilets, sand showers, a playground, and changing rooms. **Alder Lane,** entered along South Forest Beach Road at Alder Lane, offers parking and is less crowded. Toilets are also found here. Off the William Hilton Parkway, **Dreissen Beach Park** at Bradley Beach Road has toilets, sand showers, and plenty of parking as well as a playground and picnic tables. Of the beaches on the island's north, we prefer **Folly Field Beach.** Toilets, changing facilities, and parking are available.

BIKING

Enjoy Hilton Head's 25 miles of bicycle paths. There are even bike paths running parallel to U.S. 278. Beaches are firm enough to support wheels, and every year, cyclists delight in dodging the waves or racing fast-swimming dolphins in the nearby water.

Most hotels and resorts rent bikes to guests. If yours doesn't, try **Hilton Head Bicycle Company,** off Sea Pines Circle at 112 Arrow Rd. (© **800/995-4319** or 843/686-6888; www.hiltonheadbicycle. com). The cost starts at $27 per week. Baskets, child carriers, locks, and headgear are supplied. The inventory includes cruisers, BMXs, mountain bikes, tandems, and bikes for kids. Hours are daily 9am to 5pm. The company also offers free delivery and pickup.

Another rental place is **Peddling Pelican** (© **843/785-3546;** www.pelicancruiser.com), offering beach cruisers, tandems, child carriers, and bikes for kids. There's free delivery to any area hotel or resort. Cost is $15 for a full day or $25 for 3 days. Hours are 9am to 6pm daily.

CRUISES & TOURS

To explore Hilton Head's waters, contact **Adventure Cruises, Inc.,** Shelter Cove Harbour, Suite G, Harbourside III (© **843/785-4558;**

dolphin-watch cruise, which costs adults $20 and children $15.

Another outfitter, **Drifter & Gypsy Excursions,** 232 S. Sea Pines Dr., South Beach Marina (© **843/363-2900;** www.hiltonheadboat tours.com), takes its 65-foot *Gypsy,* holding 89 passengers, on dolphin watches, sightseeing cruises, and nature cruises. Call for information on what's happening at the time of your visit.

FISHING

No license is needed for saltwater fishing, but freshwater licenses are required for the island's lakes and ponds. The season for fishing off-shore is April through October. Inland fishing is good between September and December. Crabbing is also popular; crabs are easy to catch in low water from docks, boats, or right off banks.

Off Hilton Head, you can go deep-sea fishing for amberjack, barracuda, shark, and king mackerel. Many rentals are available; we've recommended only those with the best track records. The previously recommended **Drifter & Gypsy Excursions,** 232 S. Sea Pines Dr., South Beach Marina (© **843/363-2900;** www.hiltonheadboattours. com), features a 50-passenger, 60-foot drifter vessel that offers 3- to 5-hour offshore and inshore fishing excursions ranging in price from $54 to $64. The 32-foot *Boomerang* fishing boat is available for private offshore and inshore custom fishing charters lasting up to 8 hours.

Harbour Town Yacht Basin, Harbour Town Marina (© **843/671-2704;** www.harbourtownyachtbasin.com), has five boats of various sizes and prices, each available for rent. The *Hero* and the *Echo* are 32-foot ships. Their rates for a group of six are $495 for 4 hours, $750 for 6 hours, and $990 for 8 hours. A smaller four-passenger inshore boat is priced at $425 for 4 hours, $650 for 6 hours, and $850 for 8 hours. Two six-passenger boats are also available for rent, costing $550 for 4 hours, $800 for 6 hours, and $1,050 to $1,150 for 8 hours.

GOLF

With more than 20 highly challenging golf courses on the island itself, and an additional 16 within a 30-minute drive, Hilton Head is heaven for both professional and novice golfers. Some of golf's most celebrated architects—including George and Tom Fazio, Robert Trent Jones, Pete Dye, and Jack Nicklaus—have designed championship courses on the island. Wide, scenic fairways and rolling greens have earned Hilton Head the reputation of being the resort with the most courses on any number of the "world's best" lists. To receive a copy of the island's *Golf Planner,* a guide to the golf courses and golf packages on Hilton Head Island, call © **888/465-3475.** For additional information about golf on Hilton Head, go to **www.golfisland.com** or **www.hiltonheadgolf.net**.

Most of Hilton Head's championship courses are open to the public, including those at the **Palmetto Dunes Oceanfront Resort** (© 843/785-1130; www.palmettodunes.com). Its **George Fazio Course** ★, an 18-hole, 6,534-yard, par-70 course that *Golf Digest* ranked among the top 75 U.S. resort courses, has been cited for its combined length and keen accuracy. Greens fees are $58 to $130 for 18 holes. Its **Robert Trent Jones Oceanfront Course** is an 18-hole, 6,710-yard, par-72, with greens fees of $65 to $98 for 18 holes. Hours are daily from 7am to 6pm.

On Highway 278, 1 mile west of the bridge leading to Hilton Head, is **Old South Golf Links** ★★★, 50 Buckingham Plantation Dr., Bluffton (© **800/257-8997** or 843/785-5353; www.oldsouth golf.com). This 18-hole, 6,772-yard, par-72 course was recognized as one of the "Top 10 New Public Courses" by *Golf Digest,* which cited its panoramic views and settings that range from an oak forest to tidal salt marshes. Greens fees are $55 to $120, and it's open daily from 7:30am to 7pm.

Also on Highway 278 is the **Hilton Head National Golf Club,** 60 Hilton Head National Dr., Bluffton (© **843/842-5900;** www.golf hiltonheadnational.com), designed by Gary Player. The 27-hole, 6,779-yard, par-72 course has gorgeous scenery that evokes Scotland. Facilities include a full-service pro shop, driving range, and a grill. Greens fees range from $55 to $125, and it's open daily from 7am to 6pm.

Further west on Highway 278 is **Island West Golf Club,** 40 Island West Dr., Bluffton (© **843/689-6660;** www.islandwestgolf.net), which was nominated by *Golf Digest* as the best new course of 1992. With its backdrop of oaks, elevated tees, and rolling fairways, it's a challenging but playable 18-hole, 6,803-yard, par-72 course. Greens fees are $70, and it's open daily from 7am to 6pm.

HORSEBACK RIDING

Riding through beautiful maritime forests and nature preserves is reason enough to visit Hilton Head. We like **Lawton Stables,** 190 Greenwood Dr., Sea Pines Resort (© **843/671-2586;** www.lawton stableshhi.com), which offers trail rides for adults and children through the Sea Pines Forest Preserve. It costs $60 per person for a ride that lasts a bit over an hour. Riders must weigh under 250 pounds; kids 7 and under ride ponies instead of horses. The stables are open Monday to Saturday from 7:30am to 5:30pm. Reservations are necessary.

JOGGING

Our favorite place for jogging is Harbour Town at the Sea Pines Resort, 32 Greenwood Dr. (© **866/561-8802;** www.seapines.com). Go for a run through the grounds just as the sun is going down. Later, you can explore the marina and have a refreshing drink at one of the many outdoor cafes. In addition, the island offers lots of paved paths and trails that cut through scenic areas. But jogging along U.S. 278, the main artery, can be dangerous because of heavy traffic, so we'd recommend avoiding it.

KAYAK TOURS

Kayaking is one of the few ways to get an up-close view of the flora and fauna of the salt marshes. **Outside Hilton Head** (© **800/686-6996** or 843/686-6996; www.outsidehiltonhead.com) offers well-orchestrated kayak tours of various Low Country waterways and salt marshes from at least two locations on the island. Its busiest location is at 32 Shelter Cove Lane, near the Shelter Cove Marina. The 2-hour guided nature tour costs $40 for adults, and $20 for children 12 and under. After getting instructions on how to control your boat, you'll travel through the salt-marsh creeks of the Calibogue Sound or Pinckney Island National Wildlife Refuge.

A worthy competitor is **Marshgrass Adventures** (© **843/684-3296;** www.marshgrassadventures.com), featuring sailing and kayaking tours from a base at Broad Creek Marina. Every day between April and October, an experienced guide takes participants out on 2-hour kayak tours to see egrets, herons, fish, crabs, and various crawling critters. There's even the occasional dolphin. It costs $35 for adults, and $20 for children 12 and under.

NATURE PRESERVES

The **Audubon-Newhall Preserve** ★★, Palmetto Bay Road (www.hiltonheadaudubon.org/outings.htm), is a 50-acre preserve on the south end of Hilton Head Island. Here you can walk along marked trails to observe wildlife in its native habitat. Guided tours are available when plants are in bloom. Except for a scattered handful of public toilets, there are no amenities. The preserve is open from sunrise to sunset; admission is free, and it's likely that your entire time within these laissez-faire acres will be unsupervised.

Also on the south end of the island is **Sea Pines Forest Preserve** ★★, at the Sea Pines Resort, 32 Greenwood Dr. (© **843/363-4530** or 866/561-8802; www.seapines.com), a 605-acre public wilderness area with marked walking trails. Nearly all the birds and animals known to live on Hilton Head can be seen here. Yes, there are alligators, but there are also less fearsome creatures, such as egrets,

---

(Moments) **Hilton Head's Wonderful Wildlife**

Hilton Head has preserved more of its wildlife than almost any other resort destination on the East Coast.

Hilton Head Island's **alligators** are a prosperous lot, and, in fact, the South Carolina Department of Wildlife and Marine Resources uses the island as a resource for repopulating state parks and preserves in which alligators' numbers have greatly diminished. The creatures represent no danger if you stay at a respectful distance.

Many of the large **water birds** that regularly grace the pages of nature magazines are natives of the island. The island's Audubon Society reports around 200 species of birds every year in its annual bird count, and more than 350 species have been sighted on the island during the past decade. The snowy egret, the large blue heron, and the osprey are among the most noticeable.

Other animals include **deer, bobcat, otter, mink,** and a few **wild boars.** At the Sea Pines Resort, on the southern end of the island, the planners set aside areas for a deer habitat back in the 1950s.

The **loggerhead turtle,** an endangered species, nests extensively along Hilton Head's 12 miles of wide, sandy

---

herons, osprey, and white-tailed deer. All trails lead to public picnic areas in the center of the forest. The preserve is open from sunrise to sunset year-round. Maps and toilets are available.

Pinckney Island National Wildlife Refuge ★★ (© **912/652-4415;** www.fws.gov/pinckneyisland) is protected land with 115 prehistoric and historic sites. French and Spanish settlers inhabited Pinckney Island in the 1500s, with the first permanent settlement formed in 1708. The island is named for General Charles Cotesworth Pinckney, a signer of the U.S. Constitution. By 1818, more than 200 slaves were used to harvest sea-island cotton here. In 1975, the refuge was donated to the U.S. Fish and Wildlife Service. Today, it comprises four islands, including Corn, Little Harry, Big Harry, and Pinckney, the latter the largest of the islands with 1,200 acres. The islands are riddled with hiking and biking trails, and are home to large concentrations of white beaches. Because the turtles choose the darkest hours of the night to crawl ashore and bury their eggs in the soft sand, few visitors meet these 200-pound giants.

Ever present is the **bottle-nosed dolphin,** usually called a porpoise by those unfamiliar with the island's sea life. The water off Port Royal Plantation, adjacent to Port Royal Sound, is a good place to meet up with the playful dolphins, as are Palmetto Dunes, Forest Beach, and all other oceanfront locations. Barring that, consider participating in either of the kayak tours as described under "Kayak Tours," above.

The Sea Pines Forest Preserve, the Audubon-Newhall Preserve, and the Pinckney Island National Wildlife Preserve, just off the island between the bridges, are of interest to nature lovers. The **Coastal Discovery Museum** (*©* **843/689-6767**) hosts several guided nature tours and cruises. Tours, conducted weekdays, generally cost $12 for adults and $7 for children. Check the museum's event calendar at www.coastaldiscovery.org for specific dates and times; you can even reserve your tour online in advance.

ibis, herons, and egrets; you may even spot osprey nests. Two of the island's freshwater ponds were ranked among the top 20 wading bird colony sites of South Carolina's coastal plain. Alligators are also a common sight. To get here, take I-95 to S.C. exit 8; go east on Hwy. 278 toward Hilton Head for 18 miles to the refuge entrance. From Hilton Head itself, exit the island via Hwy. 278 west. The refuge, which can be visited during daylight hours, will be on your right after a 30-minute drive.

SAILING

Advanced Sail, Inc., Palmetto Bay Marina (*©* **843/686-2582;** www. hiltonheadisland.com/sailing), is a two-catamaran charter operator piloted by Captain John and his mate Jeanne. You can pack a picnic lunch and bring your cooler aboard for a 2½-hour trip—which sometimes departs in the morning but more often during the afternoon or at sunset. The cost for an excursion aboard the 53-foot-long *Pau Hana* is $32 for adults and $20 for children 11 and under. *Flying Circus,* measuring 30 feet in length, offers private 2-hour trips for up to six people priced at $220. Call for daytime special rates for fewer than six people.

H2O Sports, Harbour Town Marina (© **843/671-4386;** www. h2osportsonline.com), offers jet-skiing, parasailing, eco-tours, and water-skiing. We especially recommend their eco-tours (or "enviro-tours," as they're called by the company). Passengers head out on Zodiac inflatable boats for close encounters with wildlife, including dolphins and birds. Rates are $25 to $60 for adults and $30 to $50 for kids 12 and under.

SPA TREATMENTS

Hilton Head Island boasts a denser concentration of spas than virtually anywhere else in South Carolina. As such, you might be confronted with a barrage of publicity and brochures touting the virtue of various health-and-beauty farms, each offering a staggering array of treatments. They don't come cheaply—we urge you to compare prices and treatment options, and then, if it's possible, to reserve your spa session as far in advance as possible, since space in each of them is limited. Top choices include the **Heavenly Spa** within the Westin (© **843/681-4000;** www.starwoodhotels.com); and the **Spa Soleil** within the Marriott (© **843/686-8400;** www.hiltonheadmarriott. com). Both of these accept bookings from nonresidents of the hotels that contain them. Spas more geared to in-and-out traffic include **Faces Day Spa** (© **888/443-2237** or 843/785-3075; www.facesday spa.com); and the **Sanctuary Day Spa** (© **843/842-5999;** www. sanctuaryeurospa.com).

TENNIS

Tennis magazine included Hilton Head in its "50 Greatest U.S. Tennis Resorts." With more than 300 courts—ideal for beginner, intermediate, and advanced players—the island boasts an extremely high concentration of tennis facilities. Of its 19 tennis clubs, 7 are open to the public. A wide variety of tennis clinics and daily lessons are also available.

Sea Pines Racquet Club ★★★, Sea Pines Resort (© **843/363-4495;** www.seapines.com), was selected by the *Robb Report* as the best tennis resort in the United States. The club has been the site of more nationally televised tennis events than any other location. It has 23 clay courts, 2 lit for night play. Hotel guests get 2 hours of complimentary tennis time; after that, it costs $25 per hour.

An Excursion to Sleepy but Historic Bluffton

Despite the deep appeal of the area's sports and outdoor curriculums, history buffs might want a slower-paced morning's diversion. If that's the case, consider a few hours' excursion to a 19th-century riverfront community in Low Country that time has almost literally passed by: historic Bluffton, a town perched on the South Carolina mainland within a short drive of Hilton Head.

Bluffton's historic core remains about the way it looked in 1901. Be warned in advance not to expect palatial, aristocratic homes open to the public. Some of those were burned in 1863 during the Civil War. Most of the ones that remain are private, closed to the public, and relatively small, collectively reflecting the mercantile society of river traders who occupied them. The most impressive of the buildings is the much-weathered, carpenter Gothic Episcopal Church of the Cross, 110 Calhoun St., at the edge of the May River.

Calhoun Street has the community's densest concentration of historic homes. But for a deeper insight into just how slow and sleepy this town really is, drop into the **Heyward House,** 70 Boundary St. at the corner of Bridge Street (© **843/757-6293;** www.heywardhouse.org/hh/index). The low-slung farmhouse design of Heyward House, originally built in 1840 and later enlarged prior to 1900, was inspired by earlier planters' homes in the British West Indies. It's open for guided tours Monday through Friday from 10am to 3pm. House tours cost $5 for adults and $2 for students (children 9 and under get in free), but additional donations to the upkeep of the house are appreciated. A caretaker here will also give you a free map for a self-guided walking tour of the town as well. If you want a guided tour of town, they're available by appointment for $15. Depending on the season, there may or may not be a kitschy collection of battered memorabilia for sale somewhere along the length of Calhoun Street.

For more information about sleepy Bluffton, contact the **Old Town Bluffton Merchant Society** at © **843/815-9522** or visit www.oldtownbluffton.com.

The closest competitor to Sea Pines is the **Van Der Meer Shipyard Tennis Resort,** 116 Shipyard Dr. (© **800/845-6138** or 843/785-8388; www.vandermeertennis.com). It has about the same number of courts, equivalent prices, and well-respected teachers.

Another good place to hit balls is the **Port Royal Racquet Club,** Port Royal Plantation (© **843/686-8803;** www.portroyalgolfclub. com). With 10 clay courts and 4 hard courts, it costs $25 per hour and reservations should be made a day in advance. Clinics are $23 per hour for adults and $15 for children. Private lessons are also available for $58 per hour.

Palmetto Dunes Tennis Center, Palmetto Dunes Resort (© **843/ 785-1152;** www.palmettodunes.com), is another reliable option with 23 clay courts and 2 hard courts (some lit for night play). Hotel guests pay $25 per hour; otherwise, the charge is $30 per hour.

WINDSURFING

Hilton Head is not recommended as a windsurfing destination. Finding a place to windsurf is quite difficult, but with the plethora of other sporting activities available, no one seems to mind. One windsurfer warns that catching a tailwind at the public beaches at the airport and the Holiday Inn could land you at the bombing range on Parris Island, the Marine Corps' basic-training facility.

SHOPPING

Hilton Head is browsing heaven, with more than 30 shopping centers spread around the island. Chief shopping sites include **Pineland Station** (Matthews Dr. and Hwy. 278), with more than 30 shops and half a dozen restaurants; and **Coligny Plaza** (Coligny Circle), with more than 60 shops, food stands, and several good restaurants.

We've found some of the best bargains in the South at **Tanger Outlet Centers I and II** (© **843/837-4339;** www.tangeroutlet.com), on Highway 278 at the gateway to Hilton Head. Tanger has more than 45 factory outlets, including Ralph Lauren, Brooks Brothers, and J. Crew. Most shops are open Monday to Saturday from 10am to 9pm and Sunday from 11am to 6pm.

If you're looking for upscale boutiques, head to the **Village at Wexford,** 1000 William Hilton Pkwy. (www.villageatwexford.com), at Hilton Head's south end. One of its tenants, **Le Cookery** (© **843/ 785-7171;** www.lecookeryusa.com), is among the most comprehensive purveyors of kitchen tools and tableware in the Low Country.

WHERE TO STAY ON HILTON HEAD

Hilton Head tends to specialize in high-end rentals—mostly of upscale, ocean-fronting luxury homes and villas, with higher prices than what's available in less-desirable parts of South Carolina. But in recent years, the island's roster of lodgings has expanded to include some simple economy lodgings as well. The resort area boasts more than 6,000 villas, 3,000 hotel or motel rooms, and at least 1,000 timeshare units. Most facilities offer discount rates between November and March, and golf and tennis packages are available year-round.

VERY EXPENSIVE

Hilton Head Marriott Resort & Spa ★★   Set on 2 acres of landscaped grounds and bordering the oceanfront, this hotel's program of sports and recreation is among the best on the island, and its state-of-the-art spa (Spa Soleil) is the largest on Hilton Head. Just 10 minutes from the Hilton Head airport, the hotel's 10-story tower of rooms dominates everything around it—despite being surrounded by the much more massive acreage of the Palmetto Dunes Oceanfront Resort (p. 140). Rooms are smaller and less opulent than you might expect of such a well-rated hotel, but all are nicely furnished and supremely comfortable. Most open onto small balconies overlooking the garden or the ocean.

In the Palmetto Dunes Oceanfront Resort, Hilton Head Island, SC 29938. ⓒ 800/228-9290 or 843/686-8400. Fax 843/686-8450. www.marriott.com. 513 units. $179–$219 double; $324–$725 suite. AE, DC, DISC, MC, V. Valet parking $20; self-parking $11. **Amenities:** Restaurant; 2 bars; babysitting; coffee shop; 3 18-hole golf courses; health club; room service; 25 tennis courts. *In room:* A/C, TV, hair dryer, minibar, Wi-Fi ($10 per day).

The Inn at Harbour Town ★★★   Set within the boundaries of the Sea Pines Resort, this postmodern and upscale inn provides conventional hotel accommodations within a resort that's otherwise devoted to rentals of villas or condominiums. In their development of this inn, Sea Pines demanded an exceptionally high staff-to-client ratio. Inside the building's postmodern exterior, there's a richly upholstered, lushly paneled replica of an English-inspired country house, with heart pine floors. Although the inn isn't positioned directly beside the sea, shuttle buses haul guests back and forth. Plus, its location—just a short walk from the waterways, restaurants, shops, and entertainment of Harbour Town—and its marina more than make up for it. The hotel is proud of its four-diamond rating from AAA.

7 Lighthouse Lane, in the Sea Pines Resort, Hilton Head Island, SC 29928. ⓒ 800/732-7463 or 843/363-8100. Fax 843/363-8155. www.seapines.com. 60 units. $139–$249 double. AE, DC, DISC, MC, V. **Amenities:** Bike rentals; concierge; exercise room; outdoor pool; room service; spa; 23 tennis courts (5 lit). *In room:* A/C, TV, fridge, hair dryer, Wi-Fi (free).

The Inn at Palmetto Bluff ★★★ (Kids)   A jewel in the crown of the world-renowned Auberge Resorts, the Inn at Palmetto Bluff is an elegant, peaceful, upscale resort on the May River. Guests can stroll through the beautiful gardens, play golf on the Jack Nicklaus signature course, relax in the full-service spa, enjoy watersports like kayaking and fishing, enroll their children in the kids' camp, take art

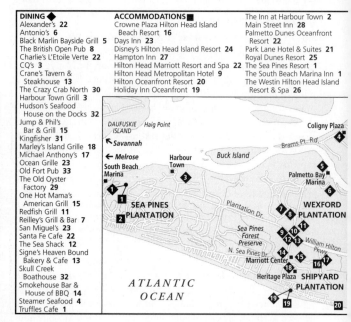

DINING ◆
Alexander's **22**
Antonio's **6**
Black Marlin Bayside Grill **5**
The British Open Pub **8**
Charlie's L'Etoile Verte **22**
CQ's **3**
Crane's Tavern & Steakhouse **13**
The Crazy Crab North **30**
Harbour Town Grill **3**
Hudson's Seafood House on the Docks **32**
Jump & Phil's Bar & Grill **15**
Kingfisher **31**
Marley's Island Grille **18**
Michael Anthony's **17**
Ocean Grille **23**
Old Fort Pub **33**
The Old Oyster Factory **29**
One Hot Mama's American Grill **15**
Redfish Grill **11**
Reilley's Grill & Bar **7**
San Miguel's **23**
Santa Fe Cafe **22**
The Sea Shack **12**
Signe's Heaven Bound Bakery & Cafe **13**
Skull Creek Boathouse **32**
Smokehouse Bar & House of BBQ **14**
Steamer Seafood **4**
Truffles Cafe **1**

ACCOMMODATIONS ■
Crowne Plaza Hilton Head Island Beach Resort **16**
Days Inn **23**
Disney's Hilton Head Island Resort **24**
Hampton Inn **27**
Hilton Head Marriott Resort and Spa **22**
Hilton Head Metropolitan Hotel **9**
Hilton Oceanfront Resort **20**
Holiday Inn Oceanfront **19**
The Inn at Harbour Town **2**
Main Street Inn **28**
Palmetto Dunes Oceanfront Resort **22**
Park Lane Hotel & Suites **21**
Royal Dunes Resort **25**
The Sea Pines Resort **1**
The South Beach Marina Inn **1**
The Westin Hilton Head Island Resort & Spa **26**

classes, or enjoy a beach excursion. (There is, however, a $25-per-day service fee per guest room to be able to use the fitness center, kayaks, canoes, and outdoor lap pool.) Accommodations include cottages, cottage suites, and village homes. Exquisitely appointed, the cottages and cottage suites have vaulted ceilings, hardwood pine floors, fireplaces, screened porches, and water views. With two to four bedrooms, full kitchens, screened porches, and luxury bed linens, the village homes are ideal for families. The Inn at Palmetto Bluff offers four dining options: the elegant **River House Restaurant,** with river views; the **May River Grill** at the May River Golf Club; **Buffalo's,** in the Village; or dining in your own cottage.

476 Mount Pilla Rd., Bluffton, SC 29910. ✆ **866/706-6565** or 843/706-6500. Fax 843/706-6550. www.palmettobluffresort.com. 77 units, 42 cottages, 8 cottage suites, 27 village homes. $475–$950 cottage; $700–$1,100 cottage suite; from $1,100 village home. AE, DC, DISC, MC, V. **Amenities:** 3 restaurants; children's camp; exercise room; outdoor pool; spa. *In room:* A/C, TV, fridge, kitchen (in village home), Wi-Fi (free).

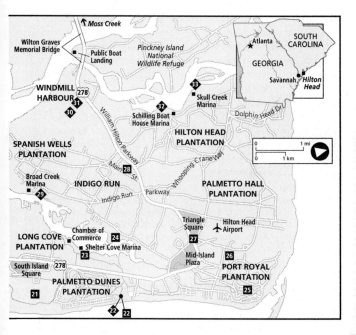

Main Street Inn ★★★ (Finds) Don't expect cozy Americana from this small, luxurious inn; it's grander and more European in its motifs than its name would imply. Designed like a small-scale villa that you might expect to see in the south of France, it combines elements from both New Orleans and Charleston, including cast-iron balustrades and a formal semitropical garden where guests are encouraged to indulge in afternoon tea. Inside, you'll find artfully clipped topiary, French Provincial furnishings, and accommodations that are more luxurious and richly appointed than those of any other hotel in Hilton Head. Despite a location that requires a drive to the nearest beach, this hotel provides a luxe alternative to the less-personalized megahotels nearby.

2200 Main St., Hilton Head Island, SC 29926. (②) **800/471-3001** or 843/681-3001. Fax 843/681-5541. www.mainstreetinn.com. 33 units. $139–$199 double. Additional person $35 extra. Rates include breakfast. AE, DISC, MC, V. Free parking. **Amenities:** Breakfast room; outdoor pool; spa. *In room:* A/C, TV, hair dryer, minibar, Wi-Fi (free).

The Westin Hilton Head Island Resort & Spa ★★ (Kids) Near the relatively isolated northern end of Hilton Head Island on 24 landscaped acres, this hotel stands out as the most child- and pet-friendly blockbuster hotel on the island. Its Disneyesque design, including cupolas and postmodern ornamentation that looks vaguely Moorish, evokes fanciful Palm Beach hotels. If there's a drawback, it's the fact that it's so obviously geared to families with children that romantically inclined couples without children in tow might not necessarily thrill to the family-friendly sweep of it all. Fortunately, there's an active and much-respected children's camp on-site for the care and attention of young'uns. Most of the guest rooms have ocean views, and are outfitted in modern interpretations of the Low Country plantation style. The hotel is also home to the elegant Heavenly Spa by Westin, a full-service spa.

2 Grasslawn Ave., Hilton Head Island, SC 29928. ✆ **800/937-8461** or 843/681-4000. Fax 843/681-1096. www.starwoodhotels.com. 412 units. $169–$429 double; $450–$1,900 suite. Children 17 and under stay free in parent's room; children 4 and under eat free. Special promotions offered. AE, DC, DISC, MC, V. **Amenities:** 3 restaurants; bar; 3 18-hole golf courses; Jacuzzi; room service. *In room:* A/C, TV, hair dryer; minibar, Wi-Fi ($13 per day).

EXPENSIVE

Crowne Plaza Hilton Head Island Beach Resort ★ Tucked away in the Shipyard Plantation (a high-end upscale resort area with private homes, golf, and tennis) and designed as the centerpiece of its 800 acres, this five-story hotel gives the Westin stiff competition. The National Audubon Society has praised its golf course for respecting local wildlife. Guest rooms are simple, yet the sheer beauty of the landscaping and the well-trained, attentive staff (dressed in nautically inspired uniforms) go a long way toward making your stay memorable. The most glamorous restaurant is **Portz,** and a good middle-bracket choice is **Brella's,** serving both lunch and dinner. Certain nights in the premier bar, **Signals,** feature line dancing and shag dancing.

130 Shipyard Dr., Shipyard Plantation, Hilton Head Island, SC 29928. ✆ **800/334-1881** or 843/842-2400. Fax 843/785-8463. www.cphiltonhead.com. 340 units. $199–$399 double; from $299 suite. AE, DC, DISC, MC, V. Free parking. **Amenities:** 2 restaurants; bar; bike rentals; exercise room; 2 pools (1 indoor); room service. *In room:* A/C, TV, hair dryer, minibar, Wi-Fi ($10 per day).

Disney's Hilton Head Island Resort ★★ (Kids) This medium-scale, cost-effective, family-conscious resort is on a 15-acre island, inland from the coast, that rises above Hilton Head's widest estuary, Broad Creek. About 20 woodsy-looking buildings are arranged on a compound. Expect lots of pine trees and fallen pine needles, garlands of Spanish moss, plenty of families with children, and an ambience that's several notches less intense than that of hotels in Disney theme parks. Characters include Shadow the Dog (a golden retriever that is the resort's mascot) and Blue Crab, a storyteller, fisherman, and musician. Part of the fun is the many summer-camp-style activities for kids with or without their parents. Guest rooms usually contain mini-kitchens, suitable for feeding sandwiches and macaroni to the little ones. **Tide Me Over** is a walk-up window serving Carolina cookery for breakfast and lunch. The resort runs a shuttle bus to and from a nearby beach at 15-minute intervals daily between 10am and 5pm.

22 Harbourside Lane, Hilton Head Island, SC 29928. ℂ **800/500-3990** or 843/341-4100. Fax 843/341-4130. http://dvc.disney.go.com. 123 units. $165–$350 studio; $260–$1,100 villa. AE, DC, DISC, MC, V. **Amenities:** 2 restaurants; bar; babysitting; exercise room; 3 outdoor pools. *In room:* A/C, TV, hair dryer, kitchenette (in most), Wi-Fi ($11 per day).

Hilton Oceanfront Resort ★

This award-winning property isn't the most prominent on the island. Many visitors, however, prefer it because of its hideaway position: tucked at the end of the main road through Palmetto Dunes, and because its rooms are, on average, a bit larger than those at any other resort on the island. In addition, a $4-million renovation, completed in 2008, adds to its appeal. The low-rise design features hallways that open to sea breezes at either end. The guest rooms offer balconies that angle out toward the beach allowing sea views from all rooms. **HH Prime,** an upmarket steak-house that looks more glamorous at night than during the day, when it evokes an upscale coffee shop, is the resort's premier restaurant. On-site are also a Pizza Hut and a much frequented, urban-looking bar and lounge, featuring live music.

23 Ocean Lane (PO Box 6165), Hilton Head Island, SC 29938. ℂ **800/845-8001** or 843/842-8000. Fax 843/341-8033. www.hiltonoceanfrontresort.com. 323 units. $139–$349 double; $359–$609 suite. AE, DC, DISC, MC, V. Parking $8–$12. **Amenities:** 4 restaurants; 2 bars; exercise room; 2 outdoor pools; room service; spa. *In room:* A/C, TV, hair dryer, kitchenette, Wi-Fi ($11 per day).

Royal Dunes Resort ★

Comfortable and clean, but bland and somewhat anonymous, this compound's three-bedroom, three-bathroom apartments have been aggressively marketed to independent investors as a timeshare investment. Whenever the owners aren't in residence, the apartments become available for rentals on the open market. They occupy a quartet of four-story buildings located on the Port Royal Plantation. Each has a washer/dryer; durable wicker, rattan, and Southern Colonial furniture; and tub/shower combinations. The resort is located at the edge of a forested greenbelt, just a 10-minute walk from the beach.

8 Wimbledon Court, Hilton Head, SC 29928. ☎ 843/681-9718. Fax 843/681-2003. www.spmresorts.com. 56 units. $195–$260 double. AE, MC, V. **Amenities:** Bike rentals; exercise room; Internet (free); 2 outdoor pools. *In room:* A/C, TV, kitchen.

MODERATE

Holiday Inn Oceanfront ★ (Kids)   The island's leading moderately priced hotel, and its oldest (dating back to 1970), this sprawling five-story building opens onto a crowded stretch of beach on the southern side of the island, directly across the road from the fast-food joints and souvenir shops of Coligny Plaza. The rooms are spacious and informally but comfortably furnished with rattan furniture and pastel colors. Unfortunately, the balconies are generally too small to actually walk out onto. Only a few of the rooms have sea views—most of them look out over parking lots and trees. Don't expect glamour here; the place is cozy, crowded, and family friendly, with a busy pool and barely enough parking. But the staff, despite many demands on their time, are genuinely concerned and helpful. In the summer, planned children's activities are offered.

1 S. Forest Beach Dr. (PO Box 5728), Hilton Head Island, SC 29938. ☎ 800/423-9897 or 843/785-5126. Fax 843/785-6678. www.hiltonhead.com. 202 units. $129–$234 double. AE, DC, DISC, MC, V. Free parking. **Amenities:** Restaurant; outdoor bar; exercise room; outdoor pool; room service; Wi-Fi (free). *In room:* A/C, TV, hair dryer.

Park Lane Hotel & Suites   Set on the eastern edge of Hilton Head's main traffic artery, midway between the Palmetto Dunes and Shipyard plantations, this is a three-story, all-suite complex in a wooded, parklike setting. The suites are functionally furnished and comfortable. Both cost-conscious families and business travelers on extended stays appreciate the simple cooking facilities in all units.

12 Park Lane (in Central Park), Hilton Head Island, SC 29938. ☎ 843/686-5700. Fax 843/686-3952. www.hiltonheadparklanehotel.com. 156 units. $79–$129 suite. Rates include continental breakfast. AE, DC, DISC, MC, V. **Amenities:** Exercise room; Jacuzzi; outdoor pool; 2 tennis courts (lit). *In room:* A/C, TV, hair dryer, kitchenette, Wi-Fi (free).

The South Beach Marina Inn ★ (Finds)   This 1986 clapboard-sided complex of marina-front buildings, within the Sea Pines Resort, offers traditional hotel-style rooms. With nautical, seafaring charm, the inn meanders over a labyrinth of catwalks and stairways above a complex of shops, souvenir kiosks, and restaurants. It is especially known for being located immediately adjacent to the Salty Dog Cafe—one of the island's most popular eateries. Each one- or two-bedroom unit is cozily outfitted with country-style braided rugs, pinewood floors, and homespun-charm decor celebrating rural 19th-century America.

232 S. Sea Pines Dr. (in the Sea Pines Resort), Hilton Head Island, SC 29920.
© **800/367-3909** or 843/671-6498. www.sbinn.com. 17 units. $65–$179 1-bedroom; $87–$186 2-bedroom. AE, DISC, MC, V. Free parking. **Amenities:** Outdoor pool. *In room:* A/C, TV, hair dryer, kitchenette, Wi-Fi (free).

INEXPENSIVE

Days Inn   The Days Inn provides easy access to the beach, golf, tennis, marinas, and shopping. The rooms are wheelchair accessible and, although unremarkable, they offer a good value for expensive Hilton Head. Families save money by using one of the grills outside for a home-style barbecue, to be enjoyed at one of the picnic tables.

9 Marina Side Dr., Hilton Head Island, SC 29928. © **800/329-7466** or 843/842-4800. Fax 843/842-5388. www.daysinn.com. 119 units. $89–$139 double; $129–$169 suite. Rates include continental breakfast. Senior discounts available. AE, DISC, MC, V. Free parking. **Amenities:** Breakfast room; outdoor pool. *In room:* A/C, TV, hair dryer, Wi-Fi (free).

Hampton Inn Hilton Head Island (Kids)   Renovated in 2007, this is one of the two or three most sought-after motels on Hilton Head, especially by families and business travelers who don't mind its lack of resort-style amenities and its straightforward, cost-effective simplicity. It's 5 miles from the Graves Bridge and the closest motel to the airport. Rooms in pastel pinks and greens are quite comfortable and well maintained. Some rooms have refrigerators. Local calls are free, and breakfast is included in the rates.

1 Dillon Rd., Hilton Head Island, SC 29926. © **800/HAMPTON** (426-7866) or 843/681-7900. Fax 843/681-4330. www.hamptoninn.com. 125 units. $124–$189 double. Children 17 and under stay free in parent's room. Rates include continental breakfast. AE, DC, DISC, MC, V. **Amenities:** Breakfast room; exercise room; outdoor pool. *In room:* A/C, TV, hair dryer, Internet (free), kitchen (in some).

Hilton Head Metropolitan Hotel (Kids)   Favored by families, this 1970s-era, five-story, white-concrete hotel is directly across the street from the island's busiest beach. Each room is configured in a bland, generic style duplicated in motels throughout the world. Virtually everything on Hilton Head is within a 15-minute drive. Expect lots of children, especially during the midsummer months.

36 S. Forest Beach Dr., Hilton Head, SC 29928. © **800/535-3248** or 843/842-3100. Fax 843/785-6928. http://hiltonheadmetropolitan.com. 140 units. $49–$139 double. Rates include continental breakfast. AE, DC, DISC, MC, V. **Amenities:** Exercise room; outdoor pool; Wi-Fi (free). *In room:* A/C, TV, hair dryer, kitchenette (in some).

VILLA RENTALS

The **Vacation Company** (© **800/845-7018;** www.hiltonhead vacationrentals.com) has been in business for almost a quarter-century and specializes in the rental of homes and villas throughout the region.

Its leading competitors include **Beach Properties of Hilton Head** (✆ **800/671-5155** or 843/671-5155; www.beach-property.com), **Hilton Head Vacation Rentals** (✆ **800/232-2463;** www.800 beachme.com), and **ResortQuest Vacation Home Network** (✆ **800/ 875-8726** or 843/785-7300; www.resortquesthiltonhead.com).

Two rental developments that we consider especially appealing are reviewed below.

Palmetto Dunes Oceanfront Resort ★ (Kids) This relaxed and informal enclave of privately owned villas is set within the sprawling 1,800-acre complex of Palmetto Dunes Plantation, 7 miles south of the bridge. Accommodations range all the way from one-bedroom condos, booked mostly by groups, to four-bedroom villas, each of the latter furnished in the owner's personal taste. This is the place for longer stays, ideal for families who want a home away from home when they're traveling. In fact, in 2003 it was ranked as the number-one family resort in the continental U.S. and Canada by *Travel + Leisure Family* and is still listed among the top 10. Villas are fully equipped and receive housekeeping service; they're located on the ocean, fairways, and lagoons. Each villa comes with a full kitchen, washer/dryer, living room and dining area, and balcony or patio. The resort opens onto a 200-slip marina.

Palmetto Dunes (PO Box 5606), Hilton Head Island, SC 29938. ✆ **800/827-3006.** www.palmettodunes.com. 500 units. $260–$3,500 per week condo or villa. Golf and honeymoon packages available. 2-night minimum stay. 50% deposit for reservations. AE, DC, DISC, MC, V. Free parking. **Amenities:** 20 restaurants; 12 bars; 3 18-hole golf courses; 28 outdoor pools; 25 tennis courts (8 lit). *In room:* A/C, TV, Wi-Fi (in some, free).

The Sea Pines Resort ★★★ Since 1955, this has been one of the leading condo developments in America, sprawling across 5,500 acres at the southernmost tip of the island. Lodgings vary—everything from one- to four-bedroom villas to opulent private homes are available when the owners are away. An additional option here is the separately recommended Inn at Harbour Town, a 60-room inn, which offers conventional hotel rooms. The clientele includes hordes of golfers because Sea Pines is the home of the Verizon Heritage golf tournament, a major stop on the PGA tour. Even if you're not a Sea Pines guest, you can eat, shop, or enjoy aspects of its nightlife.

Sea Pines (PO Box 7000), Hilton Head Island, SC 29938. ✆ **866/561-8802.** Fax 843/842-1475. www.seapines.com. 500 units. $170–$340 1-bedroom villa; $300–$385 2-bedroom villa; $320–$600 3-bedroom villa. Rates are daily, based on 3-night stay. AE, DC, DISC, MC, V. **Amenities:** 12 restaurants; 12 bars; babysitting; exercise room; 3 18-hole golf courses; 2 outdoor pools; spa; 23 tennis courts (5 lit); watersports/rentals. *In room:* A/C, TV, kitchen or kitchenette, Wi-Fi (in some, free).

Hilton Head has the dubious distinction of having the most expensive restaurants in South Carolina. What on the island might be ranked as moderate would be considered very expensive in other parts of the state.

EXPENSIVE

Marley's Island Grille ★★ (Kids SEAFOOD/STEAK   This Caribbean-themed restaurant is noted for its fresh, wood-fire-grilled seafood and steaks, accompanied by the island's best margaritas and sangria. Marley's has a fun, albeit kitschy, island vibe, and is popular with locals, vacationers, and families alike. Try the lobster tacos with rice and beans or the tortilla-crusted tilapia with jumbo lump crab salsa. Among our favorites are jerk grilled chicken and red-chili-rubbed flank steak with chimichurri sauce. After dinner, enjoy dessert next door at Marley's Ice Cream & Trading Company.

35 Office Park Rd., near Park Plaza. *C* **843/686-5800.** www.marleyshii.com. Reservations recommended. Main courses $13–$37. AE, DISC, MC, V. Sun–Thurs 4:30–10pm; Fri–Sat 5–11pm.

Michael Anthony's ★★★ ITALIAN   Nearly every critic on the island has declared Michael Anthony's the best place to eat in Hilton Head. The restaurant is family owned and operated, with hands-on attention and care paid to every detail. The exquisite menu blends traditional Italian flavors with Low Country ingredients. A local favorite is the homemade gnocchi in a sauce of porcini mushrooms with demiglace and cream. Another delectable specialty is the medallions of veal with spinach, cheese, and Italian sausage, sautéed in white wine. Don't miss the chocolate soufflé cake served with vanilla gelato. *Tip:* Michael Anthony's also has a wine bar where you can enjoy your favorite beverage or dessert or choose to have dinner—no reservations required.

37 New Orleans Rd. *C* **843/785-6272.** www.michael-anthonys.com. Reservations required. Main courses $17–$35. AE, DC, DISC, MC, V. Mon–Sat 5:30–10pm.

Ocean Grille ★ AMERICAN/STEAK/SEAFOOD   This waterfront eatery overlooking a marina is one of Hilton Head's premier restaurants. The skilled chefs specialize in fresh seafood and choice steaks, expertly prepared. First-rate appetizers include stone crab claws and coconut-fried calamari. When available, the fresh catch of the day can be grilled, broiled, blackened, or fried. The sublime sauces include lobster butter, tangerine coulis, and garlic saffron aioli. New York strip is grilled and served with buttermilk mashed potatoes.

1 Shelter Cove Lane, Shelter Cove Marina. *C* **843/785-3030.** www.oceangrill restaurant.com. Reservations recommended. Main courses $16–$35. AE, DC, MC, V. Daily 4:30–9:30pm; Sun 11am–2pm.

Old Fort Pub ★ INTERNATIONAL   Nestled within the upscale residential community of the Hilton Head Plantation on the island's northwest coast, away from most other eateries, this is one of the most consistently reliable and upscale restaurants in the Low Country. It's just a few paces from the ruin of what was commissioned by the Union army in 1862 as a fort (Fort Mitchell), and as such, some diners make it a point to traipse around the signposted footpaths. You'll eat inside connected clapboard-sided houses dating from 1973, amid candlelight and crisp napery, with views over salt marshes and estuaries. Chef Keith Josefiak prepares innovative dishes that include Vidalia onion shoots and goat cheese tarts; spring asparagus *en croûte* with prosciutto and roasted tomato vinaigrette; a succulent version of local bouillabaisse that just happens to include collards and tasso ham; crab cakes; and pork loin with chanterelles, onions, and pistachio nuts.

65 Skull Creek Dr. ⓒ **843/681-2386.** www.oldfortpub.com. Reservations recommended. Main courses $24–$38. AE, DC, DISC, MC, V. Mon–Sat 5–10pm; Sun 11am–2pm (brunch).

Redfish Grill ★ INTERNATIONAL   One of the more talked-about restaurants on Hilton Head Island, this place occupies a rambling villa that contains shopping as well as dining options. You can drop into the on-site wine shop, select a bottle, and for a $10 corkage fee, drink it with your meal. The wine shop has a few tables, and there are two postmodern, Asian-inspired dining rooms in the restaurant. The menu changes with the seasons, but might include Asian-style marinated tenderloin of beef with Thai cucumbers in a lettuce-leaf wrap; grilled seabass with a wasabi cream sauce and soy glaze on a bed of Udon noodles; seared jumbo scallops served with asparagus and lobster-studded macaroni and cheese; and two upscale and expensive burgers. One is made entirely with Kobe beef and accented with foie gras, pepper jack cheese, truffles, and port demi-glace; the other is crafted from chunks of Maine lobster mixed with shrimp. This restaurant lies in an isolated residential neighborhood inland from the sea, close to the Cross-Island Bridge.

8 Archer Rd. ⓒ **843/686-3388.** www.redfishofhiltonhead.com. Reservations recommended. Main courses $8–$12 lunch, $21–$34 dinner. AE, MC, V. Mon–Sat 11:30am–2pm and 5–10pm; Sun 5–10pm.

MODERATE

These so-called moderately priced restaurants tend to have expensive shellfish dishes. However, if you order from the lower end of the price scale, you'll find platters that cost $20 or less. Portions are usually generous, so you'll rarely need to order appetizers, which will keep your overall costs in the more affordable price range.

Alexander's ★ SEAFOOD/INTERNATIONAL One of the
most well-known independent restaurants (in other words, not associated with a hotel) on Hilton Head lies in a wood-sided, gray-stained building just inside the main entrance into Palmetto Dunes. The decor includes Oriental carpets, big-windowed views over the salt marshes, wicker furniture, and an incongruous—some say startling—collection of vintage Harley-Davidson motorcycles, none with more than 1,000 miles on them, dating from 1946, 1948, 1966, and 1993, respectively. Powerful flavors and a forthright approach to food are the rules of the kitchen. The chefs don't allow a lot of innovation on their menu—you've had all these dishes before—but fine ingredients are used, and each dish is prepared with discretion and restraint. Try the oysters Savannah or the bacon-wrapped shrimp, and most definitely have a bowl of Low Country seafood chowder. Guaranteed to set you salivating are the scallops encrusted with sun-dried tomatoes, and the bluefin crab cakes. Steak, duck, rack of lamb, and pork—all in familiar versions—round out the menu.

76 Queen's Folly, Palmetto Dunes. ✆ 843/785-4999. www.alexandersrestaurant. com. Reservations recommended. Main courses $23–$33. AE, DC, DISC, MC, V. Daily 5–10pm.

Antonio's ★ ITALIAN This island favorite, with its elegant decor and fine cuisine, continues its bold quest to duplicate the flavors of sunny Italy, and for the most part succeeds admirably. The chef is a whiz at using recipes from all the regions of Italy, although classic seafood preparations are clearly his favorite. Piano music adds to the ambience, as does a visit to the wine cellar, where you can see Hilton Head's most comprehensive assemblage of Italian *vino*. The antipasti selection is one of the area's best, and the succulent pastas include one based on fruit of the sea, with sautéed shrimp, scallops, and mussels in a tomato-and-saffron broth. Delectable veal saltimbocca appears with crispy prosciutto and creamy roasted pancetta sage potatoes.

1000 William Hilton Pkwy., in the Village at Wexford. ✆ 843/842-5505. www. antonios.net. Reservations recommended. Main courses $9–$32. AE, DC, DISC, MC, V. Daily 5:30–10pm. Closed Dec 24.

Black Marlin Bayside Grill ★ SEAFOOD Partly because of its location beside a marshy inland channel, a few steps from the most battered-looking boatyard and marina on Hilton Head Island, this is the most raffish of the "grand cuisine" restaurants of Hilton Head. Fun, with lots of salty cosmopolitan charm, and an insouciance that might remind you of Key West, it seems a world removed from the manicured, upscale conservatism of the island's secluded residential zones. Thomas Corey is the chef here, a refugee from the cold

Northeast, and an expert at crafting flavor from the fresh seafood that arrives directly from fishermen every morning at dawn. Lunch fare includes meal-size salads and at least a dozen hungryman's sandwiches, pastas, and fried seafood. Dinners are more ambitious, focusing on tuna carpaccio, tempura lobster, fish or shrimp tacos; crab-stuffed flounder, big slabs of steak, and between 7 and 10 dishes that appear only on a blackboard, based on the seafood haul brought in that day.

86 Helmsman Way, at the Palmetto Bay Marina. (✆ **843/785-4950.** www.black marlinhhi.com. Reservations not accepted. Main courses $7–$15 lunch, $13–$33 dinner. AE, DC, MC, V. Mon–Fri 11:30am–10pm; Sat–Sun 10am–2pm and 4–10pm.

Charlie's L'Etoile Verte ★★ INTERNATIONAL Outfitted like a tongue-in-cheek version of a Parisian bistro, our favorite restaurant on Hilton Head was also a favorite with former president Bill Clinton during one of his island conferences. The atmosphere is unpretentious but elegant. The service is attentive, polite, and infused with an appealingly hip mixture of Old and New World courtesy. Begin with roast portobello mushrooms and crab, and move on to tilapia sautéed in a Parmesan crust. End this rare dining experience with biscotti or a "sailor's trifle." The wine list is impressive.

8 New Orleans Rd. (✆ **843/785-9277.** www.charliesgreenstar.com. Reservations required. Main courses $8–$14 lunch, $24–$39 dinner. AE, DISC, MC, V. Tues–Sat 11:30am–2pm; Mon–Sat 5:30–9:30pm.

CQ's ★★ AMERICAN/LOW COUNTRY Onset in what was originally a 19th-century rice barn, this Harbour Town restaurant has been a Hilton Head tradition since 1973. Its extensive wine list, some 400 vintages, is one of the best on the island. Its well-thought-out menu of American classics reflects the rich bounty of South Carolina—fresh seafood, beef, and game—and also shows a French influence. To start, the Maine lobster and Boursin cheesecake with sherry butter cream is a delight. Consider yourself lucky if you arrive when game is in season, featured in such dishes as seared medallions of venison with roasted onion, shallots, leeks, and asparagus; a Madeira wine reduction adds extra special flavor.

140-A Lighthouse Rd. (✆ **843/671-2779.** www.cqsrestaurant.com. Reservations recommended. Main courses $26–$40. AE, DC, DISC, MC, V. Apr–Oct daily 5:30–10pm; Nov–Mar daily 5–9:30pm.

Crane's Tavern & Steakhouse ★ STEAK/SEAFOOD The original Crane's was launched in Philadelphia at the dawn of the 20th century and was one of the most popular taverns there until Prohibition. Always a family business, it was established by Hank Crane, who came over from Ireland, and passed down to generations of Crane sons and, now, a daughter. While other Hilton Head restaurants rush to claim the best seafood, Crane's bases its simple menu on prime beef. Each of the choicest cuts is prepared to your taste—can any trencherman cope with the whopper, 20 ounces? A 12-ounce prime rib was the best we could manage, and it was well flavored and quite succulent. The other offerings are good as well, including jumbo lump crab cakes and stuffed chicken. The sweet-potato ravioli in a molasses cream was a delightful surprise.

26 New Orleans Rd. © **843/341-2333.** www.cranestavern.com. Reservations recommended. Main courses $17–$46. AE, DC, DISC, MC, V. Daily 5–10pm. Closed Thanksgiving and Christmas.

The Crazy Crab North (Kids) SEAFOOD   Usually crowded, especially in the summer, this is the restaurant that's most likely to be patronized by locals, partly because an entire family can be fed here at relatively modest prices. In a modern, low-slung building near the bridge that connects the island with the South Carolina mainland, it serves baked, broiled, and fried versions of stuffed flounder; seafood kabobs; oysters; the catch of the day; and any combination thereof. She-crab soup and New England–style clam chowder are prepared fresh daily, children's menus are available, and desserts are a high point for chocoholics. There's a second branch of this restaurant with the same hours and virtually the same prices, at Harbour Town in the Sea Pines Resort (© **843/681-5021**).

U.S. 278 at Jarvis Creek. © **843/681-5021.** www.thecrazycrab.com. Reservations not accepted. Main courses $6–$15 lunch, $14–$33 dinner. AE, DISC, MC, V. Daily 11:30am–10pm.

Harbour Town Grill (Finds) AMERICAN   Decorated with a simple, aggressively unpretentious style that's vaguely Scottish and punctuated with occasional pieces of golfing memorabilia, this small-scale affair has views over the 9th hole and room for only about 50 diners at a time. Inside, it's sporty looking and relatively informal during the day, when most of the menu is devoted to thickly stuffed deli-style sandwiches and salads named in honor of golf stars. Dinners are more formal and more elaborate, with good-tasting dishes such as local shrimp sautéed with ginger, Vidalia onions, and collard greens; roasted rack of American lamb with white beans, spinach, and rosemary; and an array of thick-cut slabs of meat including beef, lamb, veal, and chicken.

In the Harbour Town Golf Links Clubhouse, Sea Pines. © **843/363-8380.** www. seapines.com. Reservations recommended for dinner. Main courses $9–$17 lunch, $16–$38 dinner. AE, DC, DISC, MC, V. Daily 7am–3pm and 5–10pm.

Hudson's Seafood House on the Docks ★ SEAFOOD   Built as a seafood-processing factory in 1912, this restaurant still processes fish, clams, and oysters for local distribution, so you know that everything is fresh. If you're seated in the north dining room, you'll be eating in the original oyster factory. We strongly recommend the crab cakes, the steamed shrimp, and the especially appealing blackened catch of the day. Local oysters (seasonal) are also a specialty, breaded and deep-fried. This place is an excellent choice if you're looking for an escape from the island's crowded southern tier. Before and after dinner, stroll on the docks past shrimp boats, and enjoy the view of the mainland and nearby Parris Island. Sunsets here are panoramic. Lunch is served in the Oyster Bar.

1 Hudson Rd. (go to Skull Creek just off Square Pope Rd. signposted from U.S. 278). ℭ **843/681-2772.** www.hudsonsonthedocks.com. Reservations not accepted. Main courses $6–$15 lunch, $13–$23 dinner. AE, DC, MC, V. Daily 11am–2:30pm and 5–9pm.

Jump & Phil's Bar & Grill AMERICAN   Cozy and convivial, with dining tables positioned on three sides of a large rectangular bar, this restaurant does a thriving business with 40- and 50-something owners of nearby homes and condos. It also identifies itself as the headquarters for Hilton Head's Green Bay Packers fan club. The brainchild of entrepreneurs Jump and Phil, who spent 20 years working in other restaurants before branching out on their own, it's outfitted with early-20th-century Americana, some battered antiques, and dark paneling. Food is generously portioned, reasonably priced, and unpretentious. Menu items include two-fisted versions of BLTs, Cuban sandwiches, chili dogs, tuna melts, barbecued pork, and burgers. More substantial fare includes grits with shrimp, fried oyster platters, chicken potpie, and grilled rib-eye steaks.

In the Hilton Head Plaza, Greenwood Dr. off Sea Pines Circle. ℭ **843/785-9070.** www.jumpandphilshhi.com. Reservations not necessary. Sandwiches $7–$12; main courses $11–$24. AE, DISC, MC, V. Daily 11:30am–2am.

Kingfisher ★ SEAFOOD/STEAK   This popular restaurant at Shelter Cove offers live music nightly and a panoramic view of the harbor through large picture windows in all three dining rooms. The catch of the day can be prepared several ways, including the usual grilled or blackened, but also herb-encrusted or Greek style (with tomatoes, onions, mushrooms, spinach, artichokes, and feta). Each day, different varieties of oysters are served on the half shell. Seafood selections range from a very respectable Scottish fish and chips to a Charleston-style shrimp and grits in white gravy. The seared ahi tuna comes with a *ponzu* sauce, wasabi mashed potatoes, and Asian slaw.

The filet mignon is tender and full of flavor, and for pasta lovers, the **147** chef makes a creative lasagna every day.

18 Harbourside Lane. ℭ **843/785-4442.** www.kingfisherseafood.com. Reservations recommended. Main courses $10–$40. AE, DISC, MC, V. Daily 5–10pm. Closed Dec 24–25.

The Old Oyster Factory ★ SEAFOOD/STEAK   Built on the site of one of Hilton Head's original oyster canneries, this always-popular landmark offers waterfront dining overlooking Broad Creek. At sunset, every table enjoys a panoramic view as diners sip their "sundowners." All the dishes here can be found on seafood menus from Maine to Hawaii. But the cuisine is truly palate friendly, beginning with such appetizers as a tangy kettle of clams steamed in a lemon-butter sauce, or a delectable crab cake sautéed and served in a chile-garlic tartar sauce. Will it be oysters Rockefeller (baked with spinach and a béarnaise sauce) or oysters Savannah (shrimp, crab-meat, and smoked bacon)? Almond-crusted mahimahi is among the more tantalizing main courses, as are seafood pasta and broiled sea scallops. Those who don't eat seafood can opt for a chargrilled chicken breast or a steak.

101 Marsh Rd. ℭ **843/681-6040.** www.oldoysterfactory.com. Reservations not accepted. Main courses $17–$33. AE, DC, DISC, MC, V. Daily 5–10pm (closing times can vary).

Reilley's Grill & Bar ★ **Finds** AMERICAN   This spot rarely advertises, so much of its business derives from locals, who come here after dark for hobnobbing, gossiping, or eating and drinking within the orbit of patriarch Tom Reilley, the island's ultimate food-and-beverage insider. If you can manage to pull yourself away from the mahogany and cherry-paneled bar, you'll discover that food items are the most fussed over and most sophisticated of any eatery within Hilton Head Plaza. Examples include garlic chicken pasta, grilled loin of beef with peppers and onions, pork chops stuffed with spinach and mozzarella with a Gouda cream sauce, upscale salads such as a version with warm brie and spinach, hearty sandwiches, and Asian-style chicken salad. There's also a roster of grills and a signature version of sirloin topped with an Irish whiskey peppercorn sauce and cheese grits.

In the Hilton Head Plaza, Greenwood Dr. off Sea Pines Circle. ℭ **843/842-4414.** www.reilleyshiltonhead.com. Reservations recommended for dinner. Main courses $7–$14 lunch, $10–$25 dinner. AE, MC, V. Daily 11am–2am.

Santa Fe Cafe ★ MEXICAN   The best, most stylish Mexican restaurant on Hilton Head, the Santa Fe Cafe has rustic, Southwestern-inspired decor and cuisine that infuses traditional recipes with nouvelle flair. Live music adds to the allure. Menu items are often presented in colors as bright as the Painted Desert. Dishes might include tequila shrimp, herb-roasted chicken with jalapeño cornbread stuffing and mashed potatoes laced with red chilies, grilled tenderloin of pork with smoked habañero sauce and sweet-potato fries, and worthy burritos and chimichangas.

700 Plantation Center. ✆ **843/785-3838.** www.santafecafeofhiltonhead.com. Reservations recommended. Main courses $7–$14. AE, DISC, MC, V. Mon–Fri noon–2pm and 5–10pm; Sat–Sun 5–10pm.

Skull Creek Boathouse (Kids) SEAFOOD With its nautical decor and views over salt marshes and Skull Creek, this is an appropriate venue for some fine seafood at affordable prices. From certain tables, you can see the Pinckney Island National Wildlife Refuge and the adjacent marina. Walk under a canopy of giant oaks to enjoy a drink at the Market 13 outdoor bar. Live entertainment is offered, and you can bring the kids (there's a children's menu). Plenty of fresh seafood is prepared with old Charleston flavor, including shrimp and stone-ground grits, excellent crab cakes, Southern catfish with Carolina fixin's, and the chef's own Boathouse bouillabaisse. For meat fanciers, slow-roasted baby back ribs in a sour mash sauce, served with buttermilk "smashed" potatoes and collards, seduce the palate.

397 Squire Pope Rd. ✆ **843/681-3663.** www.skullcreekboathouse.com. Reservations not necessary. Brunch items $6–$11; lunch items $9–$15; dinner main courses $16–$28. AE, DC, DISC, MC, V. Daily 11:30am–3pm and 5–9pm. Closed Christmas.

INEXPENSIVE

The British Open Pub BRITISH/AMERICAN Except for the fact that the hardworking staff speaks with a Carolina accent, you might believe you've stumbled into a remote, woodsy-looking, and unpretentious corner of Britain. And if you opt for a meal here, you'll be in good company: The town's mayor and a few of his cohorts have to some degree adopted the place as a regular hangout. Since it rarely advertises, prices remain low. Its name derives from the owners' obsession with the minutiae of the U.K.'s most famous golf tournament. There's British ale on tap, plus ever-popular versions of fish and chips, lobster potpies, shepherd's pie, and meal-size salads. As for Carolina-inspired food, we recommend the twin crab-cake platter, or perhaps the baby back barbecued ribs. Frankly, this is one of the least touristy watering holes on Hilton Head Island, and the drinks are stiff enough to ensure that locals continue to patronize it in droves.

In the Village at Wexford Shopping Center. ✆ **843/686-6736.** www.britishopen pub.net. Reservations not accepted. Main courses $8–$16. AE, DC, MC, V. Mon–Sat 11am–10pm; Sun 9am–10pm.

One Hot Mama's American Grille ★ (Kids) GRILL/BARBECUE
It's fun, it's whimsical, and its reasonably priced platters are served in a setting that evokes a mixture of a rock-'n'-roll cafe and a 1950s-era luncheonette. It's the least expensive of the eateries within "the Triangle" of Hilton Head Plaza, and the most child and family friendly. Food focuses on savory, grease-spattered ribs and barbecue dishes. The baby back barbecued ribs here are scrumptious, the pit-to-plate hand-pulled pork virtually addictive. Chargrilled steaks and chicken filets will make you call for more, and if you like fried chicken wings, this place serves them in almost 20 different variations, including a version with strawberry-jalapeño sauce. In case you're wondering who the Hot Mama is, she's Orchid, a hardworking entrepreneur whose prototype for this charming place migrated from nearby Bluffton in 2007.

In the Hilton Head Plaza, Greenwood Dr. off Sea Pines Circle. © **843/682-6262.** www.onehotmamas.com. Reservations not accepted. Main courses $8–$12 lunch, $8–$23 dinner. AE, DC, MC, V. Daily 11:30am–midnight.

San Miguel's (Kids) MEXICAN Every night since 1977 has been fiesta night here. You can have a fun evening, enjoying live music on the deck. (This eatery opens onto the same marina as Ocean Grille, p. 141.) The food is nothing to rave about, but it's substantial and freshly prepared; there's even a kid's menu. Most guests start with nachos, quesadillas, or guacamole. After that, proceed to one of the platters, such as chiles rellenos, enchiladas, or sizzling fajitas. For anyone in your party who doesn't like Mexican food, the chefs will serve a shrimp Alfredo or a New York strip steak from the grill.

9 Shelter Cove Lane, Shelter Cove Marina. © **843/842-4555.** www.sanmiguels. com. Reservations not necessary. Main courses $8–$17. MC, V. Mon–Sat 11:30am–3pm; daily 5–11pm.

Sea Shack ★ (Value) SEAFOOD This unpretentious seafood shack serves the freshest catch of the day in town; you can order it grilled, fried, or blackened. Stand at the counter and make your selection by reading the specialties on a board. Find a seat at one of the old tables, and your fresh platter will be brought to you. We like to begin with the fish soup, and the fried-oyster sandwich is a local favorite at lunch. For dinner, we prefer the grilled grouper. One of the chef's signature dishes is Caribbean jerk grouper, which you don't encounter too often; it's even been featured on the Food Network.

6 Pope Ave. © **843/785-2464.** Reservations not necessary. Main courses $6–$14 lunch, $10–$17 dinner. AE, MC, V. Mon–Sat 11am–3pm and 5–9pm.

Signe's Heaven Bound Bakery & Cafe SANDWICHES/PASTRIES Sometime in the early '70s, Signe Gardo, a refugee from Connecticut, opened this bakery. Almost 3,000 wedding cakes and countless danishes later, it's the oldest eatery under a single ownership on Hilton Head, with a roster of loyal clients. It lies in a relatively underpopulated neighborhood of private homes way, way off the island's beaten tourist track. Many come for breakfast, oohing and aaahing over Signe's signature deep-dish French toast, her breakfast polenta, and her waffles. (Rachael Ray filmed a feature story here in 2007.) Lunches focus on a half-dozen salads, a spinach-and-feta *spanikopita* pie that might have been inspired by Zorba himself, tomato or crab-cake tarts, and a steaming ration of shrimp and grits. Simple tables on an outdoor deck provide a fine setting for your meal. Few visitors can resist carting off any of the dozen-or-so homemade breads including Swiss pear, French oat and apricot, and sourdough. Delicious cakes include a Forever Valentine and a version flavored with piña coladas, coconut, and pineapple cream.

93 Arrow Rd. ✆ **866/807-4463** or 843/785-9118. http://signesbakery.com. Reservations not accepted. Main courses $6–$9. AE, MC, V. Mon–Fri 8am–4pm; Sat–Sun 9am–2pm. Closed Sun Nov–Feb.

Smokehouse Bar & House of BBQ (Kids) BARBECUE This is Hilton Head's only authentic barbecue joint, serving fine hickory-smoked meats in a casual atmosphere. There's a large outdoor deck, and takeout is available. Locals and visitors (especially families) come here nightly, raving about the man-size portions of pulled pork, sliced or pulled brisket, and barbecued chicken. The specialty is smokehouse ribs, either half or full rack. Other down-home favorites include fried catfish and award-winning chili. Beachgoers are welcome, but you must wear shoes.

102 Pope Ave. ✆ **843/842-4227.** http://smokehousehhi.com. Reservations recommended. Main courses $12–$22. AE, MC, V. Daily 11:30am–10pm.

Steamer Seafood ★ SEAFOOD/LOW COUNTRY This fun spot is suitable for the whole family. It's a casual, convivial tavern with Low Country specialties such as she-crab soup and shrimp gumbo. Many old-time Southern coastal classics are offered, including Frogmore stew (with shrimp, smoked sausage, onion, and red potatoes). The catch of the day is served grilled or blackened. The "rebel yell" rib-eye is a juicy 14-ounce slab, blackened or chargrilled, as you desire. The biggest seafood platters on the island are dished up here. After all that, dare you try the rich, creamy chocolate-peanut-butter pie or the fruit cobbler of the day?

29 Coligny Plaza (next to the Piggly Wiggly grocery store). ✆ **843/785-2070.** www.steamerseafood.com. Reservations not necessary. Lunch items $8–$37; dinner main courses $9–$37. AE, MC, V. Daily 11:30am–10pm.

Truffles Cafe ★ **Finds** INTERNATIONAL   It's no longer a gastronomic newcomer to Hilton Head, but it's garnered many fans and it remains one of our personal favorites on the island. Within the Sea Pines Center, this cafe has a dark, mostly black decor, with a large copper-topped bar, banquettes, and a menu that seems to please everybody. Start with the spinach-and-artichoke dip or coconut fried shrimp, followed by baby back ribs or grouper that's grilled and topped with a basil-Parmesan glaze. You could also try the Havana chicken with jack cheese and fresh tomato salsa, or meatloaf that's grilled with a honey-flavored barbecue sauce and Vidalia onions. Don't confuse this place with Truffles Grill on Pope Avenue, between Coligny Circle and Sea Island Circle: The Grill is newer and trendier, but many restaurant insiders swear by the original. Just know that if you come for a meal here, you'll have to pay a $5 charge to enter the Sea Island Resort itself.

Sea Pines Center, in the Sea Pines Resort. ℃ **843/671-6136.** www.trufflescafe. com. Reservations recommended for dinner. Main courses $9–$29 lunch, $12–$28 dinner. AE, DC, MC, V. Daily 11am–10pm.

HILTON HEAD AFTER DARK

Hilton Head doesn't have Myrtle Beach's nightlife, but there's plenty to keep you entertained—much of it located in hotels and resorts. Casual dress (but not swimming attire) is acceptable in most clubs.

Cultural interest focuses on the **Arts Center of Coastal Carolina,** in the Self Family Arts Center, 14 Shelter Cove Lane (℃ **888/860-2787** or 843/842-ARTS [2787]; www.artshhi.com), which enjoys one of the best theatrical reputations in the Southeast. The Elizabeth Wallace Theater, a 350-seat, state-of-the-art theater, was added to the multiplex in 1996. The older Dunnagan's Alley Theater is located in a renovated warehouse. A wide range of musicals, contemporary comedies, and classic dramas are presented. Showtimes are 8pm Tuesday to Saturday, with a Sunday matinee at 2pm. Adult ticket prices range from $45 for a musical to $75 for a play. Tickets for children 16 and under are $18 to $35. The box office is open 10am to 5pm Monday to Friday, and 10am to curtain time on performance days.

The island abounds in sports bars, far too many to document here. We recommend **Callahan Sports Bar & Grill,** 49 New Orleans Rd. (℃ **843/686-7665**), and **Casey's Sports Bar & Grill,** 37 New Orleans Rd. (℃ **843/785-2255;** www.caseyshhi.com).

Jazz Corner   Tucked away into an obscure corner of the shopping center known as the Village at Wexford, this is the closest thing to a shadowy, romantic, and permissive jazz bar on Hilton Head. No other nightclub here attracts such a diverse and noteworthy collection of jazz artists. The best way to find out who's playing is to visit the

The Triangle & How Not to Get Lost Within It

Hilton Head's hottest nightlife spot goes by many names—the Triangle, the Golden Triangle, the Barmuda Triangle, and most officially of all, **Hilton Head Plaza.** Set beside Greenwood Drive, very close to the Sea Pines traffic roundabout, the area resembles a shopping center without any shops. Instead, it contains five of the busiest nightclub venues and restaurants on Hilton Head.

Relying on word-of-mouth buzz for their ongoing success, these bars and restaurants include **Reilley's Grill & Bar, Jump & Phil's Bar & Grill,** and **One Hot Mama's American Grille** (see reviews above). In a close tie for the grungiest and least formal establishments are the **Hilton Head Brew Pub** (© 843/ 785-3900) and the **Lodge** (© 843/842-8966). Of these two, we prefer the Lodge with its pool tables. But they're all so close together that if one place isn't to your liking, you can just move on to the next one. The Brew Pub is open daily from 11am to 2am, while the Lodge is a nighttime-only affair, open daily from 7pm 'til sometime after midnight every night. None of these bars begin to get busy until after dark.

website for names and dates of upcoming gigs. Doors open nightly at 6pm, performances begin at 8pm, and intermissions are scheduled at 9:30pm. There's an on-site restaurant and a copious drink menu where many of the martinis are oversize and designed for two drinkers. In the Village at Wexford, Unit C1. © 843/842-8620. www.thejazzcorner. com.

The Metropolitan Lounge　This is the top martini bar on Hilton Head, a chic cocktail lounge like something you might find in Paris. Martinis aren't the only item on the menu. The lounge has one of the island's largest wine lists, with at least 80 different labels available by the glass. There's a light menu, featuring caviar. In chilly weather, a fireplace glows. Piano music provides a soothing ambience. Martinis cost $7 to $13. There is no cover charge. The lounge is open Tuesday to Saturday from 8pm to at least 2am. In the Park Plaza Shopping Center, off Greenwood Dr., near the Sea Pines Traffic Roundabout. © 843/785-8466. http://www.hiltonheadhotline.com/nl-metropolitan-lounge. php.

Quarterdeck　This waterfront lounge, our favorite on the island, is the best place to watch sunsets, but you can visit any time during the afternoon or evening until 2am. Try to go early and grab one of the outdoor rocking chairs to prepare yourself for nature's light show. There's dancing every night to beach music and Top 40 hits. Quarter-deck is open daily from 11am to 2am. Harbour Town, Sea Pines Plantation. © 843/671-2222. http://quarterdeckrestaurant.com.

3 ST. SIMONS ISLAND ★★

80 miles S of Savannah; 10 miles E of Brunswick

The largest of the Golden Isles, St. Simons is also the most popular for its beaches, golf courses, scenery, and numerous tennis courts. Through tunnels of ancient oaks, you can bike and drive the length of St. Simons, finding treasures at every turn. It's a vacation haven for families.

ESSENTIALS

GETTING THERE Take I-95 to Ga. 25 (the Island Pkwy.) or U.S. 17 to Brunswick, where signs direct visitors across the F. J. Torras Causeway to St. Simons Island.

VISITOR INFORMATION The **St. Simons Island Visitors Center & Chamber of Commerce,** 530 Beachview Dr. W. (© 912/638-9014; http://comecoastawhile.com), offers maps and information, particularly on beaches. It's open daily 9am to 5pm.

SEEING THE ISLAND

The best way to introduce yourself to the island is via **St. Simons Trolley Island Tours** (© 912/638-8954), which acquaints you with 400 years of history and folklore, taking 1½ hours and costing $20 for adults and $10 for children 4 to 12; tours for children 3 and under are free. Tours depart March 15 to Labor Day daily at 11am and 1pm and daily at 11am during off season.

The island's chief attraction is **Fort Frederica National Monument** (© 912/638-3639; www.nps.gov/fofr), on the northwest end of the island (signposted). Go first to the National Park Service Visitor Center, where a film and displays explain the role of the fort. There isn't much left; about all you'll see of the original construction is a small portion of the king's magazine and the barracks tower, but archaeological excavations have unearthed many foundations. The fort was constructed in 1736 by General James Oglethorpe. On the grounds is a gift shop, and walking tours can be arranged. Admission is $3 per person, free for children 15 and under. It's open from 9am to 5pm daily.

Christ Church, 6329 Frederica Rd., at the north end of the island, was built in 1820. It was virtually destroyed when Union troops camped here during the Civil War, burning the pews for firewood and butchering cattle in the chapel. In 1886, Anson Greene Phelps Dodge, Jr., restored the church as a memorial to his first wife, who had died on their honeymoon. The serene white building nestled under huge old oaks is open every day from 2 to 5pm during daylight saving time, 1 to 4pm at other times. There's no admission charge.

St. Simons Island Lighthouse Museum, 101 12th St. (☎ **912/638-4666;** www.saintsimonslighthouse.org), is a restored lightkeeper's house from 1872. You can climb its 129 steps for a panoramic view of the Golden Isles. Inside are exhibits devoted not only to the lighthouse, but also to the Golden Isles in general. But you go more for the view than the nautical exhibits. Admission is $6 for adults, $3 for children 6 to 12, and free for children 5 and under. Hours are Monday to Saturday 10am to 5pm and Sunday 1:30 to 5pm.

Scattered from end to end on St. Simons are ruins of the plantation era: the **Hampton Plantation** (where Aaron Burr spent a month after his duel with Alexander Hamilton) and **Cannon's Point** on the north; **West Point, Pines Bluff,** and **Hamilton Plantations** on the west along the Frederica River; **Harrington Hall** and **Mulberry Grove** in the interior; **Lawrence, St. Clair, Black Banks,** the **Village,** and **Kelvyn Grove** on the east; and the **Retreat Plantation** on the south end. There's a restored chapel on West Point Plantation made of tabby, with mortar turned pink from an unusual lichen. Locals say it reflects blood on the hands of Dr. Thomas Hazzard, who killed a neighbor in a land dispute and built the chapel after being so ostracized that he would not attend Christ Church.

BEACHES & OTHER ACTIVE PURSUITS

St. Simons not only attracts families looking for a beach, but it's also heaven for golfers, with 99 holes. One golfer we met who's played every hole said that each one presents a worthy challenge. Other sports include boating, inshore and offshore fishing, and water-skiing. Jet-skiing, charter fishing, scuba diving, and cruising can also be arranged at **Morning Star Marinas at Golden Isles,** 206 Marina Dr. (☎ **912/634-1128;** http://morningstarmarinas.com), on the F. J. Torras Causeway.

Neptune Park, at the island's south end, has miniature golf, a playground, picnic tables under the oaks, and pier fishing There's beach access from the park.

BEACHES   You'll find two white-sand public beaches here, foremost of which is the **Massingale Park Beach,** Ocean Boulevard. It has a county-maintained beach with a picnic area and a bathhouse. It's open with a lifeguard on duty June 1 to Labor Day, daily from 11am to 4pm. Parking is free in designated areas, and drinking is allowed on the beach but only from plastic containers (no glass). Fishing is free from the beach but allowed only from 4 to 10pm.

Another public beach is the **Coast Guard Station Beach,** East Beach Causeway, also family oriented, with a bathhouse and showers. Lifeguards are on duty from June 1 to the Labor Day weekend, daily from 11am to 4pm. Parking is free in designated areas, and fishing is permitted during nonswimming hours from 4:30 to 10pm. Drinking is allowed on the beach from plastic containers only.

Further information about beaches can be obtained from the **Glynn County Recreation Department** (© **912/554-7780;** www. glynncounty.org).

BIKE RENTALS   **Ocean Motion,** 1300 Ocean Blvd. (© **800/669-5215** or 912/638-5225), suggests that you explore St. Simons by bike and will provide detailed instructions about the best routes. The island is relatively flat, so biking is easy. Beach cruisers are available for men, women, and kids, with infant seats and helmets. Bike rentals cost $12 for 4 hours and $16 for a full day.

Fishing   Your best bet is **Golden Isles Charter Fishing,** 104 Marina Dr., Golden Isles Marina Village (© **912/638-7673;** www.golden islesfishing.com), which offers deep-sea fishing and both offshore and inshore fishing. Captain Mark Noble is your guide.

GOLF   It's golf—not tennis—that makes St. Simons Island a star attraction. Foremost among the courses is the for-guest-use-only **Sea Island Golf Club ★★★**, 100 Retreat Ave. (© **912/638-5118;** www.seaisland.com), owned by the Cloister of Sea Island. At the end of the "Avenue of Oaks" at historic Retreat Plantation, the club consists of a number of courses: the Retreat Course (9 holes, 3,260 yd., par 36), the Plantation Course (18 holes, 6,549 yd., par 72), the Seaside Course (9 holes, 3,185 yd., par 36), and the Ocean Forest (18 holes, 7,011 yd., par 72).

The club opened in 1927 and offers dramatic ocean views, adding a measure of excitement to the game. Its greatest fans mention it with the same reverence as St. Andrews, Pebble Beach, or Ballybunion. Former president George H. W. Bush liked the courses so much that he once played 36 holes a day. Seaside and Retreat are the most requested 9s, with Seaside definitely the most famous of all—known for the 414-yard no. 7. *Golf Digest* has called this hole one of the best in golf and among the toughest in Georgia. A drive has to clear a marsh-lined stream and avoid a gaping fairway bunker.

Greens fees are $150 to $175, with the cart and the caddie fee included. Clubs rent for $65. The state-of-the-art Golf Learning Center on the grounds can help improve even an experienced golfer's game. Professional instruction is available for $95 to $110 per half-hour. Also on the grounds are a pro shop, clubhouse, and restaurant. The course is open daily from 7am to 7pm.

The **Retreat Golf Club,** 100 Kings Way (© **912/638-3611;** www. seaisland.com), is an 18-hole, par-72 course of 6,200 yards—also for hotel guests only. Known for its Low Country architecture, it hosts several popular tournaments every year. The demanding course, designed by Joe Lee, features narrow fairways lined by lagoons and towering pines. Greens fees for Cloister guests are $200 to $250; cottage guests at Sea Island pay the same. Professional instruction is available for $100 to $300 per hour through arrangements made at the clubhouse and pro shop. There's also a restaurant on the premises. Play is available daily 7am to 7pm.

Sea Palms Golf & Tennis Resort, 5445 Frederica Rd. (© **800/ 841-6268** or 912/638-3351; www.seapalms.com), offers outstanding golf on its Tall Pines/Great Oaks (18 holes, 6,500 yd., par 72), Great Oaks/Sea Palms West (18 holes, 6,200 yd., par 72), and Sea Palms West/Tall Pines (9 holes, 2,500 yd., par 72) courses. Some holes nestle alongside scenic marshes and meandering tidal creeks. Reserved tee times are recommended, and cart use is required. The courses are open daily 7am to 7pm, charging greens fees of $69 and $59 after 1pm, with cart rental included. Professional instruction costs $50 for a 30-minute session, $80 for an hour.

NATURE TOURS The **Ocean Motion Surf Co.,** 1300 Ocean Blvd. (© **912/638-5225**), offers nature tours by kayak of the island's marsh creeks and secluded beaches. Featured are a 2-hour dolphin nature tour for $45 and a 4-hour wildlife tour, by request only, for $85.

SAILBOAT RENTALS **Barry's Beach Service, Inc.,** at the King and Prince Beach Hotel, 420 Arnold Rd. (© **912/638-8053**), arranges hourly, half-day, or full-day sailboat rentals, along with sailing lessons (by experienced instructors) and sailboat rides. Kayak rentals, tours, and instruction are also available.

TENNIS There are two public tennis courts on the island. The **Mallory Park Courts,** Mallory Street, has two lighted courts open year-round, and admission is free. **Epworth Park,** on Lady Huntington Drive, has two courts open 24 hours but they are not equipped with lights; it, too, is free.

In addition to the accommodations listed below, private cottages are available for weekly or monthly rental on St. Simons. You can get an illustrated brochure with rates and availability information from **Parker-Kaufman Realtors,** 22 Beachway Dr., Jekyll Island, GA 31527 (📞 **888/453-5955;** www.parker-kaufman.com). The office is open Monday to Friday 9am to 5pm and on Saturday 9am to 1pm. Vacation rental cottages can range from one to four bedrooms. Rentals begin at $625 per week in summer, lowered to as little as $490 per week off season.

Best Western Island Inn   This unassuming, brick-sided motel was built in the late 1980s, about 2½ miles from the nearest beach. The efficiencies have a kitchenette, and the guest rooms are no-nonsense, unfrilly, and economical. All rooms have well-kept bathrooms. About a dozen of them can be connected with adjoining rooms to allow families to create their own live-in arrangements.

301 Main St., St. Simons Island, GA 31522. 📞 **800/673-6323** or 912/638-7805. Fax 912/634-4720. www.bestwesternstsimons.com. 61 units. $85–$119 double; $129–$139 suite. Children 17 and under stay free in parent's room. Rates include continental breakfast. AE, DC, DISC, MC, V. **Amenities:** Breakfast room; lounge; Jacuzzi; outdoor pool. *In room:* A/C, TV, hair dryer, Wi-Fi (free).

King and Prince Beach Resort ★   This is a midsize oceanfront resort founded in 1932 by partners who were evicted from the Jekyll Island Club. Today's reincarnation of five Spanish-style buildings is a venue for frequent corporate conventions. The resort has grown and expanded over the years, and in time has attracted many famous guests. But Hugh Hefner and his Playboy bunnies haven't been seen romping around since the 1950s. The original 70 guest rooms are still here but have been restored. Even better are the newer and larger rooms with expanded bathrooms, some offering private patios or balconies. Darker woods evoke a decidedly English influence, but other brighter appointments suggest a West Indian plantation style. The condo apartments have kitchenettes.

201 Arnold Rd., St. Simons Island, GA 31522. 📞 **800/342-0212** or 912/638-3631. Fax 912/638-7699. www.kingandprince.com. 188 units. $174–$309 double; $351–$919 villa. AE, DC, MC, V. **Amenities:** Restaurant; bar; babysitting; exercise room; 5 pools (1 indoor); room service; 2 tennis courts. *In room:* A/C, TV, hair dryer, kitchenette (in some), Wi-Fi (free).

The Lodge at Sea Island Golf Club ★★   Golfers who have stayed at some of the greatest resorts in California and the Carolinas justifiably rave about this resort. A great golfing experience and first-rate accommodations combine to form this smoothly operating lodge. It doesn't pretend to have the grandeur of its sibling, the Cloister on Sea Island (see later in this chapter), but for a luxurious, casual retreat, it's hard to beat, attracting not only golfers, but also small corporate groups. Attached to one of America's premier golf clubs, the lodge has been created in the spirit of one of those private clubs in Newport or the Hamptons. Set on beautiful grounds, it overlooks Rees Jones's Plantation Golf Course, often from a private balcony with views of the fairways and ocean. An English manor-house decor prevails throughout. Whether in the hotel or in the cottages, the guest rooms are spacious and beautifully furnished, with deluxe bathrooms.

100 Retreat Ave., St. Simons Island, GA 31522. ℂ **800/SEA-ISLAND** (732-4752) or 912/634-4300. Fax 912/634-3909. www.seaisland.com. $300–$750 double; $1,600 suite; call for cottage pricing. AE, DC, DISC, MC, V. **Amenities:** 4 restaurants; 2 bars; babysitting; 3 18-hole golf courses; exercise room; Jacuzzi; room service; sauna; spa. *In room:* A/C, TV, hair dryer, Wi-Fi (free).

Saint Simons Inn ★ (Finds) Standing in the shadow of the old lighthouse, this condo hotel is for the connoisseur of offbeat lodgings. Don't be put off by the word condo. The inn operates like a regular hotel, except that each condo is individually owned by a person who renovates and decorates it to his or her own tastes. That means that each condo is unique, the most elegant being the penthouse, of course. When the owners aren't in residence, the units are rented to the general public. In a setting of palmettos and live oaks, the inn has an outdoor pool. This is an ideal place for a romantic weekend. All the condos are equipped with microwaves and refrigerators.

609 Beachview Dr., St. Simons Island, GA 31522. ℂ **912/638-1101.** Fax 912/638-0943. www.stsimonsinn.com. 35 units. $149–$179 double; $289 penthouse. Rates include continental breakfast. AE, DISC, MC, V. **Amenities:** Outdoor pool. *In room:* A/C, TV, kitchenette, Wi-Fi (free).

Sea Gate Inn Its charms and advantages are often underestimated because of its low-rise format, unpretentious entrance, and location near other, much larger hotels. Despite that, this is a well-maintained, respectable hotel whose condo units are divided into two buildings separated from one another by a quiet road that runs parallel to the sea. The more desirable (and expensive) of the two is the Ocean House, a 1985 annex built on stilts. The less-expensive, and less-desirable, guest rooms are clustered around a swimming pool, roadside-motel style. All units, each a suite, offer modest kitchenettes. Otherwise, Sea Gate lacks general amenities. The hotel, incidentally, was named after an old-fashioned ferryboat that used to ply the waters between Brunswick and St. Simons Island.

1012 Beachview Dr., St. Simons Island, GA 31522. ℂ **800/562-8812** or 912/638-8661. www.seagateinn.com. 48 units. $199–$490 suite. DISC, MC, V. *In room:* A/C, TV, kitchen.

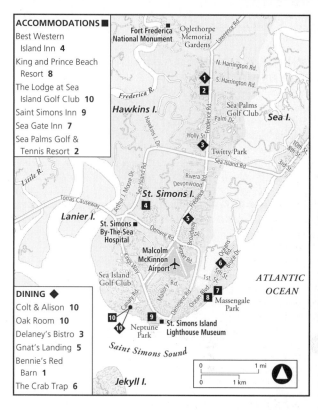

ACCOMMODATIONS ■

Best Western
  Island Inn **4**

King and Prince Beach
  Resort **8**

The Lodge at Sea
  Island Golf Club **10**

Saint Simons Inn **9**

Sea Gate Inn **7**

Sea Palms Golf &
  Tennis Resort **2**

DINING ◆

Colt & Alison **10**

Oak Room **10**

Delaney's Bistro **3**

Gnat's Landing **5**

Bennie's Red
  Barn **1**

The Crab Trap **6**

Sea Palms Golf & Tennis Resort ★★ This place imitates the older and more upscale resorts nearby. Sprawled over 800 landscaped acres, it combines aspects of a retirement community with a family-friendly resort. Most people stay 3 to 5 days. After registering in a woodsy bungalow near the entrance, you'll be waved off toward your room, to which you carry your own bags. If you're looking for maximum isolation, this place might be appropriate; otherwise, you might feel it's too anonymous. Each suite contains a kitchenette. There's a golf course on the premises and views over some beautiful marshland from many of the simply furnished units. The nearest good beach is about 4 miles away.

5445 Frederica Rd., St. Simons Island, GA 31522. (✆ **800/841-6268** or 912/638-3351. Fax 912/634-8029. www.seapalms.com. 154 units. $149–$169 double;

$219–$338 1- or 2-bedroom suite. Children 17 and under stay free in parent's room. Golf, tennis, and honeymoon packages available. AE, DC, MC, V. **Amenities:** Restaurant; bar; babysitting; 27-hole golf course; exercise room; 2 outdoor pools; 3 tennis courts (lit). *In room:* A/C, TV, hair dryer, kitchenette (in suite), Wi-Fi (free).

WHERE TO DINE
EXPENSIVE

Colt & Alison ★★ INTERNATIONAL   At the Sea Island Golf Club, this restaurant was built on the ruins of a cow barn of a plantation great house that burned down. The elegant restaurant, with its high-back leather chairs and cozy banquettes, opens onto panoramic views of the Plantation Course's 18th hole. In chilly weather, you can relax by a wood-burning fireplace. Tableside preparations are a feature of the staff, who create everything from steak au poivre to bananas foster in front of you. Chefs specialize in the best dry-aged beef on the island, along with fresh seafood. Start with the colossal shrimp cocktail or goat cheese fritters with marinated green tomatoes and smoked pecan dressing. For a main course, you can opt for various beef dishes, the herb-crusted rack of lamb, or the Southern-fried Maine lobster tails with a Jack Daniel's honey glaze. You can also dine nearby at the Oak Room (see below).

In the Lodge at Sea Island Golf Club, 100 Retreat Ave. ✆ **800/732-4752,** ext. 4353. Reservations required. Main courses $34–$52. AE, DC, MC, V. Wed–Mon 6–9:30pm. Closed Tues.

Oak Room ★ INTERNATIONAL   The sibling of Colt & Alison (see above) invites you into its oak-lined publike atmosphere with hand-painted murals, an outdoor terrace, wood-burning fireplace, and leather ceilings, opening onto views of the Plantation Golf Course. The so-called tavern menu is one of the best in East Georgia. Don't expect pub grub. Instead you're treated to such appetizers as blue crab and jalapeño hush puppies with a Cajun rémoulade or else seared foie gras with toasted cornbread and dandelion jelly. One salad is composed of buttermilk fried oysters. For your main, sample the braised pork shanks with a Parmesan polenta or the braised free-range chicken with Yukon gold potato dumplings in a chervil sauce.

In the Lodge at Sea Island Golf Club, 100 Retreat Ave. ✆ **800/732-4752,** ext. 4353. Reservations recommended. Main courses $21–$35. AE, DC, MC, V. Daily 11:30am–2:30pm and 6–10pm.

MODERATE

Delaney's Bistro AMERICAN   Local chef Tom Delaney's loyal following includes both islanders and visitors. He aims to appeal to a wide culinary taste and, in general, succeeds. In his low-rise building,

Delaney offers an array of food ranging from fresh seafood to certified Black Angus beef. The menu at lunch is light, including the usual pastas, sandwiches, and salads, as well as grilled shrimp salad and sautéed crab cakes. Tom is more ambitious at night. You might begin with a pâté of foie gras or baked goat cheese before selecting a main course such as a mixed grill (beef, veal, and lamb chop in a cabernet sauce) or veal Hannah (scaloppine topped with wild mushrooms and crab). Desserts are made fresh daily.

3415 Frederica Rd. ☎ **912/638-1330.** www.delaneysbistro.com. Reservations recommended. Main courses $9–$12 lunch, $17–$29 dinner. AE, DC, DISC, MC, V. Tues–Sat 11am–2pm and 6–10pm.

Gnat's Landing AMERICAN   This is a laid-back Key West–style place in the heart of Redfern Village. It's a family favorite in large part because of the on-site pizzeria and a kiddie menu that includes fried shrimp and chicken fingers. The joint's irreverent tone is set by its slogan: "If you like home cookin', stay home." The array of freshly made salads is among the best on the island, including a tarragon chicken salad made with chunks of chicken breast, grapes, and pecans. The real specialty of the house, worth a trip over here, is Mrs. Slappy's Seafood Gumbo. Devotees have fallen in love with this savory treat, and Gnat's Landing now ships it across the nation. Their St. Simons Stew (actually, a Brunswick stew) isn't bad, either. A wide selection of sandwiches is sold, but seafood dominates the menu. We go for the savory deviled crab.

310 Redfern Village. ☎ **912/638-7378.** www.gnatslanding.com. Reservations not needed. Main courses $3.95–$24. AE, DISC, MC, V. Mon–Sat 11:30am–2:30pm and 5:30–10pm.

INEXPENSIVE

Bennie's Red Barn ⒱ⓐⓛⓤⓔ STEAKS/SEAFOOD   Established in 1954, the place has a Southern folksiness, almost a hillbilly kind of charm. Menu items include an uncomplicated medley of food to please everyone's Southern grandmother, including fried or broiled fish, chicken, and shrimp. Steaks are sizable slabs, wood-fire-grilled and appropriately seasoned. Dinners include house salad, potato, rolls, and tea or coffee. If you're a biscuit-and-gravy kind of diner, you've arrived.

5514 Frederica Rd. ☎ **912/638-2844.** www.benniesredbarn.com. Reservations recommended Fri–Sat. Main courses $12–$32. AE, DISC, MC, V. Daily 6–10pm.

The Crab Trap Ⓚⓘⓓⓢ SEAFOOD   For the family in pursuit of coleslaw, hush puppies, and fried shrimp, the Crab Trap is the island's most popular seafood restaurant and a good buy. Forget fancy trappings—the place is downright plain. Fresh seafood is offered daily, and you can order it fried, broiled, blackened, or grilled. Appetizers include oysters on the half shell and crab soup. Boiled crab is the chef's specialty, and the seafood platter is big enough for three. For those who aren't turned on by crabs and shrimp, steaks in various cuts are also available. Heaps of battered fries come with most dishes. That hole in the middle of your table is for depositing shrimp shells and corncobs. Dress as if you're going on a summer fishing trip.

1209 Ocean Blvd. ℂ **912/638-3552.** Main courses $8.95–$27. AE, MC, V. Sun–Thurs 5–10pm; Fri–Sat 5–10:30pm. Closed Thanksgiving and Christmas.

---

4 DAUFUSKIE ISLAND ★

---

10

1 nautical mile W of Hilton Head

Rich in legend, lore, and history, Daufuskie Island is relatively cut off from the world. Lying between Hilton Head and Savannah and accessible only by boat, its heyday came in the mid–19th century when Southern plantations here produced the famous Sea Island cotton—until the boll weevil put an end to that industry. The island may be known to some readers as the setting for Pat Conroy's book *The Water Is Wide,* and it was the location for the film *Conrack.*

Half the island has remained an undeveloped wilderness of forest, marshland, and wildlife. In 1980, the other half was purchased for the development of golf courses and elegant "plantations," where people live in condos.

The 5,200-acre island is now home to about 300 permanent residents, mostly Gullahs, descendants of slaves freed after the Civil War. It was originally inhabited by the Cusabo and later the Yamacraw Indians. Indian pottery, some of the oldest in America, has been found on Daufuskie, dating back 9,000 years.

The English eventually took over the island and converted it into a plantation culture, focusing on indigo as its main export. Indigo eventually yielded to cotton plantations. After the boll weevil, an oyster-canning industry took over until it was forced out of business by the pollution of the Savannah River.

The island is a nature retreat, with thick, ancient live oaks and angel oaks along with ospreys, egrets, and other waterfowl living among the reeds and rushes.

The island's only hotel, the Daufuskie Island Resort, and its golf courses closed due to bankruptcy. It was the major source of employment for islanders. Until it reopens (if it does), Daufuskie is recommended only as a day trip.

There is only one way to Daufuskie Island, and that's by boat. See "Cruises & Tours," below.

CRUISES & TOURS

Several tempting tours are offered to Daufuskie, which has beaches, "whispering" marshes (when the wind blows through the marshes, encountering vegetation, locals think the sounds evoke whispering), ancient forests of moss-draped oaks, and two of the best golf courses in America. What it doesn't have are stoplights, crowds, and shopping centers.

The **Calibogue Cruises** ferry (© **843/342-8687**) leaves from Broad Creek Marina off Marshland Road on Hilton Head. The ferry ride is $26 per person, and the tour is $30 per person. The tour visits the Mount Carmel and First Union African Baptist churches, the Lighthouse, the Old Winery, and cemeteries dating back hundreds of years. You'll sample delicious Daufuskie Island deviled crab. Tours depart once a day Monday to Saturday (call ahead for times). You can also have the option of renting a golf cart for $50 for 2½ hours or $90 per day.

Outside Hilton Head offers two tours to Daufuskie, departing from South Beach Marina at the Sea Pines Resort (© **800/686-6996** or 843/686-6996; www.outsidehiltonhead.com). The 4½-hour tour is $85 per person (includes boat shuttle, golf cart, and guide). Once on the island, you'll board golf carts and tour historic sites including the old Baptist church, Pat Conroy's school, and other locations.

---

5 BEAUFORT ★★

---

46 miles NE of Savannah

Full of old-fashioned inns, rustic pubs, and tiny stores along the Henry C. Chambers Waterfront Park, this quaint town was the inspiration for the setting of Pat Conroy's novel *The Prince of Tides* (among other bestsellers). In fact, parts of the film were shot here, as were certain scenes from *Forest Gump* and *The Big Chill*. For its 30th anniversary, the waterfront park was rebuilt in 2010 and live bands now perform here on occasions (check local listings).

Beaufort (Low Country pronunciation: *Bew*-fort) is an old seaport with narrow streets shaded by huge live oaks and lined with 18th-century homes. The oldest house (at Port Republic and New sts.) was built in 1717. This was the second area in North America discovered by the Spanish (1520), the site of the first fort on the continent (1525), and the first attempted settlement (1562). Several forts have been excavated, dating from 1566 and 1577.

GETTING THERE

If you're traveling from the north, take I-95 to exit 33; then follow the signs to the center of Beaufort. If you're leaving from Charleston, take U.S. 17 S.; then head left on U.S. 21, and follow signs to Beaufort. From Hilton Head, go on U.S. 278 W.; after it turns into 278 Alt, exit onto S.C. 170. Follow S.C. 170 into Beaufort.

VISITOR INFORMATION

Beaufort Chamber of Commerce, 1106 Carteret St. (PO Box 910), Beaufort, SC 29901 (✆ **800/638-3525** or 843/525-8500; www.beaufortsc.org), has information and self-guided tours of this historic town. It's open daily from 9am to 5:30pm.

ORGANIZED TOURS

If you're planning to visit Beaufort in early to mid-October, contact the **Historic Beaufort Foundation,** PO Box 11, Beaufort, SC 29901 (✆ **843/379-3331;** www.historicbeaufort.org), for dates and details regarding its 3 days of antebellum house and garden tours.

A tour called the **Spirit of Old Beaufort,** 103 West St. Ext. (✆ **843/525-0459;** www.thespiritofoldbeaufort.com), takes you on a journey through the old town, exploring local history, architecture, horticulture, and Low Country life. You'll see houses that are not accessible on other tours. Your host, clad in period costume, will guide you for 1¾ hours Monday to Saturday at 10:30am, 2:30pm, and 7pm. The cost is $15 for adults and $8 for children 6 to 12. Tours depart from just behind the John Mark Verdier House Museum.

The most romantic way to see Beaufort is to take a carriage ride conducted by **Sea Island Carriage Co.** (✆ **843/525-1821;** www.seaislandcarriage.com). These rides leave from the downtown marina at Henry C. Chambers Waterfront Park, lasting 1 hour and costing $18 for adults and $7 for children 5 to 12. Sometimes you'll get an old-timer, a Beaufort native, who speaks Gullah, which makes for a very informative ride.

SEEING THE SIGHTS

John Mark Verdier House Museum, 801 Bay St. (✆ **843/379-6335**), is a restored 1802 house partially furnished to depict the life of the prosperous merchant who lived here from about 1800 to 1825. An excellent example of a Federal-style home, it was once known as the Lafayette Building because the Marquis de Lafayette is said to have spoken here in 1825. It's open Monday to Saturday 10am to 4pm. Admission is $6 for adults and $4 for children; children 5 and under are admitted free.

St. Helena's Episcopal Church, 507 New Castle St. (© **843/522-1712;** www.sthelenas1712.org), traces its origin back to 1712. Visitors, admitted free Monday to Saturday from 10am to 4pm, can see its classic interior and visit the graveyard, where tombstones served as operating tables during the Civil War.

Beaufort is the home of the **U.S. Marine Corps Recruit Depot** (© **843/228-7100;** www.mccssc.com). The visitor center (go to Building 283) is open daily from 6am to 6pm. You can take a driving tour or a bus tour (free) around the grounds, where you'll see an Iwo Jima monument; a monument to the Spanish settlement of Santa Elena (1521); and a memorial to Jean Ribaut, the Huguenot who founded Beaufort in 1562. Vehicle operators must possess a valid driver's license, vehicle registration, and proof of automobile insurance. You can expect tight security.

A worthwhile excursion from Beaufort is the 15-mile drive to the state park at **Hunting Island ★★★** (www.huntingisland.com), a lush island where the Vietnam battle scenes from *Forrest Gump* were filmed. Long a layover for sailors and pirates, including Blackbeard, the island was once a base for hunting deer. With 3 miles of natural sandy beaches—some of the most beautiful coastline in South Carolina—this 5,000-acre park is now a nature and wildlife refuge. There are showers and dressing rooms on the beach, a 200-site campground, plus cabins, a boardwalk, and nature trails, as well as a fishing pier and boat landing.

In the center of the park stands a historic lighthouse, with panoramic views. The lighthouse was rebuilt in 1875 after it was destroyed in the Civil War. To climb the 167 steps, the park (© **843/838-2011**) collects a fee of $5 for adults, $3.25 for seniors, and $3 for kids ages 6 to 15. It is open daily from 6am to 6pm.

WHERE TO STAY IN BEAUFORT
EXPENSIVE

The Beaufort Inn ★★ Built in 1897, this is the most appealing hotel in Beaufort and the place where most celebrities stay when shooting a film in town. The woodwork and interior moldings are among the finest in Beaufort, and the circular, four-story staircase has been the subject of numerous photographs and architectural awards. The guest rooms, each decorated in brightly colored individual style, are conversation pieces.

809 Port Republic St., Beaufort, SC 29902. © **888/522-0250** or 843/379-INNS (4667). Fax 843/521-9500. www.beaufortinn.com. 21 units. $159–$199 double;

$220–$299 suite; $350–$450 loft. Rates include full gourmet breakfast. AE, DISC, MC, V. No children 7 and under. **Amenities:** Room service. *In room:* A/C, TV, hair dryer, Wi-Fi (free).

Hilton Garden Inn ★   Of course, a Hilton Garden Inn is not as charming as one of the town's historic inns, but this is a find for those seeking a modern, well-maintained, and affordable place to spend the night. It lies a mile from the Historic District and is convenient for those visiting the nearby military bases such as Parris Island, just 3 miles away. The guest rooms are designed in a rather standard motel style, but they're equipped with all the basic necessities, including a large work desk and phones with voice mail and dataports. Complimentary newspapers such as *USA Today* are distributed. A freshly prepared breakfast is offered daily in the Great American Grill and drinks are served in the cozy Pavilion Lounge. Plus, an on-site pantry sells ready-to-cook meals that can be prepared in the in-room microwave oven.

1500 Queen St., Beaufort, SC 29902. ℂ **843/379-9800.** Fax 843/379-9801. http://hiltongardeninn.hilton.com. 115 rooms. $109–$229 double. AE, DC, DISC, MC, V. **Amenities:** Restaurant; bar; exercise room; outdoor pool; room service. *In room:* A/C, TV, Wi-Fi (free).

The Rhett House Inn ★★★   This inn is certainly very popular, at least with Hollywood film crews. Because it was a site for *The Big Chill, Forrest Gump,* and *The Prince of Tides,* chances are that you've seen it before. It's a Mobil and AAA four-star inn in a restored 1820 Greek Revival plantation-type home. Guest rooms are furnished with English and American antiques, and ornamented with Oriental rugs. Eight rooms contain whirlpools. The veranda is an ideal place to sit and relax as you gaze at the gardens.

1009 Craven St., Beaufort, SC 29902. ℂ **888/480-9530** or 843/524-9030. Fax 843/524-1310. www.rhetthouseinn.com. 17 units. $159–$350 double. Rates include full breakfast, afternoon tea, and evening hors d'oeuvres. AE, DISC, MC, V. Free parking. No children 4 and under. **Amenities:** Breakfast room. *In room:* A/C, TV, hair dryer, minibar (in some), Wi-Fi (free).

MODERATE

Country Inn & Suites   You can expect clean and friendly accommodations at this four-story chain hotel located 5 miles from Parris Island and 2 miles from the downtown Historic District. Perks include a business center, exercise room, indoor pool, and laundry facilities. It's a step above value chains, and a good deal for families visiting Marine recruits at Parris Island.

2450 Boundary St. (U.S. 21), Beaufort, SC 29906. ℂ **800/830-5222** or 843/379-4000. Fax 843/379-4020. www.countryinns.com. 77 units. $99–$155 double. Rates include continental breakfast. AE, DC, DISC, MC, V. **Amenities:** Breakfast room; exercise room; indoor pool. *In room:* A/C, TV, fridge, Internet (free).

DINING ◆
Blackstone's Café 10
Emily's 4
Kathleen's Grille 9
Panini's Cafe 7
Plums 8
Saltus River Grill 8

ACCOMMODATIONS ■
Best Inn 1
The Beaufort Inn 6
Country Inn & Suites 1
The Cuthbert House Inn 11
Hilton Garden Inn 1
The Rhett House Inn 3
Sea Island Inn 5
Two Suns Inn 2

The Cuthbert House Inn ★★   One of the grand old B&Bs of South Carolina, this showcase Southern home was built in 1790. It was remodeled shortly after the Civil War to take on a more Victorian aura, and its present owner, Sharon Groves, has worked to modernize it without sacrificing its grace or antiquity. Graffiti carved by Union soldiers can still be seen on the fireplace mantel in the Eastlake Room. Guest rooms are elegantly furnished in Southern plantation style, and some have four-poster beds. The inn is filled with large parlors, sitting rooms, spacious hallways, and 12-foot ceilings characteristic of Greek Revival homes. At breakfast in the conservatory, you can order such delights as Georgia ice cream (cheese grits) and freshly made breads.

1203 Bay St., Beaufort, SC 29902. © **800/327-9275** or 843/521-1315. Fax 843/521-1314. www.cuthberthouseinn.com. 7 units. $150–$259 double; $199–$269 suite. Rates include full breakfast and afternoon tea or refreshments. AE, DISC, MC, V. Free parking. **Amenities:** Breakfast room; bike rentals. *In room:* A/C, TV, fridge, hair dryer, Wi-Fi (free).

Two Suns Inn   When this place was built in 1917, it was one of the grandest homes in its prosperous neighborhood, offering views of the coastal road and the tidal flatlands beyond. Every imaginable modern convenience (at the time) was added, including a baseboard vacuum-cleaning system, an electric call box, and steam heat. Later, it became housing for unmarried teachers in the public schools. Now it's a cozy B&B. Part of the inn's appeal stems from its lack of pretension, with homey bedrooms featuring simple furnishings and neatly kept bathrooms.

1705 Bay St., Beaufort, SC 29902. (© **800/532-4244** or 843/522-1122. Fax 843/522-1122. www.twosunsinn.com. 5 units. $159–$199 double. Rates include full breakfast and afternoon cordials. AE, DISC, MC, V. Free parking. No children 11 and under. **Amenities:** Breakfast room. *In room:* A/C, TV, hair dryer, Wi-Fi (free).

INEXPENSIVE

Best Inn (Value) You'll be happiest at this local hotel chain if you know what it doesn't have: There's no restaurant, no bar, and no pool. What you do get is a cost-effective hotel room outfitted in a bland contemporary style, with solid, well-maintained furnishings. Set 2 miles north of Beaufort's commercial core, it's a worthy choice for families with children or for business travelers who simply need a no-frills place to spend the night.

2448 Boundary St., Beaufort, SC 29903. (© **800/237-8466** or 843/524-3322. Fax 843/524-7264. 62 units. $49–$85 double. Rates include continental breakfast. AE, DC, DISC, MC, V. *In room:* A/C, TV.

Sea Island Inn This is a basic two-story motel with reasonable rates for what you get. Although the rooms are nothing special, they're comfortable and well maintained. A few have sea views.

1015 Bay St., Beaufort, SC 29902. (© **800/528-7234** or 843/522-2090. Fax 843/521-4858. www.bestwestern.com. 43 units. $112–$160 double. Rates include continental breakfast. AE, DC, DISC, MC, V. **Amenities:** Breakfast room; exercise room; outdoor pool. *In room:* A/C, TV, hair dryer, Internet (free).

WHERE TO EAT IN BEAUFORT
EXPENSIVE

Emily's INTERNATIONAL This is our favorite restaurant in Beaufort, but the ambience and attitude remind us of Scandinavia. That's hardly surprising, because the bearded owner is an émigré from Sweden who feels comfortable in the South Carolina lowlands after years of life at sea. Some folks just go to the bar to sample tapas including miniature portions of tempura shrimp, fried scallops, and stuffed peppers, among at least 50 other items. The menu might also feature rich cream of mussel and shrimp soup, filet "black and white" (filets of beef and pork served with béarnaise sauce), duck with orange sauce, and a meltingly tender Wiener schnitzel. Everything is served in stomach-stretching portions.

906 Port Republic St. ℂ **843/522-1866.** www.emilysrestaurantandtapasbar.com. **169**
Reservations recommended. Main courses $16–$30; tapas $8–$19. AE, DISC, MC,
V. Mon–Sat 4–10pm (main courses served starting at 6pm).

MODERATE

Kathleen's Grille ★ (Finds) SEAFOOD/SOUTHERN   This local
eatery has plenty of Low Country atmosphere and is best known for
its fresh fish dinners. We'd go here for the Southern starters alone,
including fried green tomatoes topped with a shrimp salsa and crab
chowder. For lunch, try something from the "sandwich showcase,"
perhaps soft-shell crab or fresh grouper. Salads, including a seafood
pasta version, are made fresh daily. At night, the restaurant serves
some of the best fish platters in the area, as well as grilled shrimp and
boiled oysters. For meat lovers, there's rib-eye or pork chops, the latter
coming with a sweet-and-spicy berry glaze. One section of the menu
is reserved for "Kathleen's kids," but the offerings are so meager (fresh
boxed cereals, a hot dog), your little ones may end up nutritionally
deprived.

822 Bay St. ℂ **843/524-2500.** www.kathleensgrille.com. Reservations recommended. Main courses $7–$12 lunch, $14–$26 dinner. AE, DISC, MC, V. Daily
11am–9pm.

Panini's Café AMERICAN/PIZZA   This restaurant serves the
most savory stone-baked pizzas in this part of South Carolina. In
addition to regular pizzas, you might also want to try a "Capri," the
house specialty with spinach, sun-dried tomatoes, onions, feta cheese,
extra-virgin olive oil, and mustard aioli. The building was once a bank
and later a movie theater; an award-winning renovation has returned
the place to its former grandeur. The terrace even offers waterfront
views. In this setting, experience lunch specialties like Mediterranean
shrimp 'n' grits with pancetta polenta and an olive tomato sauté, or
the equally unique crab lasagna with mascarpone, spinach, artichoke,
and tomato couli. At dinner, main courses include a grilled lobster
and shrimp carbonara with applewood-smoked bacon, peas, asparagus, and a light Parmesan cream over capellini; and Spanish paella
with shrimp, mussels, clams, red snapper, monkfish, chorizo saffron
rice, tomatoes, onions, and garlic.

926 Bay St. ℂ **843/379-0300.** www.paniniscafe.net. Reservations recommended.
Main courses $9–$13 lunch, $10–$22 dinner; tapas $8–$12. AE, DC, DISC, MC, V.
Daily 11am–10pm. Closed Thanksgiving and Christmas.

Saltus River Grill ★★★ SEAFOOD   Saltus River Grill is the
sister restaurant to the more casual Plums in Beaufort (see p. 170),
but that's where the similarities end. Elegant and sophisticated, this
restaurant looks out over the Intracoastal Waterway and provides

spectacular scenery to match its equally spectacular menu. The building was constructed in 1787, and the restaurant was named after
shipbuilder John Saltus. Chef Jim Spratling prepares his menu with
the freshest ingredients available and produces tantalizing meat selections from the grill. You can also order from the oyster bar or the sushi
bar. Start with the steamed pork dumplings as an appetizer and follow
with a main dish of cornmeal-seared jumbo sea scallops with sweet
potato–bacon hash, warm pickled onions, and balsamic-fig molasses.
If you crave beef, order the grilled barrel-cut filet with chèvre scal-
loped potatoes, shiitake mushrooms, onion confit, and a natural
demi-glace.

802 Bay St. ⓒ 843/379-3474. www.saltusrivergrill.com. Reservations required.
Main courses $21–$32. AE, DISC, MC, V. Mon–Sat 4–10pm; Sun 10:30am–3pm
(brunch) and 4–10pm.

INEXPENSIVE

Blackstone's Café AMERICAN   This is where seemingly everybody in town gathers for breakfast. Since 1991, locals have met here
to eat and gossip. You can order such breakfast classics as shrimp
omelets or, even more authentic, shrimp 'n' grits. You can also drop
in for an informal lunch, enjoying the bustling atmosphere and the
best selection of sandwiches in town. If your kids are in tow, you can
even get a peanut butter and jelly. House specials include everything
from a smoked salmon plate to a bacon cheeseburger platter. Some
of the fresh salads are good, especially the almond chicken salad
plate or the all-white albacore tuna salad plate with feta cheese and
black olives.

205 Scott St. ⓒ 843/524-4330. www.blackstonescafe.com. Reservations not
necessary. Breakfast $5–$9; sandwiches $5–$8; house specials $8–$9. AE, DC, MC,
V. Mon–Sat 7:30am–2:30pm; Sun 7:30am–2pm.

Plums AMERICAN/SOUTHERN   Centrally located on Bay
Street on the waterfront, Plums is one of Beaufort's favorite dining
choices. This casual restaurant specializes in sandwiches, soups, and
ice cream. While filming *The Prince of Tides*, even Barbra Streisand
claimed that Plums was her favorite place in town for a cool, refreshing dish of ice cream after a long day of filming. The chicken salad
sandwich, with celery, toasted almonds, and tomato, is as delicious as
Plums's Factory Creek Shrimp Roll, with shrimp, celery, lettuce, and
spices, all piled high on a French roll. Quesadillas are another good
choice, as are heartier sandwiches like the blackened catfish sandwich.
Dinners are more elaborate, typically focusing on seafood, but the
menu frequently changes. The chef usually features a succulent pasta

studded with Georgia crab and shrimp. Desserts are luscious and
made fresh daily.

904½ Bay St. 🕐 **843/525-1946.** www.plumsrestaurant.com. Reservations not necessary. Main courses $6–$10 lunch, $15–$23 dinner. AE, DC, MC, V. Daily 11am–5pm (soups, salads, sandwiches) and 5–10pm (pasta, seafood, sandwiches).

6 SEA ISLAND ★★

11 miles E of Brunswick

The Cloister hotel, opened in 1928, is the main attraction on Sea Island. It owns the entire piece of land, which can be visited on a day trip from Savannah if you don't want to stay overnight; just allow about 1½ hours to get there. When you arrive, take a scenic drive along Sea Island Drive, also called "Millionaire's Row." Today, in addition to the hotel, the island is home to some of the most elegant villas and mansions in the Southeast. Many of Sea Island's residences are second homes to CEOs and other wealthy folks. Some can be rented if you can afford it. Call **Sea Island Cottage Rentals** (🕐 **877/732-4752;** www.seaislandcottages.com), but be prepared for very high prices.

The island was acquired by Ohio-based Howard Earle Coffin, an automobile executive, in 1925. Still owned by his descendants, the Cloister combines 10,000 acres of forest, lawn, and marshland, plus 5 miles of beachfront. It has impressed everybody from Margaret Thatcher to Queen Juliana of the Netherlands, plus four U.S. presidents, including George H. W. Bush, who honeymooned here with his wife Barbara in the 1940s.

ESSENTIALS

GETTING THERE   From Brunswick, take the F.J. Torras Causeway to St. Simons Island and follow Sea Island Road to Sea Island.

VISITOR INFORMATION   There is no welcome center. Some information is provided by the Cloister, but the hotel staff prefers to cater to registered guests.

WHERE TO STAY & EAT ON SEA ISLAND

The Cloister ★★★   Georgia's poshest retreat, this hotel has made *Conde Nast Traveler's* Gold List for 5 years in a row. Set amid the most elaborate landscaping on the coast, this vast compound between the Atlantic Ocean and the Black Banks River encompasses about 50 carefully maintained buildings, some of them massive and others on neighboring St. Simons Island. Everyone from honeymooners to golfers checks in here. The hotel offers gorgeous suites and deluxe guest rooms, all with 24-hour butler service. Other perks include luxurious Italian sheets, Bulgari toiletries, and Turkish stone bathrooms with deep-soaking tubs.

Sea Island, GA 31561. ⓒ **800/SEA-ISLE** (732-4752) or 912/638-3611. Fax 912/638-5159. www.seaisland.com. $525-$750 double; $1,350-$2,000 suite; $5,000 ultimate suite. Golf, tennis, and honeymoon packages available. AE, DC, DISC, MC, V. **Amenities:** 4 restaurants; 2 bars; babysitting; exercise club; 3 18-hole golf courses; room service; spa; 8 tennis courts (4 lit). *In room:* A/C, TV, hair dryer, minibar, Wi-Fi (free).

11

Fast Facts & Websites

1 FAST FACTS: SAVANNAH

AMERICAN EXPRESS   Cardholders can obtain assistance by calling ℂ **800/221-7282.**

AREA CODES   The area code for Savannah is 912.

AUTOMOBILE ORGANIZATIONS   Motor clubs will supply maps, suggested routes, guidebooks, accident and bail-bond insurance, and emergency road service. The **American Automobile Association (AAA)** is the major auto club in the United States. If you belong to a motor club in your home country, inquire about AAA reciprocity before you leave. You may be able to join AAA even if you're not a member of a reciprocal club; to inquire, call AAA (ℂ **800/222-4357;** www.aaaNY.com). AAA has a nationwide emergency road service telephone number (ℂ **800/AAA-HELP** [4357]).

BUSINESS HOURS   The following are general open hours; specific establishments may vary. **Banks:** Monday to Friday 9am to 3pm (some are also open Sat 9am–noon). Most banks and other outlets offer 24-hour access to automated teller machines (ATMs). **Offices:** Monday to Friday 9am to 5pm. **Stores:** Monday to Saturday 10am to 6pm, and some also on Sunday from noon to 5pm. Malls usually stay open until 9pm Monday to Saturday, and department stores are usually open until 9pm at least 1 day a week.

CAR RENTALS   To rent a car in Georgia, you need a major credit card and a valid driver's license. Sometimes a passport or an international driver's license is also required if your driver's license is in a language other than English. You often need to be at least 25 years of age, although some companies rent to younger people (often with a daily surcharge). Be sure to return your car with the same amount of gasoline that you started out with; rental companies charge excessive prices for gas. Keep in mind that a separate motorcycle driver's license is required in most states.

DENTISTS   Call **Abercorn South Side Dental,** 11139 Abercorn St. (© **912/925-9190;** www.abercornsouthsidedental.com), for complete dental care and emergencies Monday to Friday 8:30am to 3pm.

DRINKING LAWS   The legal age for purchase and consumption of alcoholic beverages is 21; proof of age is required and often requested at bars, nightclubs, and restaurants, so it's always a good idea to bring ID when you go out. Although local laws can vary, in general, no alcohol is served at bars, restaurants, or nightclubs between 4am and 12:30pm on Sunday. In addition, alcoholic beverages are not sold on Sunday in liquor stores, convenience stores, or grocery stores. Do not carry open containers of alcohol in your car or any public area that isn't zoned for alcohol consumption. The police can fine you on the spot. And nothing will ruin your trip faster than getting a citation for DUI (driving under the influence), so don't even think about driving while intoxicated.

DRIVING RULES   Speed limits are posted on Georgia highways. In addition, the law requires the driver and front-seat passengers to wear seat belts while the car is in motion. Children 4 and under must be buckled into safety seats in the back seat; those 5 to 12 must sit in the back seat if the car is equipped with air bags.

DRUGSTORES   Drugstores are scattered throughout Savannah. A good choice is **CVS,** 12012 Abercorn St. (© **912/925-5568**), open Monday to Friday 8am to 10pm, Saturday 8am to 6pm, and Sunday 10am to 6pm.

ELECTRICITY   Like Canada, the United States uses 110–120 volts AC (60 cycles), compared to 220–240 volts AC (50 cycles) in most of Europe, Australia, and New Zealand. Downward converters that change 220–240 volts to 110–120 volts are difficult to find in the United States, so bring one with you.

EMERGENCIES   Dial © **911** to report a fire, call the police, or get an ambulance. This is a nationwide toll-free call (no coins are required at a public telephone).

HOSPITALS   There are 24-hour emergency-room services at **St. Joseph Candler General Hospital,** 5353 Reynolds St. (© **912/819-6000;** www.sjchs.org), and at the **Memorial Medical Center,** 4700 Waters Ave. (© **912/350-8000;** www.memorialhealth.com).

NEWSPAPERS   The *Savannah Morning News* is a daily filled with information about local cultural and entertainment events. The *Savannah Tribune* and the *Herald of Savannah* are geared to the African-American community.

POLICE   In an emergency, call © **911.**

POST OFFICE Post offices are centrally located and open Monday to Friday 8am to 4:30pm. The main office is at 3601 Montgomery St. (📞 **912/234-8935**).

SAFETY Although it's reasonably safe to explore the Historic and Victorian districts during the day, the situation changes at night. The clubs along the riverfront, both bars and restaurants, report very little crime. But muggings and drug dealing are common in Savannah's poorer neighborhoods.

TAXES Savannah has a 7% sales tax, and a 7% accommodations tax (room or occupancy tax) on your hotel bill.

TRANSIT INFORMATION Call **Chatham Area Transit** at 📞 **912/233-5767.**

VISITOR INFORMATION You can contact the **Division of Tourism,** Georgia Department of Industry, Trade & Tourism, PO Box 1776, Atlanta, GA 30301-1776 (📞 **800/VISIT-GA** [847-4842] or 404/962-4000; www.georgia.org/travel). Ask for a calendar of events (Jan–June or July–Dec), as well as information on your specific interests. The **Savannah Information Visitor Center,** 301 Martin Luther King Jr. Blvd., Savannah, GA 31401 (📞 **912/944-0455**), is open Monday to Friday 8:30am to 5pm and Saturday and Sunday 9am to 5pm. The staff is friendly and efficient. The center offers an audiovisual presentation ($4 adults, $1 children); organized tours; and self-guided walking, driving, or bike tours with excellent maps, cassette tapes, and brochures. Tourist information is also available from the **Savannah Area Convention & Visitors Bureau,** 101 E. Bay St., Savannah, GA 31402 (📞 **877/728-2662** or 912/644-6401; www.savannahvisit.com).

WEATHER Call 📞 **912/964-1700** or visit www.weather.com.

2 AIRLINE WEBSITES

MAJOR U.S. AIRLINES
(*flies internationally as well)

American Airlines*
www.aa.com

Continental
www.continental.com

Delta Air Lines*
www.delta.com

United
www.united.com

US Airways*
www.usairways.com

INDEX

See also Accommodations and Restaurant indexes, below.

GENERAL INDEX

A
AARP, 36
Abercorn Antique Village, 104–105
Access-Able Travel Source, 35
Accessible Journeys, 35
Accommodations, 38–53. *See also*
  Accommodations Index; and
  specific destinations
    best, 4–6
    family-friendly, 42
Advanced Sail (Hilton Head),
  129–130
A Fine Choice, 108
African-American sights and
  attractions, 79–83
Aiken, Conrad, 81, 83
AirAmbulanceCard.com, 36
Air travel, 27
Alder Lane (Hilton Head), 124
Alex Raskin Antiques, 105
Alligators, 128
American Automobile Association
  (AAA), 173
American Express, 173
American Legion Post, 110–111
American Revolution, 12–13
Amick's Deep Sea Fishing, 89
Amtrak, 35
Andrew Low House, 70, 72
Antiques, 104–105
Architecture, 17–21
Area codes, 173
Armstrong College, original
  headquarters of, 96
Art, 21–22
Art galleries, 105–106
Arts Center of Coastal Carolina
  (Hilton Head), 151
Audubon-Newhall Preserve (Hilton
  Head), 127
Automobile organizations, 173

B
Bacon Park, 89, 90
Baker's Pride Bakery, 106
Barnes & Noble, 106
Bars and pubs, 111–114
Beaches, 123–124, 154–155
Beaufort, 163–171
Berendt, John, 17, 22
Bernie's River Street, 111
Biking, 87, 124, 155
Bird-watching, Hilton Head, 128
Bluffton, 131
Boat tours and cruises, 86–87,
  89–90
    Daufuskie Island, 163
    dinner cruises, 115
    Hilton Head, 124–125
Bonaventure Cemetery, 80
The Book Gift Shop, 108
Books, recommended, 22
Books-a-Million, 106
Bookstores, 106–107
Book Warehouse, 106
Business hours, 173
Bus travel, 28, 29
Byrd Cookie Company, 107

C
Calendar of events, 32–34
Callahan Sports Bar & Grill (Hilton
  Head), 151
Camping, 87
Candy, 107
Cane Grinding and Harvest
  Festival, 33
Car rentals, 28–29, 173
The Carriage House Shop, 95
Carriage Tours of Savannah, 86
Car travel, 28
Casey's Sports Bar & Grill (Hilton
  Head), 151
Cathedral of St. John the Baptist,
  75, 97

Celtic Cross, 102
Cemeteries, 79
Charlotte's Corner, 108
Chatham County Courthouse, 92
Chippewa Square, 93
Christ Church (St. Simons Island),
    154
Christ Episcopal Church, 75, 91
Christmas 1864, 34
The Christmas Shop, 108
Chuck's Bar, 114
Churches, 75–77
Churchill's Pub & Restaurant,
    111–112
City Hall, 91, 98
City Market, 30, 66–67, 104
Civil War
    architecture and, 20–21
    history of, 13–15
    sights and attractions, 78
Climate, 32
Clipper Trading Company, 105
Club One, 114
Cluskey, Charles B., 20
Coastal Discovery Museum (Hilton
    Head), 122–123, 129
Coast Guard Station Beach (St.
    Simons Island), 155
Coligny Beach (Hilton Head), 124
Colonial days, 10–12, 24–25
Colonial Park Cemetery, 79, 97
Compass Prints, Inc./Ray Ellis
    Gallery, 105
Cookware, 107

Daffin Park, 90
Daufuskie Island, 162–163
Davenport House, 98
Davenport House Museum, 72
Deen, Paula, 1, 56, 85, 107
Dejá Groove, 111
Dentists, 174
Desotorow Gallery, 105
Dinner cruises, 115
Disabilities, travelers with, 35–36
Diving, 89
Dreissen Beach Park (Hilton Head),
    124
Drinking laws, 174
Driving rules, 174
Drugstores, 174

Electricity, 174
Emergencies, 174
Emmet Park, 102
E. Shaver, Bookseller, 106–107

Faces Day Spa (Hilton Head), 130
Factors Row, 77
Factors Walk, 77
Families with children, 36–37
    accommodations, 42
    restaurants, 63
    sights and attractions, 83
Festivals and special events, 32–34
    Hilton Head, 122
Films, recommended, 22–23
First African Baptist Church, 80
First Baptist Church, 94
First Bryan Baptist Church, 80–82
Fishing, 89, 125, 155
Flying Wheels Travel, 35
Folly Field Beach (Hilton Head),
    124
Food and cuisine, 24–26
Food stores and markets, 107
Forsyth Park, 90, 96
Fort Frederica National Monument
    (St. Simons Island), 153
Fort McAllister, 78
Fort Pulaski, 78
Fort Screven (Tybee Island), 117

Gallery 209, 105
Gallery Espresso, 112
Gays and lesbians, 36, 114
Georgia Days Colonial Faire and
    Muster, 32
Ghost Talk Ghost Walk, 86–87
Gifts and collectibles, 108
Golf, 89, 122, 125–126, 155–156
Gray Line Savannah Tours, 86
Green-Meldrim House, 72, 94
Gullah Celebration (Hilton Head),
    122
Gullah Heritage Trail Tours (Hilton
    Head), 123

Haines, Connie, 24
Hamilton-Turner Inn, 97

Hansford, Danny, gravestone of, 81
Harbor Light, 102
Harbour Town Yacht Basin (Hilton Head), 125
Heavenly Spa (Hilton Head), 130
Henderson Golf Club, 89
The Herb House, 101
Heyward House (Bluffton), 131
Hilton Head, 121–153
    accommodations, 132–140
    getting around, 122
    nightlife, 151–153
    restaurants, 141–151
    shopping, 132
    special events, 122
    traveling to, 121
    visitor information, 121–122
Hilton Head Brew Pub, 152
Hilton Head Celebrity Golf Tournament, 122
Hilton Head National Golf Club, 126
Hilton Head Plaza, 152
Historic District, 29
    accommodations, 43–52
    restaurants, 57–65
Historic homes, 70–72
Historic squares, walking tour, 91–98
History of Savannah, 9–17
Hogg, John B., 20
Holiday Tour of Homes, 34
Horseback riding, Hilton Head, 126
Hospitals, 174
H2O Sports (Hilton Head), 130
Hunting Island, 165

Independent Presbyterian Church, 92–93
International Gay and Lesbian Travel Association (IGLTA), 36
Island West Golf Club (Hilton Head), 126
Isle of Hope, 118

Jay, William, 19–20
Jazz Corner (Hilton Head), 151–152
Jazz'd Tapas Bar, 112
Jazz Festival, Savannah, 33
J.D. Weed & Co., 105
Jepson Center for the Arts, 74

Jewelry and silver, 109
Jim Crow laws, 15–16
The Jinx, 111
Jogging, 89, 127
John Mark Verdier House Museum (Beaufort), 164–165
Johnny Mercer Theatre, 110
Johnson Square, 91
John Tucker Fine Arts, 106
Jones, Jacqueline, 22
Juliette Gordon Low's Birthplace, 72, 92
Juneteenth, 33

Kayaking, Hilton Head, 127
Kennett, Lee, 22
Kevin Barry's Irish Pub, 112

Lake Mayer Park, 90
Laurel Grove South Cemetery, 79
Lawton Stables (Hilton Head), 126
Le Cookery (Hilton Head), 132
Levy Jewelers, 109
Literary landmarks, 83
Live music clubs, 110–111
Low Country River Excursions, 87
The Lucas Theater, 100
Lutheran Church of the Ascension, 75–76

Marshgrass Adventures (Hilton Head), 127
Mary Calder golf course, 89
Massie Community School House, 96
Massie Heritage Interpretation Center, 83
Massingale Park Beach (St. Simons Island), 155
Mellow Mushroom, 113
Memorial Day at Old Fort Jackson, 33
Mercer, Johnny, 23, 81
Mercer Williams House Museum, 84, 85, 94–95
Mercury Lounge, 113
The Metropolitan Lounge (Hilton Head), 152

Midnight in the Garden of Good and Evil, 17, 22, 23, 64, 95
    Bonaventure Cemetery, 80
    Mercer Williams House, 84
    sights associated with, 84–85
Money and costs, 34–35
Monterey Square, 95
Morning Star Gallery, 106
MossRehab, 35
Murphy, Christopher P. H., 22
Museums, 73–74
Music, 23–24

Nature preserves, Hilton Head, 127–129
Nature tours and watches, 89–90
    St. Simons Island, 156
Neighborhoods in brief, 29–31
Neptune Park (St. Simons Island), 154
Nicholsonboro Baptist Church, 82
Nightlife, 110–115
    Hilton Head, 151–153
Norris, John, 20
North beach (Hilton Head), 124

Obelisk, 102
O'Connor, Flannery, 83, 96
Oglethorpe, James Edward, 10–11, 18
Oglethorpe Mall, 104
Oglethorpe Square, 97
Old Fort Jackson, 78
Old South Golf Links (Bluffton), 126
Old Town Trolley Tours, 86
Olympic Yachting Cauldron, 102–103
Outdoor activities, 87–90
Outside Hilton Head, 127
Owens-Thomas House and Museum, 73, 97

Palmetto Dunes Oceanfront Resort (Hilton Head), 126, 132
Pinckney Island National Wildlife Refuge (Hilton Head), 128–129
Plantation Sweets Vidalia Onions, 107
Police, 174

Port Royal Racquet Club (Hilton Head), 132
Post office, 175

Quarterdeck (Hilton Head), 152–153
Quarterman, Leonora, 21

Rainfall, average, 32
Ralph Mark Gilbert Civil Rights Museum, 82
Ray Ellis Gallery, 105
Reconstruction, 15–16
Recreational parks, 90
Regency style, 19–20
Reid, Irene, 24
Restaurants, 54–68. *See also*
    Restaurant Index; and *specific*
    destinations
        best, 6–8
        City Market area, 66–67
        family-friendly, 63
        Historic District, 57–65
        riverfront, 54–57
Retreat Golf Club (St. Simons Island), 156
Riverfront District, 29, 103
    accommodations, 38–42
    restaurants, 54–57
River's End Campground and RV Park, 87
River Street, 104
River Street Sweets, 107
The Riverwalk, walking tour, 98–103

Safety, 175
Sail Harbor, 90
Sailing, 90, 129–130
St. Helena's Episcopal Church (Beaufort), 165
St. Julian Street, 101
St. Patrick's Day Celebration on the River, 32
St. Phillip Monumental A.M.E. Church, 82–83
St. Simons Island, 153–162
St. Simons Island Lighthouse Museum, 154
Sanctuary Day Spa (Hilton Head), 130

180 SATH (Society for Accessible Travel & Hospitality), 35

Savannah Convention & Visitors Bureau, 100

Savannah Cotton Exchange, 100

Savannah Festival Factory Stores, 104

Savannah History Museum, 74

Savannah Irish Festival, 32

Savannah Jazz Festival, 33, 110

Savannah Mall, 104

Savannah Music Festival, 33

Savannah National Wildlife Refuge, 88

Savannah Oak RV Resort, 87

Savannah's Candy Kitchen, 107

Savannah Smiles, 113

Savannah Symphony Orchestra, 110

Savannah Theatre, 110

Savannah Tour of Homes & Gardens, 33

Savannah Walks, 86

Scuba diving, 89

Sea Island, 171–172

Sea Island Carriage Co. (Beaufort), 164

Sea Island Golf Club (St. Simons Island), 155–156

Sea Palms Golf & Tennis Resort (St. Simons Island), 156

Sea Pines Forest Preserve (Hilton Head), 127–128

Sea Pines Racquet Club (Hilton Head), 130

Seasons, 32

Second African Baptist Church, 82

Senior travel, 36

17 Hundred 90 Lounge, 113

Ships of the Sea Maritime Museum, 74

Shopping, 104–109, 132

ShopSCAD, 108

Sights and attractions, 69–87

    African-American, 79–83

    Beaufort, 164–165

    Tybee Island, 116–119

Silver, Murray, 22

Simply Silver, 109

Skidaway Island State Park, 87

South Forest beach (Hilton Head), 124

Spa Soleil (Hilton Head), 130

Spa treatments, Hilton Head, 130

Specialized travel resources, 35–37

Spirit of Old Beaufort, 164

Sports and outdoor activities, 87–90

Steele, Joe, 23

Tanger Outlet Centers I and II (Hilton Head), 132

Taxes, 175

Taxis, 29, 122

Telfair Museum of Art, 74

Telfair Square, 92

Temperatures, average, 32

Temple Mickve Israel, 76

Tennis, 90, 130, 156

Tours, organized, 84–87, 164. *See also* Boat tours and cruises

Train travel, 27–28

Transportation, 28–29

Trinity United Methodist Church, 76

Troup Square, 97

True Grits, 108

The Trustees' Garden, 102

Tybee Island, 116–120

Tybee Lighthouse, 117

Tybee Marine Center, 119

Tybee Museum, 117

U.S. Custom House, 73, 99

U.S. Marine Corps Recruit Depot (Beaufort), 165

Van Der Meer Shipyard Tennis Resort (Hilton Head), 131

Verizon Heritage PGA Tour and Tournament (Hilton Head), 122

Victorian District, 31, 67

Vietnam War Veterans Memorial, 102

Village at Wexford (Hilton Head), 132

Village Craftsmen, 106

Villa rentals, 139–140, 171

Visitor information, 175

Walking tours

    guided, 86

    self-guided, 91–103

The Washington Guns, 99

Weather, 175

Wesley, John, bronze statue of, 100
Wesley Monumental United
    Methodist Church, 77
Wet Willie's, 114
Wheelchair accessibility, 35–36
Williams, Jim, gravestone of, 81
Windsurfing, Hilton Head, 132
Winefest (Hilton Head), 122
Wormsloe Plantation, 118
Wright Square, 92

Yamacraw Bluff, 98

ACCOMMODATIONS

AVIA Savannah Hotel, 38
The Azalea Inn, 45
Ballastone Inn, 43
Baymont Inn & Suites, 52
The Beaufort Inn, 165–166
Bed & Breakfast Inn, 51
Best Inn (Beaufort), 168
Best Western Island Inn (St. Simons
    Island), 157
Catherine Ward House Inn, 45–46
The Cloister (Sea Island), 171–172
Country Inn & Suites (Beaufort),
    166
Crowne Plaza Hilton Head Island
    Beach Resort, 136
The Cuthbert House Inn (Beaufort),
    167
Days Inn (Hilton Head), 139
Disney's Hilton Head Island Resort,
    136–137
Dresser Palmer House, 48
East Bay Inn, 48
Eliza Thompson House, 48–49
Fairfield Inn by Marriott, 51–52
Foley House Inn, 46
Forsyth Park Inn, 49
Four Points by Sheraton Historic
    Savannah, 43
The Gastonian, 43–44
Hamilton-Turner Inn, 44
Hampton Inn Hilton Head Island,
    139
Hampton Inn Historic District,
    49–50
Hilton Garden Inn (Beaufort), 166
Hilton Head Marriott Resort & Spa,
    133

Hilton Head Metropolitan Hotel,
    139
Hilton Oceanfront Resort (Hilton
    Head), 137
Hilton Savannah DeSoto, 46
Holiday Inn Oceanfront (Hilton
    Head), 138
Homewood Suites by Hilton, 52–53
Howard Johnson's Admiral Inn
    (Tybee Island), 119
Hyatt Regency Savannah, 40
The Inn at Harbour Town (Hilton
    Head), 133
The Inn at Palmetto Bluff (Hilton
    Head), 133–134
The Kehoe House, 44–45
King and Prince Beach Resort (St.
    Simons Island), 157
The Lodge at Sea Island Golf Club
    (St. Simons Island), 157–158
Main Street Inn (Hilton Head), 135
The Mansion on Forsyth Park, 40
Marriott Riverfront Hotel, 40–41
The Marshall House, 50
The Mulberry Inn, 47
Ocean Plaza Beach Resort (Tybee
    Island), 119
Olde Harbour Inn, 41–42
Palmetto Dunes Oceanfront Resort
    (Hilton Head), 140
Park Lane Hotel & Suites (Hilton
    Head), 138
Planters Inn, 50
The President's Quarters, 47
The Rhett House Inn (Beaufort),
    166
The River Street Inn, 42
Royal Dunes Resort (Hilton Head),
    137–138
Saint Simons Inn, 158
Sea Gate Inn (St. Simons Island),
    158
Sea Island Inn (Beaufort), 168
Sea Palms Golf & Tennis Resort (St.
    Simons Island), 159–160
The Sea Pines Resort (Hilton Head),
    140
The South Beach Marina Inn
    (Hilton Head), 138–139
Staybridge Suites, 51
Thunderbird Inn, 52
Two Suns Inn (Beaufort), 167–168
The Westin Hilton Head Island
    Resort & Spa, 136

182 The Westin Savannah Harbor Golf
     Resort & Spa, 41
Whitaker-Huntingdon Inn, 47–48
Wingate Inn, 53

RESTAURANTS

Alexander's (Hilton Head), 143
Alligator Soul, 66
Antonio's (Hilton Head), 143
Back in the Day, 62
Barnes Restaurant, 62–63
Belford's, 66
Bennie's Red Barn (St. Simons
     Island), 161
Black Marlin Bayside Grill (Hilton
     Head), 143–144
Blackstone's Café (Beaufort), 170
The Breakfast Club (Tybee Island),
     119–120
The British Open Pub (Hilton
     Head), 148
Broughton & Bull, 57–58
Casbah, 60
Cha Bella, 60
Charlie's L'Etoile Verte (Hilton
     Head), 144
Chart House, 54
Clary's Café, 63–64, 96
Colt & Alison (St. Simons Island),
     160
CQ's (Hilton Head), 144
The Crab Shack (Tybee Island), 120
The Crab Trap (St. Simons Island),
     161–162
Crane's Tavern & Steakhouse
     (Hilton Head), 144–145
The Crazy Crab North (Hilton
     Head), 145
Delaney's Bistro (St. Simons
     Island), 160–161
Elizabeth on 37th, 67
Emily's (Beaufort), 168–169
Garibaldi's, 56
Gnat's Landing (St. Simons Island),
     161
Harbour Town Grill (Hilton Head),
     145
Hudson's Seafood House on the
     Docks (Hilton Head), 146
Johnny Harris Restaurant, 68
Jump & Phil's Bar & Grill (Hilton
     Head), 146

Kathleen's Grille (Beaufort), 169
Kingfisher (Hilton Head), 146–147
The Lady & Sons, 56
MacElwee's Seafood House (Tybee
     Island), 120
Marley's Island Grille (Hilton Head),
     141
Masada Café, 64
Michael Anthony's (Hilton Head),
     141
Moon River Brewing Company, 67
Mrs. Wilkes' Dining Room, 63, 64–65
Oak Room (St. Simons Island), 160
Ocean Grille (Hilton Head), 141
The Olde Pink House Restaurant, 59
Old Fort Pub (Hilton Head), 142
The Old Oyster Factory (Hilton
     Head), 147
One Hot Mama's American Grille
     (Hilton Head), 149
Outback Steakhouse, 61
Panini's Café (Beaufort), 169
Pearl's Saltwater Grille, 61
Pirates' House, 101
The Pirates' House, 61–62
Plums (Beaufort), 170–171
Redfish Grill (Hilton Head), 142
Reilley's Grill & Bar (Hilton Head),
     147
Ruan Thai, 65
Saltus River Grill (Beaufort),
     169–170
San Miguel's (Hilton Head), 149
Santa Fe Cafe (Hilton Head),
     147–148
Sapphire Grill, 58
Sea Shack (Hilton Head), 149
700 Drayton Restaurant, 58–59
17 Hundred 90, 59–60
Shrimp Factory, 57
Signe's Heaven Bound Bakery &
     Cafe (Hilton Head), 150
Six Pence Pub, 65, 94
Skull Creek Boathouse (Hilton
     Head), 148
Slicers Deli, 100
Smokehouse Bar & House of BBQ
     (Hilton Head), 150
Steamer Seafood (Hilton Head),
     150
Truffles Cafe (Hilton Head), 151
Tubby's Tank House, 57
Wall's, 63, 65

—— NOTES ——